The Relationship between Human Development, Exports and Foreign Direct Investments in Emerging Europe

Polish Studies in Economics

Edited by Ryszard Kokoszczyński

Volume 2

PL ACADEMIC RESEARCH

Jan Jakub Michałek
Michał Brzozowski
Andrzej Cieślik
(eds.)

The Relationship between Human Development, Exports and Foreign Direct Investments in Emerging Europe

PL ACADEMIC RESEARCH

Bibliographic Information published by the Deutsche Nationalbibliothek
The Deutsche Nationalbibliothek lists this publication in the Deutsche Nationalbibliografie; detailed bibliographic data is available in the internet at http://dnb.d-nb.de.

This publication was supported by the University of Warsaw.

Cover Design: © Olaf Gloeckler, Atelier Platen, Friedberg

Library of Congress Cataloging-in-Publication Data

The relationship between human development, exports and foreign direct investments in emerging Europe / Jan Jakub Michalek, Michal Brzozowski, Andrzej Cieslik (eds.). — 1 Edition.
pages cm. — (Polish studies in economics, ISSN 2191-8848 ; volume 2)
Includes bibliographical references and index.
ISBN 978-3-631-62566-8 (Print) — ISBN 978-3-653-01883-7 (eBook) 1. Economic development—Europe, Eastern. 2. Economic development—Europe, Central. 3. International economic relations. 4. Europe, Eastern—Economic conditions—21st century. 5. Europe, Central—Economic conditions—21st century. 6. Europe, Eastern—Social policy—21st century. 7. Europe, Central—Social policy—21st century. I. Michalek, Jan Jakub. II. Brzozowski, Michal. III. Cieslik, Andrzej.
HC244.R4345 2013
337.43—dc23

2013017073

ISSN 2191-8848
ISBN 978-3-631-62566-8 (Print)
E-ISBN 978-3-653-01883-7 (E-Book)
DOI 10.3726/978-3- 653-01883-7

Peter Lang – Frankfurt am Main · Bern · Bruxelles · New York · Oxford · Warszawa · Wien

www.peterlang.de

Table of contents

Preface

Even a small difference in growth rates can lead to a significant change in quality of life within a single generation. However, inducing economic growth is not an easy task. The state can exercise a wide range of policies that can only indirectly lead to the desired results in terms of income growth and social welfare improvement. To that end, countries may use different economic policies and opening up to international trade and financial flows is just one of these roads that many nations have undertaken. Not surprisingly, the problem of the relationship between growth and trade and foreign direct investment has already been thoroughly studied and established in the literature. In contrast, the originality of our book lies in an analysis of the social factors conducive to enhancing trade and FDI, thus increasing welfare and economic convergence. In fact, the opening up of a given country may not be sufficient to intensify international trade and investment flows efficiently. Therefore, we believe that the effects of economic openness depend on the level of human development. We want to verify whether human and social development has a positive impact on international trade and incoming foreign investment. So far this point of view has not been analyzed in the literature despite its importance as often underlined by policy-makers.

Most of the authors of this book work at the Faculty of Economic Sciences at the University of Warsaw. Fragments of the empirical studies discussed in chapters 3, 4, 5 and 6 were presented at Polish and international conferences. We would like to thank the many discussants who reviewed our research with consideration and a high degree of criticism.

With this book, we would like to contribute to the discussion on the inconsistency between the policy of economic openness and human development. In particular, we would like to verify if a higher level of human development is necessary for the success of the policy of economic openness. We hope that the results of our research presented in the book will provide substantial recommendations in the context of the challenges facing the economic and social policies of Poland. We also hope that this book will be a contribution to the discussion on the role of social factors in an open economy.

1 Human development and internationalization of the economy

Michał Brzozowski, Andrzej Cieślik, Jan J. Michałek

1.1 Introduction

Over the past two decades since the collapse of the communist system in the countries of Central and Eastern Europe (CEEC) deep social and economic changes have taken place.[1] Most of the countries in this group can now be considered as advanced economies fully open to international trade and foreign direct investment. The countries that joined the European Union have demonstrated long-term convergence with Western European countries. Although, their development so far has not been uniform, the new EU member states can be described as successful fast-growing economies, especially in comparison with the countries of the former Soviet Union that liberalized and opened their economies to a smaller extent. The uneven pace of transition in Central and Eastern Europe, reflected in the different rates of economic growth and the different strategies with respect to the internationalization of their economies, led to differences in the pace of human development between countries in this region.

The main objective of this book is to analyze the interactions between various aspects of human development and the internationalization of the economy. In particular, we have studied the potential impact of human development on international trade and foreign direct investment (FDI), which in turn may stimulate economic growth and result in an improved quality of life. In our analysis of the relationship between human development and country position in terms of trade and Foreign Direct Investments (FDI) we had to deal with many challenges

The concept of human development goes far beyond the material standards of living as measured by GDP per capita or quantity of consumption per capita. It also includes a number of other elements of quality of life, such as the

1 CEE countries include: Albania, Armenia, Azerbaijan, Belarus, Bulgaria, Croatia, Czech Republic, Estonia, Georgia, Hungary, Kazakhstan, Kyrgyzstan, Latvia, Lithuania, Moldova, Mongolia, Poland, Romania, Russian Fed., Slovakia, Slovenia, Tajikistan, Turkey, Turkmenistan, Ukraine, Uzbekistan. Several countries were excluded from the analysis because of "instability": Bosnia and Herzegovina, Macedonia, Montenegro, Serbia and Kosovo.

availability and quality of education, inequality of income, access to health care, the scope of civil liberties and issues of gender equality. From the point of view of an economist examining the economic consequences, human development is inextricably linked to investments in human capital. The main difficulty stems from the fact that there is no precise common definition of human development and it is difficult to quantify this phenomenon.

Human development is about creating an environment in which people can develop to their full potential and lead productive, creative lives in accordance with their needs and interests, and thus improving the usage of human capital. This definition of human development is accepted by both liberal and socio-democratic economists and politicians because it is akin to postulating the "equality of chances" for everybody.

In attempting to quantify the economic implications of human development, we utilized a frequently-used measure, the Human Development Index (HDI). We assumed, following the *Human Development Report*, that a prerequisite for a society to be considered as highly-developed is to achieve not only a high level of income but also a high level of education and health. In addition, we assumed that an important element of human development is also a low level of income inequalities and discrimination on gender grounds. Moreover, a highly-developed society should also guarantee its members a high level of civil rights.

The countries of Central and Eastern Europe (CEE) that underwent the transition witnessed multidimensional changes in their levels of human development. These changes were progressive, although in the initial period of transformation there was a clear setback in income level, and in some countries also in the level of education.

The economic transition led to a decline in GDP in all of the countries of the region, ranging from 20 to over 50 percent, depending on the country. The decrease in income was most visible in two groups of transition countries: Southern Europe and the newly independent states arising after the dissolution of the Soviet Union. In the first of these groups of countries, the income indicator used for the construction of the HDI fell in the years 1990-1995, by more than 10%, while in the second group it fell by almost 20%. In the countries of southern Europe, a drop in the education index of about 10 percent was reported. At the same time in the post-Soviet States, a slight decline in life expectancy was also observed.

At the same time, income differences within countries increased and a completely new phenomenon - unemployment - emerged. In the non-market economy job security was guaranteed to all persons of working age, while subsidies for basic goods and social transfers, primarily aimed at retirees, contributed to income equalization and poverty elimination within the society.

Both the education and health care systems were organized and financed by the state and universal access to the healthcare system was without a doubt one of the major achievements of the CEE countries. The state had full control over educational policy and guaranteed universal access to primary and secondary education, however, access to tertiary higher education, was limited due to ideological and financial constraints.

The accumulation of human capital slowed down as a result of a reduction in government spending on social policies. The initial phase of the transformation forced some people to seek access to private health care systems and private tertiary education. However, access to private health care systems and private tertiary education was limited by rising income inequalities. As a result, the erosion of human capital occurred across the region.

The socio-economic situation among the 11 EU new member states (NMS) was slightly better in comparison with other CEE countries.[2] However, even in those countries, spending for social purposes declined as a percentage of GDP. These negative trends were reversed in the late 90s, which coincided with a clear economic recovery in most transition countries. Increasing GDP was accompanied by an increasing share of the state budget being devoted to social spending. With the improving economic situation, the level of human capital in the past 10 years has begun to grow. This has been supported by the stabilization of income distribution and inequality at the levels close to those observed in OECD countries (see ILO 2008).

The starting point for our analysis is that, in the case of transition economy countries, human development is a factor affecting foreign trade and FDI. Certainly, there is a question on the direction of the causal relationship between the openness of the economy and human development. One could argue that the liberalization of international trade and capital flows may affect human development. The opening up to international trade and capital flows from the rest of the world, especially from developed countries, combined with price liberalization and privatization, was one of the foundations of the transition. Therefore, because the integration of the economies of the region into the global economy was relatively recent, while the accumulation of social capital began long before the period of transition, we will examine the impact of human development on trade and FDI and not the other way round.

Moreover, both the accumulation of human capital in the form of a higher quality of education and health and increasing wealth are processes taking place

2 The new member states of the EU include: the Czech Rep., Estonia, Lithuania, Latvia, Poland, Slovakia, Slovenia and Hungary, which joined the EU in 2004, Bulgaria and Romania which joined the EU in 2007, and Croatia which joined the EU in 2013.

slowly and to a smaller extent are shaped in the CEE countries by the current inflow of FDI or trade flows. It should be emphasized that the existence of causality running from the openness of the economy to human development should not cast doubt on our results. The transition countries, in terms of the level of human development, differed from their new foreign partners significantly less than in terms of the internationalization of their economies. Therefore, it can be argued that in the CEE countries human development preceded the opening of their economies.

1.2 The impact of human development on trade and FDI: Literature review

The analysis of the relationship between human development and economic openness is important and no previous studies for transition countries have been made. We attempt to fill the gap existing in the literature by postulating that human indicators may have an impact on international trade and FDI. Before presenting the results of our empirical research for the CEE countries, it is worth reviewing the existing literature on other countries. This will allow us to take a broader perspective on the role of human development in the internationalization processes of the economies of the CEE countries.

1.2.1 Human development and international trade

According to some theoretical models of international trade, human capital is an important factor in determining the pattern of trade flows. Human capital usually refers to the stock of skills and knowledge embodied in the ability to perform labour so as to produce economic value. It includes the skills and knowledge gained by a worker through education and experience. According to Gary Becker (1964), human capital is similar to "physical means of production", such as factories and machines. One can invest in human capital (via education, training, medical treatment) and one's output depends partly on the rate of return on the human capital one owns. Human capital, therefore, directly affects the size of production and, like physical capital, depreciates over time and sometimes specifically, i.e. related to a specific job.

The human capital literature often distinguishes between "specific" and "general" human capital. Specific human capital refers to skills or knowledge that are useful only to a single employer or industry, whereas general human capital (such as literacy), is useful to all employers. Our study is related to the analysis of general human capital, important for all companies, although in the broader context of human development. In the case of an open economy, on the one hand, human capital can be transferred from abroad by international trade, and on the other, domestic human capital accumulation can encourage exports.

The importance of human capital, usually interpreted in the narrow sense of the level of education and skills, is included in both traditional and new trade theories. A higher level of human capital has a positive effect on the productivity of labour, and thus, also on the competitiveness of firms and sectors, and consequently their ability to export.

The latter relationship is particularly clearly shown in the classical trade theory. According to the theory of David Ricardo, comparative advantage is determined by differences in the productivity of a homogeneous workforce in different sectors of the economy. Differences in productivity – which are exogenously given in the Ricardian theory – may result from the differences in the endowments of physical and human capital. According to this theory, countries export products produced in those sectors of the economy where the relative productivity compared to other countries is higher and import goods produced in sectors with relatively low levels of productivity.

Dornbusch, Fischer and Samuelson (1977) in a more formal model in the Ricardian tradition, extended to many goods, analyzed the relative importance of average levels of labour productivity at a national level for international trade flows. In their model, a higher average level of labour productivity in the country, resulting from physical capital and / or human abundance, leads to lower prices and export growth. Consequently, it leads through the trade balance to relatively higher real wages in the country with the higher level of labour productivity. Thus, labour productivity is the main determinant of both sectorial and bilateral trade flows in the Ricardian model.

Many economists tested the importance of the productivity differences in the Ricardian model as the main determinant of international trade flows. Examples of the early studies include the work of Balassa (1963, 1986) and Horiba (1979). Most of them have shown that in the classical model, sectorial labour productivity has some influence on the export specialization of countries. This result was confirmed by Golub and Hsieh (2000), who conducted a detailed econometric analysis of sectorial and bilateral trade flows between countries.

However, the importance of human capital in the development of international trade cannot be analyzed in a direct way in the Ricardian model because the only variable that is included in this model is the exogenously determined level of sectorial labour productivity. The importance of human capital, as a direct factor determining the size of trade flows, has been included in extensions of the neoclassical trade theory that take into account a larger number of factors of production. According to the factor abundance theory, the differences in relative factor endowments determine the structure of comparative advantages and affect trade flows. In other words, a country that is relatively rich in one factor should specialize in the production and export of goods that require relatively large amounts of this factor.

In a pioneering study, the empirical validity of the predictions of the Heckscher-Ohlin (HO) model in its most basic form with two factors of production: physical capital and labour, Leontief (1954), obtained a result that contradicted predictions of the theory known in the economic literature as the Leontief paradox. Since then, a number of empirical studies, which verified the importance of the extended neoclassical model by Vanek (1968), took into account a larger number of factors of production, including the role of human capital.

In particular, Leamer (1984) shows that in addition to other factors such as capital, land and raw materials, the supply of skilled labour has a significant impact on the size and structure of international trade in the selected OECD countries. A later study by Bowen, Leamer and Sveikauskas (1987) provided a weak support of the neoclassical trade theory. Trefler (1995) made an alternative test of the Hecksher-Ohlin-Vanek theory, taking into account differences in factors' productivity between countries. His results were more in line with the predictions of the theory in comparison with the results of Bowen, Leamer and Sveikauskas (1987).

In the latest strand of the theory of international trade, mainly represented by the Melitz (2003) model, firms differ in terms of their labour productivity which determines their export decisions. The level of labour productivity may in turn depend on the resources of human and social capital. It can therefore be expected that a higher level of human development is positively associated with higher productivity of human capital and thus can have a positive impact on the productivity of companies and their export decisions. This means that the greater resources of skilled labour may be factors contributing to the increase in exports of heterogeneous firms.

Since the publication of the Melitz (2003) model, numerous empirical studies have been made using firm-level data. In particular, they studied whether higher productivity of labour increases the likelihood of a decision to start exporting. Most of the empirical research confirmed this prediction. The examples include studies by Bernard and Wagner (1997) for Germany, Bernard and Jensen (1999) for the U.S., Clerides and others (1998) for Colombia, Mexico and Morocco, and Castellani (2002) for Italy.

Similar studies for the countries of the Visegrad Group: the Czech Republic, Slovakia, Poland and Hungary, and separately for Poland were made by Cieslik,

Michalek and Michalek (2012 a, b). Their analysis showed that labour productivity was positively related to the probability of exporting.

On the other hand, empirical studies also looked at other factors that could influence the export decisions of companies. They also analyzed other factors affecting export performance. For example, they showed that a higher proportion of skilled workers, as well as a higher percentage of college graduates among the total number of employees increases the probability of exporting, regardless of the sector in which the company operated (EFIGE 2010; Cieslik, Michalek and Michalek 2012 a, b). Therefore, it might be interesting to analyze whether or not a higher stock of human capital in the country can positively affect the export performance of individual companies and entire economies.

1.2.2 Human development and FDI

The recent strand in the literature on FDI brings human capital into the fore. In the international trade theory which endogenizes multinational firms under assumptions of imperfect competition and scale economies in production, the importance of human capital is stressed in vertical FDI models. Zhang and Markusen (1999) focused on skilled labour as one of the main determinants of costs of investing abroad. Although unskilled labour in the assembly process is employed by multinationals, minimal levels of skilled labour must be drawn from the host economy in order to set up a plant abroad. If the relative endowments in skilled and unskilled labour diverge significantly, the scarcity of the skilled labour required to establish a plant in the host economy becomes prohibitive and no FDI takes place.

The results of empirical research are far from clear-cut, which is partly due to the difficulties in gauging, without a measurement error, the level of human capital.[3] Nunnenkamp and Spatz (2003) compiled data from US FDI stocks in 166 countries and found the positive and statistically significant impact of the average years of schooling in both 1995 and 2000. The regression analysis of FDI in 165 countries between 1980 and 1999 in Akin and Vlad (2011) revealed that the relationship between educational attainment and FDI seems to be negative for high income countries but it switches to positive in the middle income group.

---

3 For a comprehensive review of the early literature, Miyamoto (2003) is strongly recommended.

Agosin and Machado (2006) employ the UNDP's education index which couples both the rate of investment in and the level of basic education. It is equal to the weighted average of the adult literacy rate (two thirds) and the combined gross school enrolment rate (one third). Applying several panel data estimation methods to the data set collected for more than 100 countries in 1990, 1996 and 2002, they supported the view that education is amongst the primary determinants of FDI flows.

The importance of the stock and flow of human capital for FDI flows to 36 developing countries over the period 1980-1994 was scrutinized by Noorbakhsh *et al.* (2001). The secondary school enrolment ratio is a measure of the flow of investment in human capital and two variables were taken by the authors to quantify the stock of human capital, namely the mean years of secondary and the sum of the mean years of secondary and tertiary education in the working age population. The coefficients of all three measures of human capital are positive and statistically significant and the effect of human capital on FDI inflows was estimated to be considerably larger when the last three years 1991-1994 were added to the regression, suggesting an upward trend in its importance across time.

The availability of skilled and educated labour proxied by the percentage of government spending going to education turns out to be insignificant in Ismail's (2009) study of the determinants of inward FDI into 8 ASEAN economies. The ratio of total federal government education development expenditure to GDP was found by Tsen (2005) to attract FDI in the long-run in Malaysia. By contrast, Cheng and Kwan (2000) appraised three alternative proxies for labour quality in their analysis of the determinants of FDI in 29 Chinese regions from 1985 to 1995 but none proved to be significant.

Firms contemplating direct investment abroad face a two-stage decision process. Firstly, they decide how much they have to invest. Secondly, they must also decide whether to carry out the new investments at all. Razin *et al.* (2008) in their study of the determinants of bilateral FDI flows among 62 countries over the period 1987-2000 found that differences in average years of schooling in educational attainment discourage the decision to invest abroad but they do not influence the magnitude of FDI once the decision to invest is taken.

Access to skilled labour is considered to be a major advantage of Central European countries in the competition for FDI. This view was corroborated by Carstensen and Toubal (2004) who measured skills as the fraction of medium and higher education workers in the relevant labour force. The estimated coefficient for this indicator was positive and statistically significant in all specifications. Authors conjectured that the importance of skills in Central

Europe stems from their influence on the ease of the adaptation to a Western business culture.

Majeed and Ahmad (2008) recognized the fact that the concept of human capital goes beyond education and embraces good health. In their analysis of FDI determinants in 23 developing countries from 1970-2004, health expenditure was found to be a significant attractor of multinationals and the effect of illiteracy was negative but insignificant. Alsan *et al.* (2006), who conducted a panel data analysis of 74 industrialized and developing countries from 1980-2000, also detected the strong and positive influence of population health on FDI in low and middle-income countries.

The documented evidence on the role of gender inequality is very scarce. A noticeable exception is the work by Busse and Nunnenkamp (2009) who assessed the importance of gender inequality in education as a determinant of FDI. On theoretical grounds, the authors point to the twofold effect of gender disparities on host countries' attractiveness for FDI. On the one hand, an educational attainment gap between sexes may stimulate efficiency-seeking FDI. Low-skilled and therefore low-wage labour may offer a cost advantage to investors. On the other hand, low-wage unskilled labour is not necessarily cheap in terms of unit labour costs. The benefits of low compensation costs may be completely outweighed by low productivity of less educated workers. Both arguments are relevant for cost-oriented or vertical FDI.

Since the impact of gender inequality in education on FDI is theoretically ambiguous, the results of empirical investigation merit special attention. The analysis of Busse and Nunnenkamp seeks to explain bilateral FDI flows from 28 source to 77 host economies and covers the period 1978-2004. Gender disparity in education is measured by the ratio of male to female years of schooling at all levels of education or at specific, namely primary, secondary and tertiary levels of schooling. The average number of years of schooling of both sexes taken together in the population aged 25 and above, as well as the mean years of schooling of both sexes at all levels of education separately, were shown to be strongly and positively associated with FDI flows. All coefficients on education inequality, at all levels of education, were statistically significant and negative. The robustness tests revealed that discouraging effects of gender disparity on FDI are confined to middle income developing host countries and to investors from developed countries.

1.3 Research hypotheses

Our research is focused on the relationship between human development, trade and foreign direct investment. This book starts with a descriptive analysis of major trends in human development using various indicators for the independent CEE countries in the 1980-2010 period. The concepts of human development and human capital are multidimensional and the way they affect foreign trade and FDI is complex. We believe that the qualitative analysis of the major trends must be accompanied by quantitative research. Therefore, a more formal econometric analysis is presented in the second part of this book.

Our study concerns the determinants of the level of human significance for the volume of trade in goods and FDI inflows. We treat trade and FDI variables as independent variables while the explanatory variables include the set of variables measuring different aspects of human development in the regression analysis. In order to study the role of human development, regression analysis based on static and dynamic techniques is used. Among the explanatory variables we focus on measures of human development such as general human development indexes constructed by the United Nations (Human Development Index, the Gender-related Development Index).

The main objective is to assess the impact of the aggregate measures of human development and their components such as: the level of education, income inequality, gender inequality on the openness of the economy: foreign direct investment and international trade in the region of Central and Eastern Europe.

In the following chapters we present the results of our empirical investigation concerning the relationship between various measures of human development, trade and foreign direct investment in the CEE countries. In particular, we try to verify a number of research hypotheses:

- a higher level of Human Development Index (HDI) is positively associated with larger trade and foreign direct investment flows;
- higher levels of particular HDI components: education, life expectancy and incomes per capita indexes increase the volume of trade flows and FDI inflows;
- a higher level of female participation in human and economic development, as proxied by the gender inequality measure: Gender Empowerment Measure (GEM), as well as its components that assess the level of political and economic participation by women, is positively associated with intensified trade and foreign investment;

- the impact of higher inequality within societies, represented by a higher value of Gini coefficient, might be twofold. First, large differences in income levels may result in smaller trade and lower FDI (Sen 1976).4 On the other hand, the opposite impact might be expected, as argued by Stark (2006), when a larger inequality of incomes prompts a search for higher status, additional work, and therefore promotes additional effort, more production, trade and investment;
- more civil freedom within a society, as measured by lower values in the index of civil liberties, should be positively associated with the development of trade and FDI.

The most aggregate measure of human development is the HDI (Human Development Index). One of the main components of this indicator is per capita income, which is an approximation of the standard of living. However, the popular view is that human development is not only the dimension of income, because other components of the index include the dimensions of education and health. Therefore, this index consists of three elements: (i) life expectancy at birth, which is an approximate measure of the quality of health, (ii) education index, which measures the level of education of the society, both current and anticipated, and (iii) the level of GNI per capita, which is a synthetic measure of standard of living.

An important aggregate measure of human development is also the Gini index, which measures income inequality in society. The higher the Gini index value, the higher the income or consumption disparities in society.

Another measure of economic and social inequality with respect to gender is the Gender Empowerment Index (GEM). It measures: (i) inequality in political life (as measured by the proportion of women in parliament), (ii) inequality in decision-making (the percentage of women among legislators, senior officials and managers), and (iii) economic inequality (income of women as a percentage of the income of men). In this case, the higher the value in the GEM index, the smaller the degree of social and political discrimination against women.

The last measure used in our study is the level of civil liberties, compiled by the non-governmental organization, Freedom House. These liberties allow individuals and the whole society to participate in political life, through an appropriate system of representation and elections. They measure the functioning of the rule of law, which is important not only for dealing with

---

4 In Sen's framework, social welfare is the mean income of the group multiplied by one minus Gini coefficient. This formulation gives two rationales for income redistribution: the pursuit of social justice and the securing of efficiency.

potential social conflicts, but also for the appropriate functioning of the economy.

The structure of the book is as follows. Chapter 2 discusses the previously mentioned measures of human development in greater detail. We start with the most popular aggregate measure of human development, the Human Development Index Human Development Index (HDI). Then, we discuss supplementary measures of human development which take into account other dimensions of human development, such as income disparities, gender equality and civil liberties. Finally, using those indices, we analyze the changes in the level of human development in Central and Eastern Europe. These changes were particularly pronounced after the beginning of transition in the early 1990s. At that time, there was the opening of the economies of the countries of Central and Eastern Europe.

Then we move to the main part of the study, i.e., the econometric analysis of the role of social factors affecting trade and foreign direct investment. In Chapter 3, we examine the relationship between different aspects of human development and international trade. The study of aggregate trade flows is based on the gravity equation derived from theoretical trade models assuming incomplete specialization in production. In Chapter 4, we perform a similar analysis using firm level data on the companies from the CEE countries based on the Melitz (2003) model of a heterogeneous firm.

In Chapter 5, we analyze the relationships between various aspects of human development and foreign direct investment. The dependent variable is the amount of long-term foreign capital inflow at two levels of aggregation. Firstly, we estimate the regression in which the dependent variable is the total inflow of FDI in a large group of countries. The theoretical basis for the specification of estimated equations is the theoretical models of vertical and horizontal direct investment. Secondly, we analyze bilateral FDI flows between developed and Central European countries belonging to the European Union. The gravity model constitutes the basis for the estimated regressions. In Chapter 6, we present the analysis of the importance of foreign capital flows for individual firms in transition economies using microeconomic data.

2 Measures of human development

Jan J. Michałek, Dagmara Mycielska, Agnieszka Pugacewicz

2.1 Introduction

In this chapter, we present and discuss the key properties of different indicators of human development. As there is no unique and commonly accepted definition of human and social development, measuring human development can impose several problems and misunderstandings. In the literature, a large number of indicators of human and social development can be found. In this chapter, we restrict our attention to the main indicators and discuss their limitations. Moreover, we also analyze the level of human and social development of CEECs measured with the indicators discussed below.

We start by presenting the most widely used aggregate indicator, the Human Development Index (HDI) and its three constituent components: income index, life expectancy index and education index. Then, we discuss the specific indicators measuring income inequality and gender discrimination. In particular, we describe a well-known Gini index, as well as other gender related inequality indices such as the Gender Development Index (GDI), the rate of economic and political equality (Gender Empowerment Measure, GEM), and a gender based index of inequality (Gender Inequality Index, GII). Finally, we also present other measures related to human development such as indices of civil liberties and political rights. In order to take into account a geographical dimension of the data context, we present indicators for selected countries that are divided into several regional groups.

In our study, we use the most acknowledged indicators that have been developed by the United Nations Development Program (UNDP). Most of the data is presented in subsequent editions of Human Development Reports (HDR) and available at the UNDP website. Therefore, in this chapter we describe the main indicators and rely heavily on technical notes attached to the different HDR issues.

When selecting an indicator of human development, one should take into account the nature of the research and the purpose of the analysis for which the index is going to be used. For example, an aggregate human development index gives an overall picture of the level of human development in a specific country; however, it does not provide a lot of information on the extent of gender discrimination in the society.

2.2 The Human Development Index and its components

The Human Development Index (HDI) is a well-known composite indicator that measures the level of human and social development. The concept of HDI is based on the assumption that the level of GDP per capita cannot be the only measure of social well-being, let alone social development. Therefore the composite index was proposed, which measures in a synthetic way, various aspects (dimensions) of the level of human development of a given country.

The HDI measures - in a synthetic way - the level of human development using three sub-indices (so called dimension indices): (i) the life expectancy index, which is a rough measure of quality of life, (ii) the education index that is based on average years of schooling, and (iii) the income index, which expresses the standard of living.

The first version of the HDI has been heavily criticized since its publication in the Human Development Report.[5] In our study, we use the latest form of the HDI that was introduced in 2010. The significant changes introduced in 2010 in the HDI calculation applied to the procedure of the aggregation, as well as the formulas for the dimension indices. Therefore, we present in detail the aggregate 2010 HDI and sub-indices and we describe how they differ from those previously used.

As it was mentioned, the HDI is based on three dimension indices. Life expectancy is defined as the life expectancy at birth, assuming that the living standards will remain unchanged throughout the child's life. The life expectancy is often regarded as the most synthetic measure of quality of life and the quality of social and health care of a given country. This is based on the notion that living in a better environment (a cleaner environment, better social infrastructure and health care system, improved housing, etc.) results in a healthier and longer life. In some studies, life expectancy is supplemented or replaced by the infant mortality rate per 1000 live births. It shows the probability of dying between birth and the age of one year. This indicator mainly reflects the basic living conditions of the population and the quality of the health care system and thus has less synthetic character. The data on life expectancy for Human Development Reports is taken from UNDESA (2009).

The second HDI component, the education index, measures a country's average achievement in fostering access to education and access to knowledge. In previous editions of the HDRs, the education index was created as a

5 E.g. Noorkbakhsh (1998), Decanq and Lugo (2009).

combination of the level of literacy among adults and the combined index of access to primary, secondary and higher education, expressed as a percentage of the population in the official age group corresponding to the given level of education. Since 2010, the literacy rate has been excluded from the index calculation as it is a very simple dummy variable that only determines whether an adult is literate or not. Therefore, it is quite an imprecise measure of the quality of human capital of a given country.[6]

Starting from 2010, the education index is based on the expected number of years that a person spends in school and on the average number of years spent in school by adults over 25 years of age. The first variable is usually significantly greater than the other. This index is based on the reasonable assumption that a longer period of education leads to higher qualifications and thus increases a country's human capital resources. However, differences in the quality and efficiency of national education systems make this improved measure still an imperfect one. The data for the education index come from the Barro and Lee (2010) database and a database elaborated by the UNESCO Institute for Statistics.

The last HDI component, the income index, was also modified in 2010. Previously, the income index was based on the level of GDP per capita, which measures the value of goods and services produced per capita in a given country. Currently, the index is based on gross national income (GNI, Gross National Income), which measures the income earned by residents of a given country, taking into account the net income from abroad. It is commonly accepted that the GNI is a better measure than GDP, especially for countries for which a large part of the population gains its income abroad. The GNI data comes from the World Bank database (up to 2009) and the International Monetary Fund for 2010.

Another change in the HDI formula relates to a method of aggregation. In previous editions of the HDR, the HDI had been calculated as an arithmetic mean of sub-indices with different weights for dimension indices. Since 2010, the geometric mean has been used with the same weights for each dimension index. The HDI is thus calculated using the following formula:

$$I_{HDI} = I_{life}^{\frac{1}{3}} \times I_{edu}^{\frac{1}{3}} \times I_{inc}^{\frac{1}{3}}, \qquad (2.1)$$

---

6 For example, for twelve developed countries the literacy rate was 99%, which means that the differences between those countries in terms of that aspect of social development were practically immeasurable.

where I_{HDI} – HDI index, I_{life} – life expectancy index, I_{edu} – education index, I_{inc} – income index.

The general formula for the dimension indices is as given:

$$I_{d,i,t} = \frac{V_{i,t} - V_{min}}{V_{max} - V_{min}}, \qquad (2.2)$$

where $I_{d,i,t}$ – dimension index for the *i-th* country (eg, life expectancy or education) in year t, V_i – current value of a given variable for the *i-th* country in year t, V_{max} and V_{min} are the maximum, and respectively, minimum value of a given variable. This normalization allows for the transformation of indicators expressed in different units to the unit-less quantities taking values between 0 and 1.

The determination of the maximum and minimum values for the dimension indices was modified in 2010 as well. The maximum value is the highest observed value in the time series, whereas the minimum values were set arbitrarily at the specific levels.

This new method of selecting the minimum and maximum values used for the dimension indices can lead to some misinterpretations. In particular, even if the actual values of given variables for a given country have not changed, the application of different minimum and maximum values of the sub-indices would result in changed indices' values. This, in turn, may be misinterpreted as a real change in the level of human development of the country.

Changes made in 2010 improved to some extent the quality of the indices but they also affected the values of indices for a given country and thus the HDI ranking. One can point out several shifts in the countries' HDI ranking as a result of the new method of aggregation. Present values of sub-indices are lower than previously calculated ones and the largest changes in the relative level of the HDI occurred in countries with highly differentiated sub-indices, i.e. with highly asymmetrical levels of development in different dimensions. Those changes resulted mainly from using the geometric instead of the arithmetic mean in the aggregation formula.

The new dimension indices and the new aggregated HDI - have been calculated for the period 1980 to 2010 for 169 countries. For the period covering years 1980-2000, average indices are calculated for each five-year period (i.e. for the year 1980, 1985, 1990 and 1995) and starting from 2000 for each subsequent year. We use these indices in the empirical analysis described in next chapters.

The data for the HDI sub-indices are provided by different renowned institutions and researchers (such as Barro and Lee). Countries for which all or some of the data needed for the construction of sub-indices were missing, were excluded from the analysis. However, these are usually small countries, which have no impact on global trade and foreign direct investment flows.[7] The available data on dimension indices and the HDI allows for building a fairly long panel study and formulating conclusions about the long-term impact of human development on international trade and FDI.

Our analysis concentrates on Central and Eastern European countries (CEECs). In particular, we discuss the data for the following countries: Albania, Armenia, Azerbaijan, Belarus, Bulgaria, Croatia, the Czech Republic, Estonia, Georgia, Hungary, Kazakhstan, Kyrgyzstan, Latvia, Lithuania, Moldova, Mongolia, Poland, Romania, the Russian Fed., Slovakia, Slovenia, Tajikistan, Turkey, Turkmenistan, Ukraine and Uzbekistan. We present the human indicators for specific countries and for various regional sub-groups. The changes in the level of human indicators in the CEECs are compared with the evolution of human development in some other reference regions such as the OECD, the EU, Southern Europe, and the former soviet republics.

Firstly, we present the HDI values calculated for 2011 for Central, Eastern and Southern Europe and post-Soviet republics as well as Mongolia and Turkey (see Table 2.1). The countries in this sample can be divided into three groups according to their HDI values. The UNDP defines the countries of "very high human development" as those for which the HDI value is greater than or equal to 0.793. This group consists of EU member states.[8]

Table 2.1: Estimated values of HDI in 2011 for 26 selected countries, divided into groups of very high, high and medium levels of human development

Very high		High		Medium	
Country	HDI	Country	HDI	Country	HDI
Slovenia	0.884	Romania	0.781	Turkmenistan	0.686
Czech Republic	0.865	Bulgaria	0.771	Mongolia	0.653
Estonia	0.835	Belarus	0.756	Moldova	0.649
Slovakia	0.834	Russia	0.755	Uzbekistan	0.641
Hungary	0.816	Kazakhstan	0.745	Kyrgyzstan	0.615
Poland	0.813	Albania	0.739	Tajikistan	0.607
Lithuania	0.810	Georgia	0.733		
Latvia	0.805	Ukraine	0.729		

7 Omitted countries for which the data was missing are: Antigua and Barbuda, Bhutan, Dominica, Eritrea, Grenada, Cuba, Lebanon, Occupied Palestinian Territories, Saint Vincent and the Grenadines, Samoa, the Seychelles and Vanuatu.

8 Including Croatia, that became an EU member on July 1, 2013.

Croatia	0.796	Armenia	0.716		
		Azerbaijan	0.700		
		Turkey	0.699		

Source: Human Development Report 2011. Notes: a very high level of human development is defined for values: 0.943 (Norway) ≥ HDI ≥ 0.793 (Barbados), the high level of human development: 0.783 (Uruguay) ≥ HDI ≥ 0.698 (Tunisia), the medium level of human development: 0.698 (Jordan) ≥ HDI ≥ 0.522 (Bhutan), the low level of human development: 0.51 (Solomon Islands) ≥ HDI ≥ 0.286 (Congo).

The second category, reported as countries with a high level of human development, consists of the majority of countries from our sample. For these countries, the HDI values are lower than or equal to 0.783 but greater than or equal to 0.698. In this group, there are two EU-member countries (Romania and Bulgaria), Russia, a few of post-Soviet countries, Albania and Turkey. The HDI values lower than 0.698 in 2011, representing a medium level of human development, were observed in four post-Soviet republics of Central Asia: Turkmenistan, Uzbekistan, Kyrgyzstan and Tajikistan, as well as in Mongolia and Moldova. All countries in our sample represent a fairly high level of human development.

The present ranking of countries is important, but we should also look at the evolution of human development indices over a longer period of time. The available data covers the period from 1980-2010 (see Figure 2.1). In the case of all the analysed countries, the HDI indices increased between 1980 and 2010. For Poland, and other *CEE* countries that became members of the European Union (CEEC-UE), the values of the HD indices were increasing. The growth of HD indices was also observed in many countries in Eastern Europe (*EE*, that is Turkey and post-Soviet Asian republics such as Armenia, Azerbaijan, Belarus, Georgia, Kazakhstan, Kyrgyzstan, Mongolia, Russia, Tajikistan, Turkmenistan, Ukraine, Uzbekistan) and Southern Europe (*SE*, namely Albania, Croatia and Moldova), however these countries experienced a clear breakdown resulting from the political and social transformation that occurred in early 1990's.

Figure 2.1 suggests that these countries were gradually overturning the loss in human and social development levels, as it took several years to recover from the shock caused by the communist system collapse and transition to the market economy. Afterwards, starting from 2000, all countries and regions have experienced continuous growth in social and human development. A temporary downturn related to the economic crisis occurred in 2009 and affected simultaneously almost all groups of countries including the OECD states. It can be pointed out that for all countries the difference between the CEECs and OECD countries in terms of the human development level is slowly decreasing.

The "catching up" phenomenon is mainly visible in the case of the CEEC-UE countries as these countries experienced only a slow-down of HDI growth in the early 1990s.

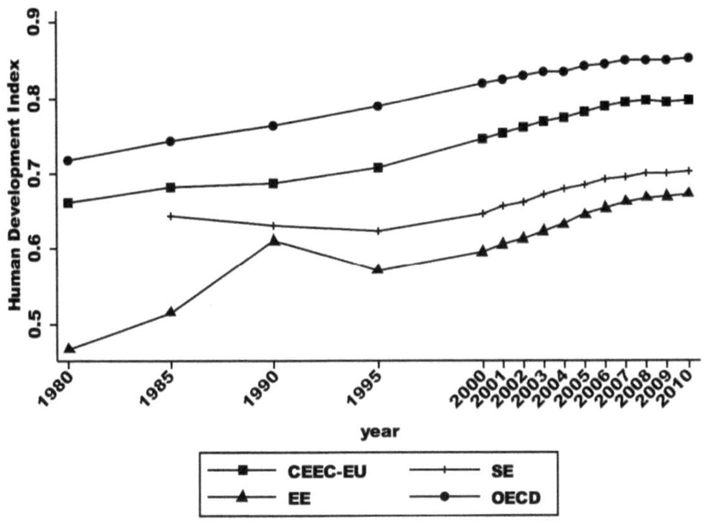

Fig. 2.1: *Human Development Index (HDI) in selected regions, 1980-2010; source: own calculations based on UNDP data*

The HDI is an aggregate measure of human development. It is worth analysing its components which are the three key elements of this development: life expectancy (life expectancy index), achievements in education (education index) and the level of national income per capita (income index). We discuss these indices in detail in the next sections.

2.2.1 Life Expectancy Index

Life expectancy, which is a component of the HDI, may have values between 0 and 1, where 1 is assigned to the country with the highest life expectancy. For example, the maximum life expectancy reported in the 2010 HDR was 83.2 years in Japan. In the HDR 2011, the maximum was set at 83.4 years, again the value observed for Japan in 2011. However, the minimum value of life expectancy is somewhat arbitrarily set at 20 years. This value was based on historical evidence, which showed that if the life expectancy falls below this threshold, a given society can no longer reproduce.[9] Lower values can occur only in the short term, during exceptional periods of crises or wars. The minimum value observed in a sample of 1980-2010 was 39 years in Afghanistan.

Increasing life expectancy is regarded as a sign of improving public health, usually related, among other things, to an improvement in the health care system and better nutrition within the population. This index measures the estimated life expectancy for a child born in a given year. For the majority of the analysed countries, an upward trend can be observed (see Figure 2.2 below). For the Eastern European countries (EE), a temporary decrease in the life expectancy is reported for the period of 1985-1995. During that period the index value for the Central and Eastern European members of the EU was constant at the higher level. Steady growth in life expectancy for all the regions was observed in the last decade.

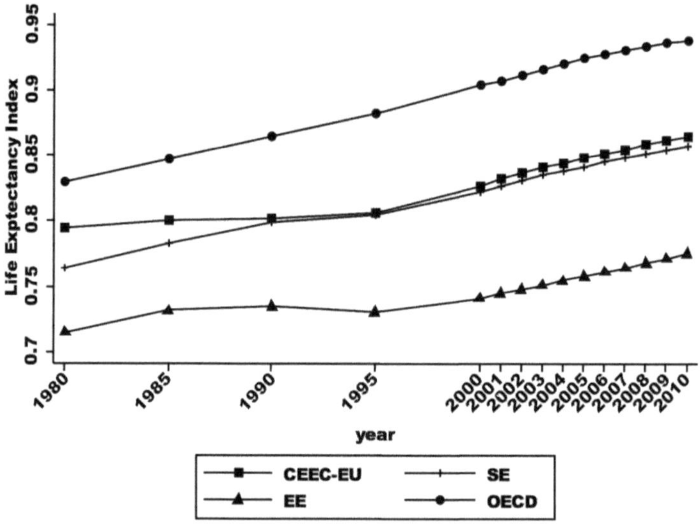

Fig. 2.2: *Life Expectancy Index in selected regions, 1980-2010; source: own calculations based on UNDP data*

9 Maddison (2010), Riley (2005).

2.2.2 Income Index

The formula for the income index is slightly different than for life expectancy and uses the natural logarithms of the maximum and minimum values. This allows for elimination of possible relative distortion of the index value, as absolute values of the Income Index are much higher than in case of the other two indices, i.e. life expectancy and education. The income index is therefore calculated as follows:

$$I_{inc,i,t} = \frac{ln(V_{i,t}) - ln(V_{min})}{ln(V_{max}) - ln(V_{min})}. \qquad (2.3)$$

In previous editions of the HDR, the maximum value for the income index was set at \$ 40,000 PPP, which corresponded to the highest value in the mid-1990s. As a consequence, in 2007 13 countries reported income levels higher than this value, which reduced the diversity of income indices. Therefore, as it was mentioned earlier, from 2010 onwards the maximum and minimum values are the highest and the smallest actual values found in the sample of countries covered by the analysis. For example, in the 2010 HD Report the maximum income (GNI) value was set at \$ 108,211, representing income in the United Arab Emirates in 1980. But in the 2011 edition of the HD Report, the maximum value was set at \$ 107,721, which corresponded to the GNI per capita of Qatar in 2011. The minimum value in the 2010 edition of the HD Report was set at \$ 163 (or 45 cents a day), which corresponds to the value of Zimbabwe's per capita income in 2008. In the 2011 HD Report, the minimum reference level was fixed arbitrarily at \$ 100.

The data points to a higher dispersion of the income index values then for other HDI components (see Figure 2.3). The highest values are reported for the relatively richest OECD countries and for those countries the index values are not lower than 0.7 for the entire period.

The income index levels for the CEEC-EUs (including Poland) were about 10 percentage points lower than for OECD countries on average. A slight decrease can be observed for the years 1985-1995, but again that could be the consequence of the economic slowdown, after the collapse of the system of centrally planned economies.

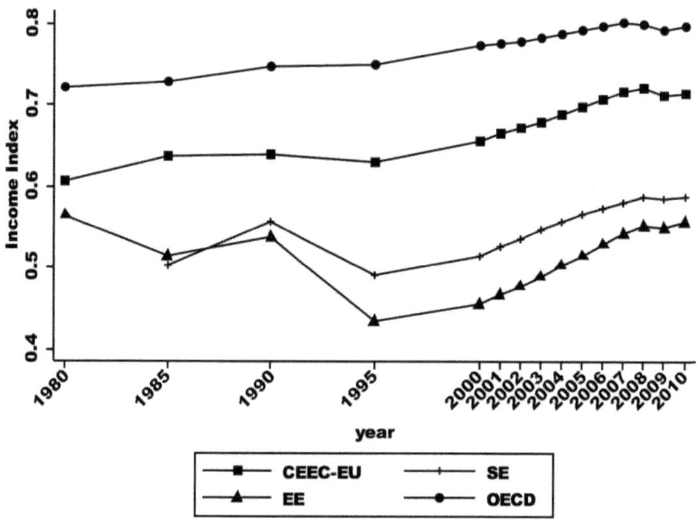

Fig. 2.3: *Income Index in selected regions, 1980-2010; source: own calculations based on UNDP data*

2.2.3 Education Index

The education index, which is a rough measure of the human capital in a given country, is calculated as the geometric mean of two indicators that measure the expected years of schooling and the mean years of schooling. It is assumed that the minimum values for both, i.e. the expected years of schooling and the mean years of schooling, are equal to zero. The observed maximum value for the expected years of schooling was over 20 years in Australia in 2002 (HDR, 2010). In the 2011 edition of the HDR, authors set an arbitrary value of 18 years. The maximum values for the mean years of schooling of adults over 25 years was 13.2 years in the 2010 HDR (the United States in 2000) and 13.1 years in the 2011 HDR (the Czech Republic in 2005).

Access to education, as measured by the UNDP education indices, gives a fairly consistent picture of human capital development in the whole region of Central and Eastern Europe (see Fig. 2.4). The difference between the OECD and the CEEC-EU countries in terms of education visibly decreased, especially in the first decade of XXI century, when the index value for both groups of countries exceeded 0.8.

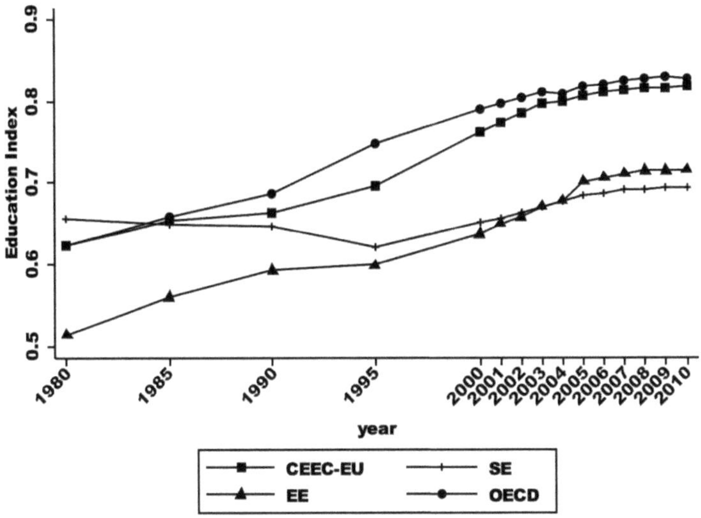

Fig. 2.4: *Education Index in selected regions, 1980-2010; source: own calculations based on UNDP data*

It is worth noting that at the beginning of the analysed period (i.e. 1980-1985), the countries of Southern Europe reported the highest levels in the education index (0.66). Then, like in the case of the HD Index, the transformation process brought a decrease in the indices to approximately 0.60 in 1995. In the following years, a gradual improvement has been observed and the levels of the Education Index in Southern Europe reached the levels of the Eastern European countries. The data for the latter point to the surge in access to education as the average value of the index increased from about 0.5 in the early 1980s to over 0.7 in the 2000s.

As the data show, access to education in the OECD and the CEEC-EU countries did not decrease significantly after the beginning of the transformation process as it was observed for the other two HDI sub-indices. The short-term decline was observed only in Eastern and Southern Europe. Starting from the mid-1990s, for all analysed countries the index showed an upward trend, but after a decade of fairly stable and fast growth the index values dropped for almost every group of countries in the sample. In the following years, education indices slowly returned to the previous levels in 2009.

In many economic analyses, educational attainment is regarded as a measure of human capital, which may positively affect the level of exports and the inflow of foreign direct investment. We analyse this relationship, in quantitative terms, in the following chapters.

The data shows that all CEE countries experienced a surge in human and social development. They managed to restore the levels of human development that had decreased temporarily during the political reforms and transition from centrally planned to market economies in the early 1990s. During the last decades, the CEE countries recorded further increases in both the HDI and its components. Now, all countries in our sample are reported by the UNDP to be countries with a "very high" or "high" level of human development, with a few exceptions of former soviet republics that still report a "medium" level in the HDI.

At the same time, CEECs have made substantial progress in trade policy and international financial flow liberalization. International trade and foreign direct investment visibly increased and became the important engines of economic growth in those countries. Therefore, it is interesting to verify whether or not the development, in terms of human and social capital, fostered the international trade and foreign capital inflow of the CEE countries.

2.3 Other measures of human development

The aggregated HDI measures human development in three different dimensions but does not reflect other factors that can have a significant impact on the level of social well-being. The income and other disparities within a society can play a crucial role in the perception of well-being and evaluation of human development in a given country. The HDI masks discrepancies between the rich and the poor, women and men, in terms of access to education, health and a decent standard of living. It may happen that the country's HD index achieves high values despite the fact that people within the same society experience large disparities in opportunities. This is why the analysis of performance in terms of the HDI is frequently complemented by other indices measuring different aspects of human inequalities. Therefore, in the following sections, we will discuss some detailed indicators measuring income inequalities and social discrimination in terms of origin, gender and political system.

2.3.1 Gini index

According to many economists, the existence of disparities in income and consumption within a population affects the society's wellbeing as well as its economic performance. Even if the rate of economic growth is relatively high, the uneven distribution of income between individuals may be considered as deprivation and a lack of social justice, despite the higher average income and standard of living. Thus, social and income inequality is a slightly different and broader concept than poverty or income per capita, as it concerns the income distribution within a society, rather than just average values.

The best known measure of inequality is the Gini index. It measures inequality in the frequency of income distribution.[10] The Gini index can therefore be regarded as a representation of the expected differences between two units or households randomly chosen from the population. The Gini index is calculated in relation to the Lorenz curve graph as the area between the curve and the uniform distribution. The index ranges from 0 to 1 and a higher value means a higher inequality between individuals or households. In order to calculate the Gini index, it is necessary to define the variable to which the inequality refers to (income, consumption, etc.), the part of population that it affects, the statistical unit (individuals/households) and the weighting scheme. The Gini indices are reported mainly by two sources. The first is the World Income Inequality Database (WIID2) - a result of collaboration between the UNDP and the UN University (World Institute for Development Economics Research), UNU-WIDER. Another source of the Gini indices is the database of the World Bank; the World Development Indicators. Although both databases are prepared by acknowledged institutions, there are some weaknesses that demand careful evaluation and great caution in the interpretation of the results of analyses carried out on the basis of data derived from those two sources.

The major shortcoming of the Gini index is that the index values are not calculated on the basis of uniform methodology: they refer to different definitions of the variable that measures inequality (e.g. income, consumption), population, and statistical unit. So in reality the databases contain a mix of different Gini indices that are not fully comparable in an international context and even within a given country. For example, in some cases the index value covers the whole country and sometimes only the capital or major cities.

---

10 In this sense, the Gini index reflects the quantitative theory of relative deprivation but it is also a statistical measure of volatility. In contrast to the variance, which is based on the square of the difference between the two observations, the Gini index is defined on the basis of the absolute differences.

Similarly, the definitions of income used in the index calculation are heterogeneous: total income, disposable income, consumption, expenditure, etc. In addition, data differs with regards to the population (for example, the whole population, only employees, households of a certain size, only people over 15 years of age etc.) or comparative scale. All those differences make the observations for different years, even for a given country, hardly comparable.

Of course, the application of a uniform definition for calculation of indices would reduce drastically the number of available observations and thus would have a negative impact on the quality of empirical results. On the other hand, the use of the full database may result in misleading conclusions and thus the outcomes of the econometric analysis should be interpreted with great caution.[11]

For the analyses presented in the following chapters, we used the widest possible definition of the Gini coefficient in order to get the largest possible number of observations. We have to note that despite the acceptance of different index definitions, many values of Gini indices are still missing, which also weaken the quality of the empirical results. The data coverage for all countries and for the years 1980-2009 only slightly exceeds 10 percent. Bearing this in mind, below we describe the data on the Gini index that was used in our empirical analysis.

During the 1990s, the Gini index levels have increased in the majority of the countries that underwent the transformation (Figure 2.5). This upward trend represents a polarisation of incomes. Income disparities were reduced only in the case of three countries: the Russian Federation, Kazakhstan and Slovenia. Despite this change, the level of income inequalities in the case of Russia remains among the highest in the region.

In addition to the regional cross country-analysis, we compare income inequalities within regions. In the next section we present the data for the following regions: Central Europe (the Czech Republic, Croatia, Poland, Romania, Slovakia, Slovenia, and Hungary), Eastern Europe (Belarus, Moldova, Russia, and Ukraine), South-Eastern Europe (Albania, Bulgaria, Bosnia and

---

11 The problems with the quality of the Gini indices can be illustrated in the example of Azerbaijan. The lowest index value for this country was reported for 2005 and equalled to 0.1683. This is somewhat surprising, considering the fact that this value is several times lower than the indications for developed countries, characterized by a relatively low level of the Gini index. But it raises additional concerns when it is contrasted with the values for Azerbaijan for other years. In 1995, the Gini index was 0.3496, in 2001 it rose to 0.365, then declined in 2005 to 0.1683, and then almost doubled to 0.3371 in 2008. This simple example shows that the use of the Gini index in empirical studies even for a single country and certainly in an international context could be problematic.

Herzegovina, and Macedonia), Central Asia (Kazakhstan, Kyrgyzstan, Tajikistan, Turkmenistan, and Uzbekistan) and Transcaucasia (Armenia, Azerbaijan, and Georgia). We present income disparities in those countries in comparison to Polish Gini indices.

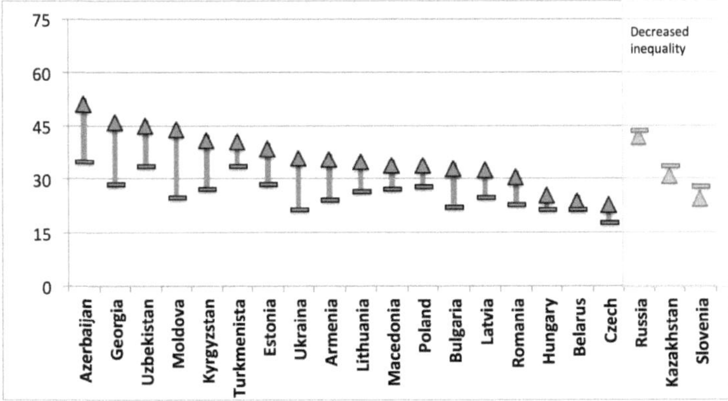

Fig. 2.5: *Gini index - a comparison for 1990 and 2000 in countries of Central, Eastern and Southern Europe and former Soviet Republics; source: ILO (2008), page 11; note: the dash denotes the value of the Gini index in 1990, the arrow - in 2000*

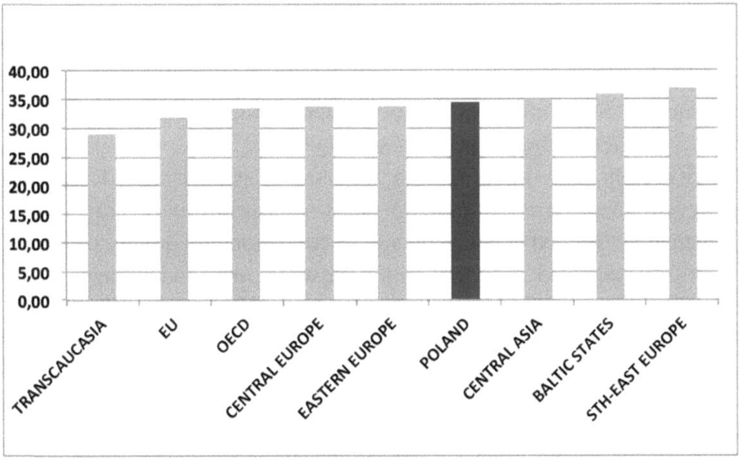

Fig. 2.6: *Average Gini index in selected regions and Poland, 2000-2008; source: own calculations based on WDI data*

We use the regional and Polish average levels of the Gini index calculated for years 2000-2008 (Figure 2.6). As already discussed, the Gini index varies from 0 to 1 (or zero to 100 percent). A higher Gini index value indicates a greater inequality of income and consumption among individuals or households in a given country or a group of countries.

It may be noted that the average Gini indices are greater than 25 percent and do not exceed 40 percent. In the case of Poland, the index is relatively high and equals to 34.45%. This value is close to the average level for other OECD countries and the Central European and Eastern European countries. The Baltic states are characterized by a slightly higher level on the Gini index (36.03%). The highest income inequalities were observed in South-Eastern Europe (Albania, Croatia, and Moldova) with the average Gini index equal to 37.06%.

The lowest average value and thus the smallest income inequalities can be observed in the Transcaucasian countries (Armenia, Azerbaijan, and Georgia), for which the average Gini index equals to 28.95 percent. However, as discussed in the section on the quality of the Gini index, it might be biased by an unreliable level reported by Azerbaijan – only 16.8% in 2005.

2.3.2 Gender – related measures of inequality

Many studies demonstrate that gender discrimination can significantly limit access to education, job opportunities, health care etc. In this section, we discuss three basic indicators of gender development: the Gender-related Development Index (GDI, social discrimination based on gender), an index of economic and political equality for women, the Gender Empowerment Measure (GEM) and its successor – the Gender Inequality Index (GII).

The first indicator, the GDI, is a measure of gender-related inequality in human development. It is a synthetic index measuring the average change in three dimensions: life expectancy, access to education and quality of life, but all sub-indices are adjusted for inequalities between men and women. It can be pointed out that the GDI is basically the HDI, adjusted for gender discrimination. The GDI takes values from 0 to 1. A higher value of the indicator reflects a lower inequality between the sexes. The levels of the GDI are very close to the value of the HDI for a given country and the correlation between these two indices exceeds 0.99.[12] This is the reason why both indices should not be used as explanatory variables in the same regression.

12 Own calculations for 2006.

The GDI calculation is similar to the HDI with the partial indices calculated separately for men and women. This method of aggregation leads to a situation where the existence of unequal treatment based on gender decreases the value of the sub-indices. The aggregate value of the GD index is calculated as the average of the three dimension indices, adjusted for gender inequality. Thus, the presence of differences in gender discrimination results in the lower value of the GDI than the HDI value for a given country. This pattern is observed for all the countries included in the sample.

It should be noted, however, that in principle, the GD index is not a measure of gender inequality in the strict sense. As mentioned, this is just the HDI adjusted for differences between the values of partial indices, calculated separately for the two sexes. And since the difference between the HDI and GDI values is low, it can create an incorrect impression that there is little difference in the human development of women and men.

Several other weaknesses of the GDI have been pointed out.[13] The Income sub-index, adjusted for gender, ignores the disparities between the sexes in quality of food, quality of housing and quality of clothing (Klasen, 2006). Additionally, the construction of this index does not reflect the inequalities within a household. For example, the income index can create a false impression that the unpaid work, which in many communities is the domain of women, does not contribute to human development. Due to the fact that accurate data on income levels classified by gender are not available, the index is based on the estimated relationship between wages for women and men in the non-agricultural sector, which also does not reflect precisely the measure of income disparity between the sexes.

The last remark refers to life expectancy. Statistically, women tend to live longer, which is biologically determined. It is not clear whether this should be regarded as a manifestation of gender inequality, or should be treated as an acceptable difference. In addition, the share of women in the population can be modified by the artificial control of the population structure by the abortion of female foetuses or the negligence shown to female babies in some cultures.

The GDI variable has a right-skewed distribution: the average value of the index for the whole sample in 2007 was 0.732, while the median was 0.77. The lowest value of the index was 0.308 (for Niger) and the highest was 0.966 (for Australia).

The GDI was introduced in 1995. In the same edition of the HDR, the authors introduced another indicator that measures directly gender equality – the

13 HDR (2006), p. 16.

Gender Empowerment Measure (GEM). This index has been used by us in Chapter 3, as it relates to economic and social discrimination against women, which can have a potential impact on the production and export of individual countries.

The GEM measures the inequality of gender in three dimensions: economic participation and decision-making, political participation and power over economic resources. Political participation is measured by the percentage of seats held by women in national parliaments. Economic participation and decision-making is measured by the percentage shares of women and men among legislators, senior officials and managers. The last dimension is based on the estimated income earned by women and men (in PPP US dollars).

Similarly to other indices, GEM is normalized to 1. A higher value in the GEM is associated with a higher participation of women in economic and political life, which can be treated as a lower level of discrimination of women. The values of the GEM are highly differentiated amongst countries. The lowest value in 2007 was found for Yemen (0.135) and the highest for Sweden (0.909).

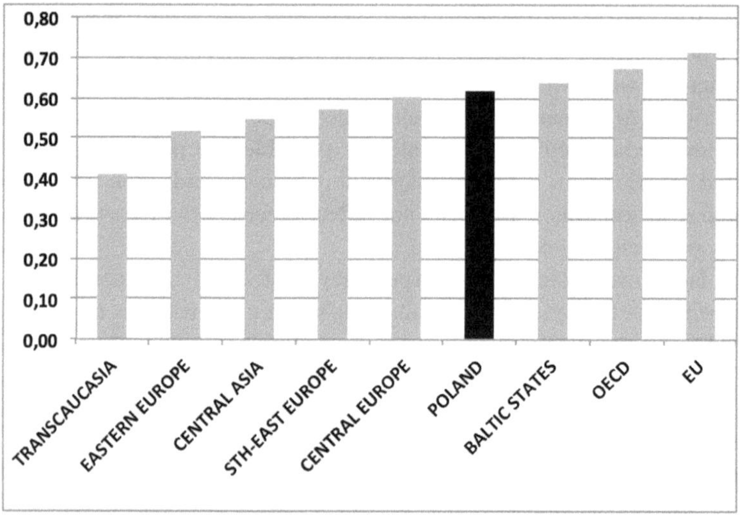

Fig. 2.7: Average rate of economic and political equality of women (GEM) in selected regions and groups of countries, and in Poland, 2000-2008; source: own calculations based on UNDP data

The income index that measures the income inequality is the weakest point of the GEM. Firstly, the value of this GDI component is calculated based on the earned income that excludes the value of housekeeping. Secondly, the aggregated GEM depends heavily on the income index, and can show a misleadingly low value for a country with a high level of gender equality, but at the same time a low level of income. Therefore, the weaknesses of the income index may distort the aggregated GDI.

Another drawback of the GEM is the limited data coverage. For example, the 2003 data covered 70 countries and for the next year the number of observations raised to 78 countries. Later on, this number increased gradually up to 110 observations in 2007. The use of this indicator in the empirical studies can therefore significantly reduce the size of the sample and thus affect the quality of the estimated parameters.

The following charts (Figures 2.8-2.11) show levels of the GEM index components. In terms of access to legislative power, the highest percentage of women in parliament is reported for the EU and OECD countries (23-24%), while in the group of transition countries, this index does not exceed 20 percent (Figure 2.8).

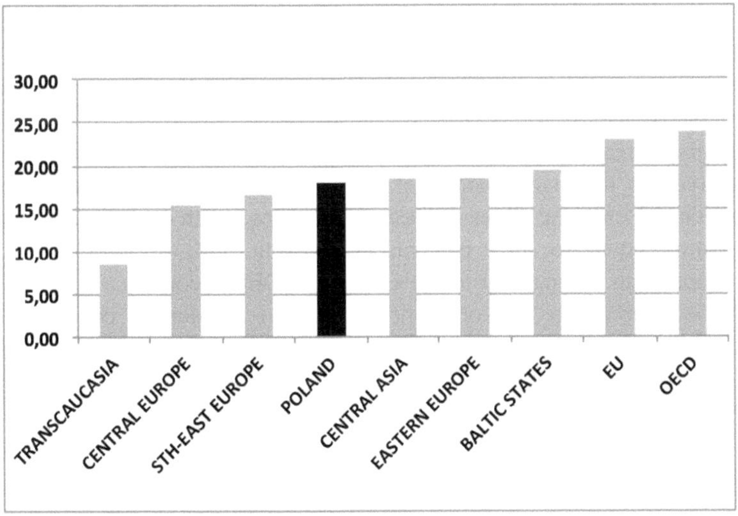

Fig. 2.8: Average share of women in parliament seats in selected regions and groups of countries, and in Poland, 2000-2008; source: own calculations based on UNDP data

Women in the Baltic states participate quite intensively in parliament activities (19.5 percent). In Eastern European and Central Asian countries about 18.5 percent of parliamentary seats were taken by women. Poland, where the relevant rate equals to 18 percent of all seats, grants wider access for women to parliament in comparison to the average 15.37 percent, for the whole of Central Europe. Female discrimination is highest in the case of the Transcaucasian countries, only 8 percent of the parliamentary seats are taken by women. In general, female participation in parliament in the CEECs is slightly lower in comparison to the OECD developed countries with the exception of the Transcaucasian countries, where low values probably reflect culture differences.

The second sub-index of the GEM is access for women to executive and managerial positions (Figure 2.9). The highest index levels were observed in Eastern Europe, where the index reached 38.7 percent, and in Baltic states (38.3 percent).

It also seems that women's access to leadership positions in Poland has been relatively high (35 percent), especially in comparison to the other CEE countries such as the Czech Republic (29 percent) or Slovakia (28 percent). On average, women have held 31.3 percent of high-level positions across the European Union, and this result is close to the average rate in Central and Southern Europe, as well as in the OECD countries. The lowest percentage of women in executive and managerial positions was observed in the case of the Transcaucasian countries (24.3%), which again might be the consequence of cultural differences.

A very different picture emerges when we view gender equality from the perspective of the participation of women in professional and technical occupations. Here, the Transcaucasian countries, with an average rate of participation equal to 59.3 percent, demonstrate a lower level of gender discrimination in comparison to the EU or the OECD countries (Figure 2.10). The highest percentage of women holding expert positions is observed in the Baltic states (67.7 percent, reaching even 71 percent in the case of Lithuania), while the lowest values are observed in the European Union, where the average equals 53.7 percent.

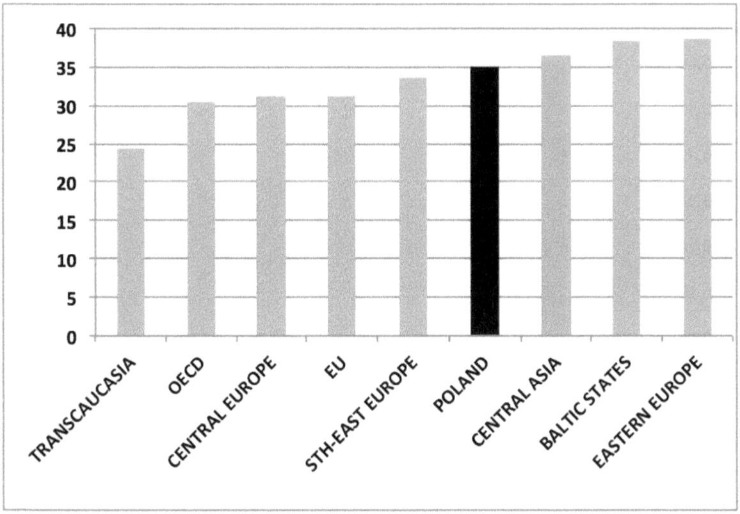

Fig. 2.9: *Average share of women in the executive posts in selected regions and groups of countries, and in Poland, 2000-2008; source: own calculations based on UNDP data*

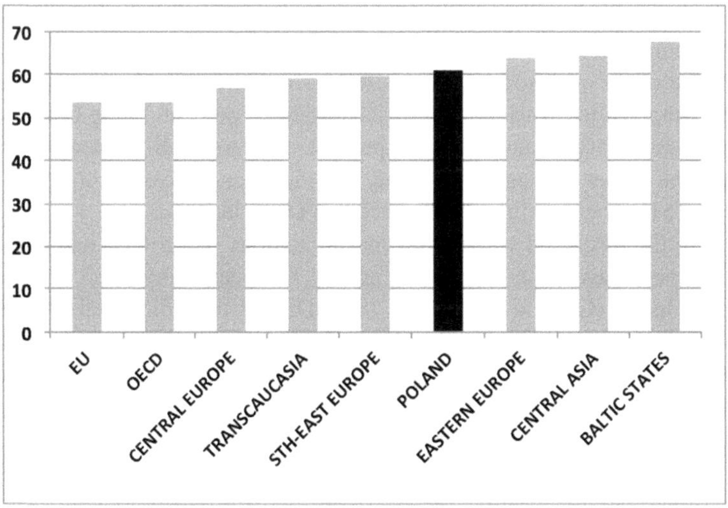

Fig, 2.10: *Average share of women holding professional and technical positions in selected regions and groups of countries, and in Poland, 2000-2008; source: own calculations based on UNDP data*

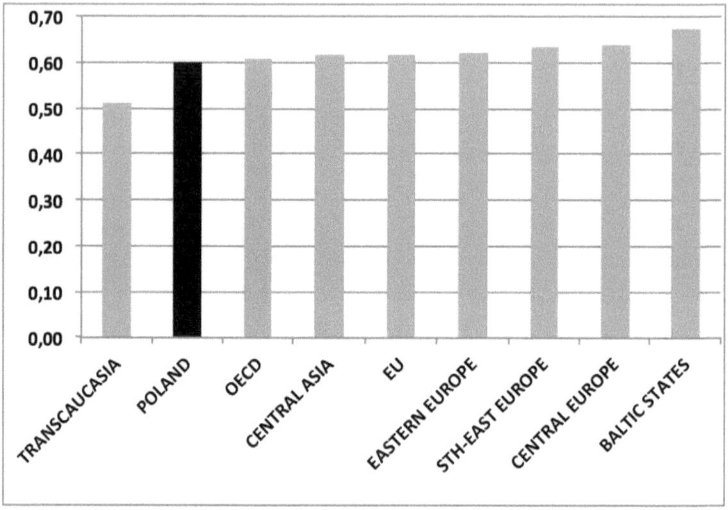

Fig. 2.11: *Average share of women's income as compared to men's income in selected regions and groups of countries, and in Poland, 2000-2008; source: own calculations based on UNDP data*

The last GEM component relates to gender income inequalities (see Fig. 2.11). In case of the analysed countries and regions the ratio between men and women incomes does not exceed 70 percent.

In most of the analysed regions, as well as in Poland, the average income of women compared to men's income stays close to 60 percent. In the Baltic states, the percentage is higher and equals 67 percent. The largest differences in income between the sexes are again reported for the Transcaucasia countries – an average of 51 percent, with only 33 percent in Georgia.

Due to the discussed weaknesses and limitations of the GDI and the GEM indices, a new measure of gender inequality has been introduced; the Gender Inequality Index (GII). In contrast to the GDI and the GEM indices, the GII shows that income is not the only aspect that matters for inequality and social exclusion. As noted, discrimination may limit women's freedom in many dimensions: education, employment, careers or access to medical care. The significance of these restrictions on human development is measured by the GII.

The GII measures the negative effects of discrimination in three dimensions: women's reproductive health, empowerment and the labour market. The GII value should be interpreted as the loss in human development resulting from the existence of inequality between the sexes in all dimensions. The index ranges from 0 (where women and men are equal) to 1 (where women experience inequality in all dimensions). For example, the average value of the index for the entire sample of countries is 0.492, which means that the difference between the achieved and possible to obtain level of human development is 49.2 percent. The GII reaches 31 percent for Europe and 61 percent for sub-Saharan Africa. Sweden reported the lowest value in the index (4.9 percent) and the highest was reported for Yemen (76.9 percent). The data shows that women's reproductive health has the strongest impact on the aggregated index value.

The average values of GII for different groups of countries, calculated for the period 2000-2008, are presented in Figure 2.12.

The GII data was not available in the case of Turkmenistan, Uzbekistan, Belarus, Bosnia and Herzegovina and Macedonia. The lowest levels of gender discrimation were observed in the European Union, the OECD countries and in Poland. In these regions and countries, the average GII level was close to 0.3 from 2000-2008. The most substantial discrimination on the grounds of gender was recorded in the countries of Transcaucasia as well as in Central Asia. The GII in those regions exceeded 0.5 and in the case of the South-Eastern Europe countries, the index equalled 0.48.

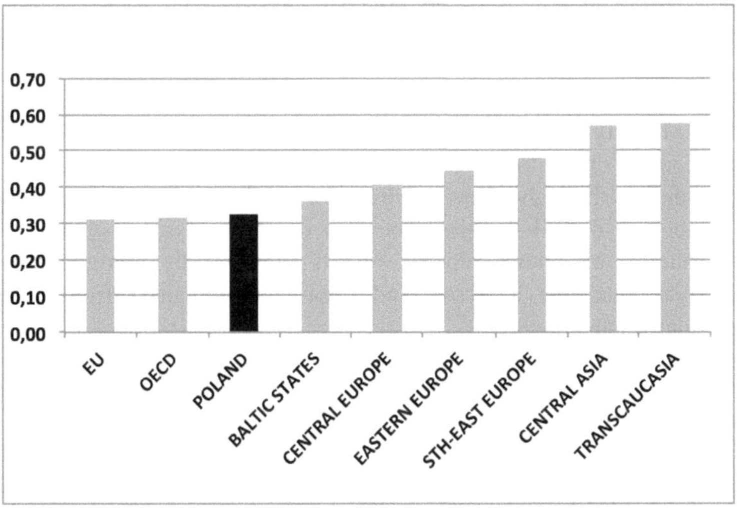

Fig, 2.12: Average index of inequality based on gender (GII) in selected groups of countries, and in Poland, 2000-2008; source: own calculations based on UNDP data

Comparing GII values to the previously discussed GEM results, the European Union and the the OECD countries are characterized by relatively low levels of gender discrimination, while in the post-Soviet Caucasus countries, the discrimination is much higher. Meanwhile, the countries of Central Europe and the Baltic states exhibit a relatively low level of discrimination based on gender.

2.3.3 Political rights and civil liberties indices

Countries in Central and Eastern Europe have undergone deep political and economic transformation after the collapse of the Soviet Union. The increased level of political and civil liberties in these countries had a positive impact on their economic development. An acknowledged measure of political freedom was introduced and reported by Freedom House. This survey provides annual evaluations of the state of freedom in all countries. Political rights allow for free participation in the political process, including the right to vote freely in legitimate elections, to join political parties and organizations, and to compete for public office. It seems that the most important is the right to vote for representatives who will have an effective influence on social policy and economic development. Civil liberties, in turn, protect individuals against excessive interference from the state in their private lives. Among the civil liberties being assessed, there is the freedom of expression and belief, personal autonomy, property rights and secrecy of correspondence.

Each country or territory is assigned a numerical rating on a scale of 1 to 7, where 1 indicates the highest level of freedom and 7 - the lowest one. A similar rating is applied to civil liberties. The data for the analysis is obtained from various sources, e.g. news reports, reports prepared by non-governmental organizations, academic analyses, and information obtained from visits to various countries and regions.

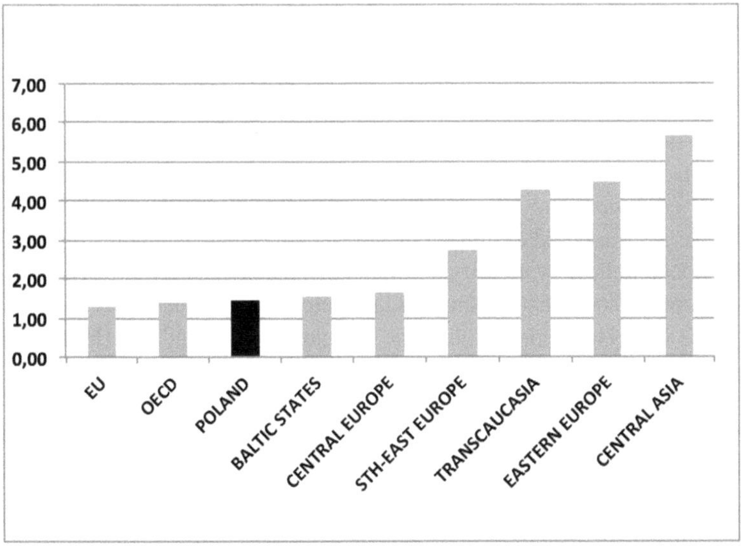

Fig. 2.13: *Average freedom index in selected regions, groups of countries, and in Poland, 2000-2008; source: own calculations based on the Freedom House Political Rights, 2009; notes: ranking from 1 to 7, where 1 indicates "most free" and 7 means "least free", from the point of view of civil liberties in a given country or region*

The average values of freedom indices, calculated for 2000-2008, are presented in Figure 2.13. The countries considered to be free, from the civil liberties point of view, are the Central European countries and the Baltic states. The values of the index vary from 1.44 (Poland) to 1.67 (average for the Baltic states) and are slightly above the average for the "most civilly and politically free" regions like the European Union (1.29) and the OECD (1.39). In the case of South-Eastern Europe, the index reaches 2.72 and that region is classified as "partly free". Less free, in terms of civil liberties, are the Transcaucasian and Eastern European countries, with the average indices reaching 4.26 and 4.50 respectively. In our sample, Central Asian countries revealed the lowest levels of civil liberties, and the average value of those countries is equal to 5.64.

2.3.4 Other indices used in analyses of human development

One of the phenomena that might have a significant negative influence on human and social development is poverty. Poverty does not only refer to income. It also reflects a lack of opportunities and possibilities, even at a basic level, including access to education and the health care system. From the economic policy perspective, such a broad definition of poverty is crucial, as it helps the design of a proper social policy, by identifying the factors that contribute to poverty.

Measures of social exclusion, that take into account other aspects of poverty, are indices of social deprivation – the Human Poverty Indices (HPI). The HP indicators have been published since 1997. In contrast to the HDI, which takes into account the level of income, the HPI rather focus on other aspects of poverty: lower life expectancy, lower quality of education or limited access to public and private goods. These measures show the position of disadvantaged people or people deprived of public rights within a society. There are two separate indices for developing countries (HPI-1) and for developed countries (HPI-2). In both cases, poverty is measured in three dimensions:

- The length and quality of life - the risk of dying at a relatively young age: measured by the calculated probability at birth that death occurs before the age of 40 (HPI-1), or 60 (HPI-2).
- Knowledge - exclusion due to illiteracy or lack of communication skills, as measured by the adult illiteracy rate (HPI-1), or as a percentage of adults (aged 16-65) within the limits of writing and reading (HPI-2).
- A decent standard of living - measured as the percentage of people living below the poverty line, or in the case of HPI-1, as lack of access to adequate economic provisioning. This dimension is measured in the HPI-1 as the average of two indicators: the percentage of the population not using an improved water source and the percentage of children underweight for their age. The HPI-2 includes an additional area of social exclusion measured by the long-term unemployment rate (the percentage of the labour force that has been unemployed for at least 12 months).

An important advantage of these indicators is that they complement the definition of poverty that was largely monetary. However, some significant weaknesses and limitations of the two indexes should also be pointed out.

A major limitation of the HPI that is associated with the construction of the index is the adoption of arbitrary and different targets for different groups of countries. In the case of life expectancy, the introduction of two age limits suggests that increased mortality between 40 and 60 years is acceptable in developing countries, whereas for the developed countries that would be treated as a serious deprivation to a long and healthy life.[14] Unintentionally, this has introduced a value judgment into the index of what is understood to be a "decent" life for a given country. Similarly, the introduction of different measures of the second dimension, i.e. knowledge, gives the impression that in the case of developed countries, the problem of illiteracy does not exist and social exclusion is the result of a low level of communication skills. On the other hand, in the case of developing countries, functionally illiterate adults are not considered deprived if they can read and write at a very low level.

The third weakness is that the index is not weighted by the percentage of the population actually affected by poverty. While analysing the potential level of social deprivation, this indicator does not reflect the differences between the countries where this problem affects a relatively small number of people and the countries where this is a problem involving a large part of the society.

There are several drawbacks restricting the possibility of the effective use of the HPI in empirical research. Firstly, the HPI-2 index is based on data with a very low frequency. Secondly, this data has a low variance and tends to vary relatively little amongst countries, so the index may have poor explanatory power. Thirdly, because of differences in definitions, indices should be applied separately for developing countries and developed countries, making it impossible to obtain general, cross-country conclusions.

Since 2010, the HP indices were replaced by the broader measure of the multidimensional poverty index (Multinational Poverty Index, MPI). This index, like the HPI, identifies poverty in a much broader sense than just a monetary one. Poverty is measured at a household level in three dimensions: health care, education and standard of living. In contrast to the HPI, the MPI reflects how many people experience deprivation and measures the intensity of the poverty. Importantly, the index can be split down into components that can be used to show the differences in social exclusion levels for different social groups, regions, etc.

The MPI consists of 10 variables categorized into three dimensions. First, health and medical care are measured by two indicators: malnutrition and infant mortality. Specifically, for each household, it is reported if at least one member of the household suffers from malnutrition or at least one child died (those are dummy variables). In the case of education, it is reported if at least one member of the household completed five classes and if there is at least one child of school age in the household who does not attend school. The last dimension, a

---

14 HDI (2008), p. 5.

decent standard of living, includes: access to electricity, drinking water, sanitation, housing and the lack of a car with the possession of another good: bicycle, motorcycle, radio, refrigerator, telephone and TV. It is assumed that households with index values higher than 33.3 percent are treated as affected by poverty.

The MPI had the highest value for Niger in 2006 (0.64) and lowest for the United Arab Emirates in 2003 (0.002). The major weakness of the MPI dataset is that there is only one observation per country included in the database and the observations are reported for different years. Hence the possibility of using the multidimensional poverty index as an explanatory variable in empirical research is very limited so far.

In planning our research, we wanted to analyse the impact of poverty on trade and FDI. It appeared, however, that due to the incomparability of the HPI-1 and HPI-2 indices, an estimation carried out for all countries was impossible. On the other hand, there are so few observations for the MPI that it is impossible to obtain statistically reliable results. Despite those constraints, we decided to present a complete description of the indicators of human development even if they cannot be directly used in our analysis.

As mentioned, there are indicators that can be used as measures of various aspects of social and human development. However, the data availability is frequently limited. In particular, the composite indices are sometimes based on unavailable data at a household level.

2.4 Summary

In Chapter 1, we showed that human and social development can be defined in many ways. Similarly, there are a number of indicators measuring various aspects of human development. In this chapter, we discussed some of them, including the most well-known indices presented in the Human Development Report. We focused our attention on the most important aggregated indicator, the HDI. Furthermore, we presented indices that measure income inequality and gender-related discrimination: the Gini index, the GDI, the GEM and the GII. We discussed the indicators that highlight other aspects of human development, such as poverty (the HP index), civil liberties and political rights (the Freedom Index). We supplemented the presentation of indices by drafting a picture of the socio-economic situation in the countries of Central and Eastern Europe. In the next chapters, we will analyze the impact of human development on international trade and foreign direct investment, using the above discussed indices.

The analysis carried out for the CEE countries during the period 1980-2010 shows that the level of human development, both in terms of income and education, and quality of life, is gradually increasing. We have also observed a fairly significant temporary drop in the human development of the CEE countries during the early period of political and economic transformation. The negative impact of transformation was reflected, in particular, in the periodic decline of the income and education indices, especially in the case of the former Soviet republics and the countries of Southern Europe.

We also pointed out some similarities between Poland and other EU countries in the period 2000-2008. Firstly, all the above mentioned countries report similar levels of income inequality measured by the Gini index, which is about 35 percent on average. Secondly, the level of political rights and civil liberties was also close to the EU and the OECD average, placing Poland amongst the "freest" countries. The third dimension of comparison referred to social and gender-related inequalities. We compared the aggregate GII and GEM indices, as well as the average participation of women in parliament, high-level positions, and professional positions, and by analyzing men and women's incomes. While the overall level of inequality in Poland measured by the GII is close to the value of the European Union and the OECD countries (average 30 percent), the proportion of women in parliament, which can be treated as the measure of real involvement of women in political and economic life, was lower by 5 percentage points (on average). The Baltic states, Central Asia and Eastern Europe have indices quite similar to the reference countries. On the other hand, the access to management positions and job opportunities for women in the CEE countries is better in comparison to the average for the EU and the OECD countries. For all analyzed countries, gender-related income inequality was noticeable, as women's earnings generally do not exceed 70% of the average men's earnings.

The data presented clearly shows increasing human and social development in the CEE countries. Those countries experienced the economic slowdown associated with the political reforms and transition from the centrally planned to the market economies in the early 1990s. During the next decades, they managed to rapidly restore previous levels of human development and recorded further significant improvement in human and social development, and in reducing gender discrimination.

At the same time, the CEECs liberalized their trade policies, promoted integration and recorded a rapid expansion of international trade and inflow of FDIs. Those two elements, reflecting the growing internationalization of their economies, contributed to economic growth in the CEECs. In the next chapters, we will verify whether growing human and social development could also contribute to the expansion of international trade and foreign capital inflow to the CEE countries.

The possibilities of using the above described indices in empirical research are frequently restricted by the incompleteness of the data. Missing data was reported for both periods and countries included in the databases. Thus, in some cases, the number of observations can dramatically decrease for certain indicators, such as the Gini index.

We are aware of serious limitations in conducting the empirical research based on the human development indicators. Firstly, in principle, all aggregated indicators contain a component that refers to the per capita income level: i.e. the average for the whole society. The aggregate index value can thus be heavily biased by the income level, which also means that the two explanatory variables, i.e. HDI and GDP per capita, cannot be used in the same regression.

Secondly, the construction of composite indicators requires a set of data that is missing for some countries and periods. What's more, in many cases, the quality of information is questionable, which may impair the quality of the composite index. That is why we recommend caution while comparing various indices between countries, and even between years for a given country. We believe that despite those shortcomings, the human development indices can be used in empirical testing and are useful in formulating more general conclusions, based on statistical and econometric analyses.

3 Human development and aggregate exports: A country level analysis

Andrzej Cieślik, Jan Jakub Michałek, Jerzy Mycielski

3.1 Introduction

In this chapter, we investigate the relationship between human development and international trade flows. The role of human capital has been stressed by both the traditional and the new trade theory. The traditional Ricardian trade theory predicts that differences in technology at a country level create the basis for international comparative advantage and affect trade flows. Similarly, the role of labour productivity is stressed by the latest strand of the new trade theory initiated by Melitz (2003) that focuses on firm heterogeneity and shows that export decisions are based on labour productivity at a firm level. However, both traditional and new trade theories treat labour productivity both at a country and at a firm level, as an exogenous variable. However, in our view, labour productivity may depend on the stock of human and social capital. Therefore, we can expect that a higher level of human development may be positively associated with the efficiency of human capital, and thus may positively affect firm productivity and wages, and therefore affect their decisions to export.

The main goal of this paper is to study the role of human development in increasing international trade using the theory consistent with the gravity model. The structure of this paper is as follows. In Section 2, we present the analytical framework and discuss data explanatory variables. In Section 3, we present estimation results. Section 4 summarizes and concludes with policy recommendations and directions for future studies.

3.2 Analytical Framework

Empirical gravity equations have been widely used to study a whole range of spatial interactions in economics for half a century. In particular, it has been most often applied to study the determinants of bilateral trade flows and to assess the impact of various forms of regional economic integration. The gravity equation in its most basic form postulates that the amount of trade between two countries increases in their sizes, as measured by their national incomes, and decreases in the cost of transport between them, as measured by the distance between their economic centers.[15]

Although the gravity equation in its basic form does a pretty good job at explaining bilateral trade with just the size of trading partners and distances between them, there is still a huge variation in trade that it is unable to explain. Therefore, in order to improve the performance of the gravity equation in empirical studies of bilateral trade flows, it has also been common to specify it in a more general form that also takes into account the impact of other factors that may affect trade. One of the most frequently used variables to augment the baseline gravity equation is per capita income.

The first formal justification for the inclusion of the per capita income variables was provided by Bergstrand (1989, 1990) who concentrated on the demand-side. He assumed complete specialization in production and in order to provide the theoretical justification for the use of per capita incomes in his estimating equations, he had to depart from the standard assumption of homothetic and identical preferences across countries. Instead, he assumed non-homothetic preferences in the manner of Markusen (1986). However, his approach was not very successful empirically. More recently, Cieślik (2009) demonstrated how the augmented gravity equation can be derived from a variety of models based on both neoclassical and monopolistic competition approaches that assume incomplete specialization in production and provided a supply-side justification for the inclusion of per capita income variables. According to him, income per capita variables proxy for the differences in relative factor endowments between trading partners.

Per capita incomes constitute an important component of the HDI and will be used as one of main explanatory variables in the disaggregated analysis of components of the HDI. In our specification, in addition to the standard gravity variables, we use arable land per capita as a measure of relative factor endowments. Moreover, we also control for changes in trade policy that occurred during the period covered by our sample that reflect multilateral as well as regional trade liberalization. Our estimating equation used to study the determinants of bilateral trade flows, specified in the logarithmic form, is as follows:

$$lnExports_{ijt}=\alpha_0+\alpha_1 rep\_lnGDP_{it}+\alpha_2 part\_lnGDP_{jt}+\alpha_3 rep\_lnGDP\_pc_{it}+$$

15 This relationship closely resembles Newton's (1687) law of universal gravitation which states that every particle in the universe attracts every other particle with a force that is proportional to the product of their masses and inversely proportional to the square of the distance between the particles.

$$+\alpha_4 part\_lnGDP\_pc_{jt}+\alpha_5 lnDistance_{ij}+\alpha_6 contig_{ij}+\alpha_7 EU_{ijt}+\alpha_8 col\_1945_{ij}+$$
$$+\alpha_9 GATT\text{-}WTO_{ijt}+\alpha_{10} OECD_{ijt}+\alpha_{11} comlang_{ij}+\alpha_{12} rep\_Land_{it}+$$
$$+\alpha_{13} part\_Land_{jt}+\alpha_{14} rep\_post\_comm+\alpha_{15} part\_post\_comm+$$
$$+\alpha_{16} europe\_agreement\_eu_{ijt}+\alpha_{17} eu\_europe\_agreement_{ijt}+\xi Z_{ijt}+c_{ij+}+\gamma_t+\varepsilon_{ijt}$$

where:

- $Exports_{ijt}$: bilateral exports between country i and j in period t depending on model specification; data expressed in current US dollars for exports and volume of trade (gross exports, gross trade) (WITS);
- rep_lnGDP_{it}: log of GDP in reporting country *i* in period *t* measured in current US dollars (WDI);
- $rep\_lnGDP\_pc_{it}$: log of GDP per capita proxying for the wage level in reporting country *i* in period *t* measured in current US dollars (WDI);
- $part\_lnGDP_{jt}$: log of GDP in partner country *j* in period *t* measured in current US dollars (WDI);
- $part\_lnGDP\_pc_{jt}$: log of GDP per capita proxying for the wage level in partner country *j* in period *t* measured in current US dollars (WDI);
- $Distance_{ij}$: geographic distance between principle cities measured using the great circle formula[16], proxy for trade costs (CEPII);
- $contig_{ijt}$: dummy variable that has an impact on trade cost and takes value 1 if there is a common border between countries *i* and *j* and 0 otherwise;
- rep_Land_{it}: log of arable land *per capita* in reporting country *i* in year *t* expressed in hectares per person;
- $part\_Land_{jt}$: log of arable land *per capita* in partner country *j* in year *t* expressed in hectares per person;
- EU_{ijt}: dummy variable that takes value 1 if both countries are members of the European Union in period *t* and 0 otherwise;
- $europe\_agreement\_eu_{ijt}$: dummy variable that takes value 1 if reporter (country *i*) is the member of the Europe Agreement and partner (country *j*) is a member of the European Union in period *t* and 0 otherwise;
- $eu\_europe\_agreement_{ijt}$: dummy variable that takes value 1 if reporter (country *i*) is the member of the European Union and partner (country *j*) is a member of the Europe Agreement in period *t* and 0 otherwise;
- col_1945_{ijt}: dummy variable that takes value 1 if there is a colonial link after 1945 between the reporting and partner countries in period *t* and 0 otherwise;

16 The great circle formula which uses longitudes and latitudes of the most important cities. See Head and Mayer (2002) for more details.

- *GATT-WTO*$_{ijt}$: dummy variable that takes value 1 if both countries are members of the WTO in period *t* and 0 otherwise;
- *OECD*$_{ijt}$: dummy variable that takes value 1 if both countries are members of the OECD in period *t* and 0 otherwise;
- *comlang*$_{ijt}$: measure of cultural compatibility that affects trade cost; dummy variable that takes value 1 if at least 9 percent of population in both countries shares a common language;
- Z_{ijt}: vector of human development variables that affect labour productivity and price indexes in country *i* and country *j* in period *t*. The detailed description of these variables is provided below;
- c_{ij}: individual country-pair specific effect that may be fixed or random depending on model specification;[17]
- γ_t: time specific effect;
- ε_{ijt}: error term.

We examine the role of aggregate human development indicators included in *Z* such as HDI and GEM as well as detailed measures reflecting various forms of human inequalities:

- *hdi*: Human Development Index, elaborated by UNDP (HDI);
- *incomex*: index of GNI per capita;
- *edux*: index of education;
- *lifex*: index of expected number of years at birth.
- *civil_liberties*: degree of civil rights, measured by the civil liberties index (Freedom House);
- *gem*: gender empowerment measure (HDI);
- *income*: estimated earned female income (female; HDI);
- *legis*: female legislators, senior officials and managers as a percentage of total (HDI);
- *prof*: female professional and technical workers as a percentage of total (HDI);
- *seats*: seats in parliament held by women as a percentage of total (HDI).

---

17 Our empirical specification includes an unobserved effect cij that can be often correlated with explanatory variables. In the case of the fixed effects estimator, some of the explanatory variables that do not change over time become the part of the fixed effect. In the case of the random effects estimator, the individual effect becomes the part of the joint error term that can be defined as: $v_{ijt} = c_{ij} + \varepsilon_{ijt}$.

We have taken logs of all the variables listed above before using them as explanatory variables. In particular, we try to verify a number of research hypotheses:

- a higher level in the Human Development Index (HDI) is positively associated with larger trade;
- a higher level of female participation in human and economic development, as proxied by the gender inequality measure: Gender Empowerment Measure (GEM), as well as the components that assess the level of political and economic participation of women, is positively associated with intensified trade;
- more civil freedom within a society, as measured by lower values in the index of civil liberties, should be positively associated with the development of trade;
- a higher value in the life expectancy index and lower rates of infant mortality (a proxy for the quality of the healthcare system and a reflection of the level of human development) should be associated with larger international trade;
- a higher level in the education index, measuring the average and expected years of schooling, is positively associated with higher levels of international trade.
- a lower level of income inequalities is positively associated with higher levels of international trade.

To verify those hypotheses we use two data samples: the panel covering all countries and years 1980-2010, and for the limited 2007-2008 period for which detailed measures reflecting various forms of social inequalities were available. In our study, we used the bilateral trade exports of all countries that were treated as reporters, with all other countries, that were treated as partners, excluding the smallest countries.[18] The complete description of the dataset and data sources used in our study is provided in below.

The data on social and human development was obtained from the last edition of the Human Development Indices (2008), prepared by the United Nations Development Programme. Data on civil rights was collected from the Freedom House database (www.freedomhouse.org).

In our analyses, we used a sample of over 150 countries (depending on the data availability). The smallest economies, with a population of less than 200 000 inhabitants, were excluded from the sample. In the panel analysis, we treated the OECD, MENA, and CEE countries as reporters, whereas we treated

18 The smallest economies with a population of less than 200 000 inhabitants were excluded from our sample.

as partners all other countries (including the aforementioned countries) that were in our sample. In the cross section analysis the sample covered all the countries with the exception of the smallest economies.

Macroeconomic data was obtained from the World Development Indicators (WDI) 2009 database published on CD-ROM by the World Bank in Washington. Trade data comes from the WITS (World Integrated Trade Solution) database, compiled jointly by the World Bank, WTO and UNCTAD. Data on distance comes from the CEPII (Centre d'Etudes Prospectives et d'Informations Internationales) database. Zero observations for trade flows are omitted in the WITS database. In order to avoid confusing omitted observations with the cases when trade was not reported to the WTO by the exporting country, the following procedure was used. If a given country in a given year reported export to any country then missing observations for trade flows between this country to other countries were set to zero. Otherwise, we decided that the country in question did not provide trade information to the WTO in a given year and in this case the observations are just missing. The same procedure was used in the case of imports.

In order to take into account zero trade observations, we estimated our equations using the procedure suggested by Silva and Tenreyro (2006) based on the Poisson model with fixed effects. The FE Poisson estimation procedure is based on a conditional maximum likelihood (ML) estimator suggested by the Hausman et al. (1984) paper. This allows us to verify the robustness of our previous results (Cieślik, Michałek and Mycielski, 2012) obtained using the standard panel data analysis where the FE estimator was the preferred estimation procedure. A well-known consequence of using the FE method is that all the variables that are time invariant in the sample used are omitted in our regressions.

In cases when the within (over time) variation was too small to utilize the FE model, we used the population averaged (PA) Poisson regression with the unstructured working matrix and general estimation equations (GEE) of Liang and Zeger (1986) to find the estimates of the parameters in the Poisson model. This estimation method exploits conditional expectation and variance, implied by the form of the Poisson model, to estimate parameters and can be interpreted as an analogue of the RE method used for linear models.

In our estimations, we always used the maximum number of observations available. An unfortunate consequence of this rule is that the higher the number of explanatory variables, the smaller the number of observations used in the regression, because missing values for additional variables are limiting the sample which can be used. In case of the PA Poisson regression, some observations were dropped from the sample because this estimation procedure cannot exploit observations for country-pair with only one non-missing observation.

As it is often suggested that the heteroskedasticity is present in trade data, we are using the Huber/White robust variance matrix in all estimations except for the ones in which we are using the Arellano-Bond estimator. To save space, the coefficient for time specific dummies and country specific dummies are omitted in the tables of regression results.

One of the most important problems in our analysis is the direction of the causality between trade flows and human development. The direction usually considered in the literature is from trade to human development. The standard argument is that as trade is mutually beneficial, it should increase social welfare and hence enable trading countries to follow social oriented policies. However, it is also possible that advances in human development are influencing a country's trading potential. Therefore, we can also expect that the advances in human development can cause increases in trade flows.

In order to test this hypothesis, we used the well-established concept of Granger (1969) causality. According to this approach, there is causality between human development and exports, if it is possible to better predict the changes in future exports with the use of past indices of human development rather without them. The null hypothesis is that human development is not a Granger cause of exports. Moreover, in addition to studying causality from human development to exports we also studied the traditional direction of causality from exports to human development as increasing exports may result in improved human conditions. To study two-way causality, we used a two-equation VAR system with one lag estimated using the Arellano-Bond (1991) estimator. For the years 1980-1999, the values of the HD index were published every 5 years. Since then, it has been published every year. In order to use a sample that extends over time for as long as possible, the VAR model was estimated using data for 5 years periods for the years 1980-2010, the lag included in the model is then a 5 year lag.

3.3 Estimation results

We will present two sets of estimation results. First, we will discuss the general results for the period 1980-2010 obtained using the Poisson model with fixed effects. Then, we will present estimation results obtained using the random effects estimator for the latest two years: 2007 and 2008, for which the data for the extended set of social indicators was available.

3.3.1 Results for the period 1980-2010

We start by estimating the benchmark gravity model for the whole world for exports using the Poisson model with fixed effects. Our specification for the estimating equation includes firstly the HDI as the most general variable measuring the level of human development, having controlled for the extended set of gravity variables: GDP and land per capita approximating the factor proportions in the trading countries. Moreover, we include trade policy variables such as membership in the OECD, EU, and GATT-WTO.

The benchmark estimation results for the whole sample of countries are presented in columns (1) in Table 3.1. In our results, the estimated parameters for reporters should be interpreted as accompanying characteristics of exporting countries, while the parameters for partners as accompanying characteristics of importing countries.

Table 3.1: Exports and the HDI and its components – results for 1980-2010 (standard errors in parentheses)

	All countries	CEE with all countries	CEE only	All countries	CEE with all countries	CEE only
Main	1	2	3	4	5	6
rep_lnGDP	0.581***	0.375***	-0.240**	0.433***	0.304**	-0.188
	(0.041)	(0.097)	(0.119)	(0.047)	(0.123)	(0.130)
part_lnGDP	0.664***	0.282***	0.048	0.612***	0.297***	0.081
	(0.035)	(0.092)	(0.131)	(0.038)	(0.107)	(0.144)
lrep_Land	0.020	-0.175	-0.310	-0.027	-0.234	-0.377*
	(0.068)	(0.250)	(0.255)	(0.069)	(0.242)	(0.219)
lpart_Land	0.016	0.207	-0.729**	-0.009	0.195	-0.740***
	(0.057)	(0.364)	(0.289)	(0.057)	(0.364)	(0.280)
OECD	0.191*	0.139***	-0.058	0.247**	0.126***	-0.131
	(0.105)	(0.047)	(0.103)	(0.115)	(0.046)	(0.110)
EU	0.165***	0.105***	0.143***	0.180***	0.101***	0.141***
	(0.033)	(0.040)	(0.055)	(0.034)	(0.039)	(0.054)
GATT-WTO	0.233***	-0.123***	-0.150***	0.164***	-0.127***	-0.107**
	(0.039)	(0.039)	(0.049)	(0.036)	(0.039)	(0.050)
europe_agreement_eu	-0.068*	0.096**	-0.101*	-0.077*	0.102**	-0.112**
	(0.041)	(0.047)	(0.059)	(0.039)	(0.046)	(0.052)
eu_europe_agreement	0.068**	-0.132***	0.090**	0.064*	-0.130***	0.060
	(0.034)	(0.040)	(0.042)	(0.033)	(0.040)	(0.040)

lrep_hdi	2.695***	2.210**	1.122			
	(0.457)	(1.041)	(1.372)			
lpart_hdi	1.323***	0.900	3.885**			
	(0.360)	(0.938)	(1.536)			
lrep_incomex				2.512***	1.695**	-0.054
				(0.346)	(0.788)	(0.853)
lrep_edux				0.592***	0.349	-0.281
				(0.214)	(0.763)	(0.812)
lrep_lifex				-1.551***	0.218	4.851
				(0.571)	(2.228)	(3.420)
lpart_incomex				1.172***	0.095	1.225
				(0.179)	(0.704)	(0.925)
lpart_edux				0.234	0.186	0.148
				(0.205)	(0.387)	(0.800)
lpart_lifex				-0.372	1.808	6.949**
				(0.288)	(1.368)	(2.861)
N	182931	29805	5093	182931	29805	5093
N_g	19025	3077	521	19025	3077	521

- *** denotes statistical significance at the 1% level,- ** denotes statistical significance at the 5% level, * denotes statistical significance at the 10% level.

The estimated parameter on our key variable of interest – the HDI displays the positive sign and is statistically significant at the 1 per cent level in the case of reporter (exporting) and partner (importing) countries. Thus, exports are positively associated with the level of human development. The standard gravity variables in most cases display the expected signs and are statistically significant. For example, the positive values of the estimated parameters on the GDP variables of both exporting and importing countries show that exports are bigger between larger countries. The positive values of the parameters on trade policy variables suggest that membership in the EU, OECD, and GATT-WTO promotes exports. Moreover, the Europe Agreements promoted old EU countries' exports to CEE countries, while they restricted the level of exports from the CEE to the EU countries. The land per capita variables were not statistically significant.

In columns (2) and (3), we present the estimation results obtained for the same set of variables but estimated for the smaller samples of countries, including CEE countries that trade with the rest of the world and among themselves, respectively. The results presented in column (2), obtained for exports of CEE countries to the rest of the world, show that the level of human development is statistically significant at the 5 per cent level only for the reporting country. Thus, the exports of CEE countries are positively associated with the level of human development. The results presented in column (3), obtained for exports of CEE countries among themselves, show that the level of human development is statistically significant at the 5 per cent level only for the partner country. The remaining trade theory and policy variables are, in the majority of cases, statistically significant, although in some cases they display unexpected signs.

In columns (4)-(6) we present the estimation results where we split the HDI into its constituent components. The results are like in columns (1)-(3), obtained for exports of all countries, exports of the CEE countries to the rest of the world and exports of the CEE countries amongst themselves, respectively. The results obtained for the whole world displayed in column (4) show that income indexes are statistically significant at the 1 per cent level for both reporter and partner countries. The education index, reflecting the average and expected years of schooling, is statistically significant at the 1 per cent level only for the reporting country. The life expectancy index is statistically significant at the 1 per cent only in the case of the reporting country and surprisingly displays a negative sign. In the case of the results obtained for the CEE exports to the rest of the world displayed in column (5), the income index for the reporting country is the only statistically significant variable at the 5 per cent level. While the results obtained for exports of the CEE countries amongst themselves reported in column (6) show that the only statistically significant variable is the life expectancy index for the partner country. The lower level of statistical significance in the case of regressions for the CEE trade with the world and amongst themselves might be due to the significantly smaller number of observations compared to the full sample.

To study the robustness of our estimation results, we repeated the analysis by adding an additional variable reflecting the level of civil liberties in reporting and partner countries. The estimation results are reported in Table 3.2. The particular columns of Table 3.2 are the direct counterparts of the columns in Table 3.1.

Table 3.2: Exports, the HDI and civil liberties – results for 1980-2010 (standard errors in parentheses)

	All countries	CEE with all countries	CEE only	All countries	CEE with all countries	CEE only
Main	1	2	3	4	5	6
rep_lnGDP	0.582***	0.362***	-0.252**	0.422***	0.278**	-0.228*
	(0.042)	(0.091)	(0.119)	(0.046)	(0.114)	(0.129)
part_lnGDP	0.662***	0.256***	0.019	0.603***	0.266**	0.056
	(0.036)	(0.095)	(0.129)	(0.038)	(0.111)	(0.144)

lrep_Land	0.013	-0.282	-0.314	-0.046	-0.330	-0.390*
	(0.069)	(0.251)	(0.241)	(0.071)	(0.246)	(0.219)
lpart_Land	0.006	0.120	-0.797***	-0.023	0.108	-0.803***
	(0.057)	(0.378)	(0.289)	(0.056)	(0.375)	(0.279)
OECD	0.186*	0.173***	-0.010	0.235**	0.157***	-0.082
	(0.105)	(0.050)	(0.092)	(0.113)	(0.048)	(0.104)
EU	0.164***	0.139***	0.093	0.161***	0.135***	0.080
	(0.037)	(0.046)	(0.069)	(0.037)	(0.046)	(0.067)
GATT-WTO	0.233***	-0.103***	-0.155***	0.162***	-0.114***	-0.118**
	(0.040)	(0.038)	(0.043)	(0.036)	(0.039)	(0.046)
europe_agreement_eu	-0.110***	0.073	-0.072	-0.115***	0.081	-0.081
	(0.038)	(0.054)	(0.067)	(0.037)	(0.054)	(0.066)
eu_europe_agreement	0.041	-0.155***	0.055	0.030	-0.149***	0.036
	(0.034)	(0.054)	(0.043)	(0.032)	(0.054)	(0.045)
rep_civil_liberties	-0.005	0.083**	0.014	-0.037**	0.094***	0.012
	(0.016)	(0.036)	(0.037)	(0.015)	(0.034)	(0.037)
part_civil_liberties	-0.002	0.001	-0.053	-0.013	-0.000	-0.047
	(0.012)	(0.037)	(0.035)	(0.012)	(0.036)	(0.032)
lrep_hdi	2.687***	2.756***	0.307			
	(0.459)	(1.065)	(1.413)			
lpart_hdi	1.331***	1.029	4.395***			
	(0.359)	(1.004)	(1.575)			
lrep_incomex				2.546***	1.866**	0.216
				(0.343)	(0.773)	(0.901)
lrep_edux				0.581***	0.722	-1.016
				(0.216)	(0.799)	(0.707)
lrep_lifex				-1.773***	-0.404	4.362
				(0.583)	(2.257)	(3.378)
lpart_incomex				1.207***	0.197	1.346
				(0.177)	(0.749)	(0.941)
lpart_edux				0.223	0.255	0.339
				(0.202)	(0.409)	(0.910)
lpart_lifex				-0.413	1.442	6.341**
				(0.283)	(1.442)	(3.028)
N	179781	27822	4598	179781	27822	4598
N_g	18736	2899	476	18736	2899	476

- *** denotes statistical significance at the 1% level,- ** denotes statistical significance at the 5% level, * denotes statistical significance at the 10% level.

The estimated parameter on the civil liberties variable in the reporting country was not always statistically significant and its sign was not always in line with expectations. The expected negative sign meaning that a higher level of civil liberties is associated with bigger exports was reported only in the case of the full sample with the decomposed HDI. The unexpected positive sign on the civil liberties variable was reported in the case of CEE countries exporting to the rest of the world. The estimated parameter on the civil liberties variable in the partner country was never statistically significant. The addition of the civil liberties variables did not change, however, our previous conclusions concerning the role of the HDI and its components. Moreover, in almost all cases, the estimated parameters on the standard gravity variables were not affected.

The role of income inequalities for international trade flows is analyzed in Table 3.3. Here, in addition to the HDI and civil liberties, we also included the Gini index as an additional explanatory variable.

Table 3.3: Gini and exports – results for 1980-2010 (standard errors in parentheses)

	All countries	CEE with all countries	CEE only	All countries	CEE with all countries	CEE only
Main	1	2	3	4	5	6
rep_lnGDP	0.014	-0.153	-0.207	-0.016	0.092	0.052
	(0.136)	(0.273)	(0.299)	(0.152)	(0.279)	(0.293)
part_lnGDP	0.721***	0.463**	0.319	0.637***	0.419**	0.259
	(0.150)	(0.189)	(0.248)	(0.153)	(0.206)	(0.255)
lrep_Land	-0.460	-0.535	-0.532	-0.404	-0.278	-0.291
	(0.284)	(0.384)	(0.410)	(0.277)	(0.320)	(0.340)
lpart_Land	-0.212	-1.507**	-1.473**	-0.259	-1.648**	-1.686**
	(0.468)	(0.626)	(0.675)	(0.482)	(0.728)	(0.776)
OECD						
EU	0.256	0.034	-0.003	0.038	-0.114	-0.157
	(0.159)	(0.133)	(0.132)	(0.194)	(0.166)	(0.169)
GATT-WTO	0.162*	-0.099	-0.077	0.163**	-0.058	-0.042
	(0.088)	(0.113)	(0.120)	(0.080)	(0.093)	(0.096)

europe_agreement_eu	-0.238	-0.126	-0.108	-1.484***	-0.686***	0.067
	(0.204)	(0.127)	(0.128)	(0.260)	(0.219)	(0.149)
eu_europe_agreement	0.114	0.117*	0.060	1.526***	0.786***	
	(0.127)	(0.065)	(0.076)	(0.158)	(0.172)	
rep_civil_liberties				-0.012	0.010	-0.008
				(0.065)	(0.072)	(0.076)
part_civil_liberties				-0.053	0.033	0.021
				(0.056)	(0.050)	(0.053)
rep_gini	0.013	-0.005	-0.003	0.016	0.006	0.010
	(0.011)	(0.009)	(0.009)	(0.010)	(0.008)	(0.008)
part_gini	-0.018*	-0.027***	-0.024***	-0.017*	-0.025***	-0.022**
	(0.010)	(0.009)	(0.009)	(0.010)	(0.009)	(0.009)
lrep_hdi	3.574	-0.381	-0.116	2.562	-7.955	-8.347
	(2.600)	(5.313)	(5.518)	(2.823)	(5.495)	(5.577)
lpart_hdi	-3.159	-3.682	-1.524	-2.268	-3.311	-0.622
	(2.204)	(3.237)	(4.105)	(2.175)	(3.559)	(4.315)
N	2559	1072	579	2363	927	493
N_g	1054	434	228	980	381	199

- *** denotes statistical significance at the 1% level,- ** denotes statistical significance at the 5% level, * denotes statistical significance at the 10% level.

The estimated parameter on the Gini variable displays an expected negative sign and is statistically significant only for the partner country in all estimated equations. Thus, a lower level of income inequality in the importing country is positively associated with a higher level of trade flows. The inclusion of the Gini variable affects the statistical significance of all other variables. In particular, the HDI and the civil liberties variables lose their statistical significance. This however, can be related to a large reduction in the number of observations used in the regression due to the high number of missing observations for the Gini variable.

In addition to the robustness of our estimation results, we also studied causality between human development and exports, as well as causality between exports and human development for all countries in our sample, using a bivariate VAR framework. In the VAR model, we included one lag only as the

Arellano-Bond test for autocorrelation does not reject the null of no autocorrelation for all lags except the first one. The results of the two-way Granger causality tests are reported in Table 3.4. In column (1), we report the estimation results for causality between human development and exports, while in column (2), for causality between exports and human development, respectively.

Table 3.4: Two-way Granger causality tests (standard errors in parentheses)

	HDI on exports	Exports on HDI
L.lGross_Exp	0.2318***	0.0003***
	(0.0226)	(0.0001)
L.rep_lnGDP	-0.0621	0.0105***
	(0.0915)	(0.0006)
L.part_lnGDP	-0.1010	-0.0001
	(0.0777)	(0.0006)
L.rep_lnGDP_pc	0.0026	-0.0088***
	(0.0768)	(0.0005)
L.part_lnGDP_pc	0.0105	-0.0004
	(0.0682)	(0.0006)
L.EU	-0.1154***	-0.0068***
	(0.0328)	(0.0006)
L.GATT-WTO	0.1102**	0.0014***
	(0.0468)	(0.0004)
L.rep_hdi	5.7682***	0.3449***
	(0.7700)	(0.0067)
L.part_hdi	0.7444	0.0020
	(0.5853)	(0.0054)
_cons	2.7485***	0.4207***
	(0.5161)	(0.0048)
N	23700	23961

- *** denotes statistical significance at the 1% level,- ** denotes statistical significance at the 5% level, * denotes statistical significance at the 10% level.

The estimated parameter on the lagged value of the HDI for the reporting country shown in column (1) is statistically significant, which indicates that the null hypothesis of no causality is clearly rejected for the exporting country. This result confirms the view that human development as measured by the HDI is the Granger cause of exports. Similarly, the estimated parameter value on the lagged value of exports reported in column (2) is also statistically significant, which indicates that the null hypothesis of no reverse causality is clearly rejected for the exporting country. This means that exports also increase human development as measured by the HDI. Therefore, we demonstrated that there is a two-way causality. Hence, the standard way of analysing the impact of exports on human development is confirmed, but in addition to this, there is also the positive impact of human development on exports.

3.3.2 Results for the period 2007-2008

In addition to the estimation results obtained for the longer panel, we also present the results obtained for the shorter period of 2007-2008 using the PA Poisson model. This method was used because for such a short period of time, the time variation was too small to use the FE method. The main advantage of this set of results is that they include another measure of human development that was not available for the earlier years of our sample. This measure is the GEM (Gender Empowerment Measure), a composite index to evaluate gender inequality based on three basic dimensions of empowerment — political participation, decision-making and power over economic resources.

Gender inequality in political participation is measured here by the percentage of seats held by women in national parliaments (*seats*). The inequality in economic participation and decision-making power is to be captured by two explanatory variables: the percentage share of women and men among legislators (*legis*), senior officials and managers as well as the percentage share of women and men in professional and technical fields (*prof*). Finally, the power over economic resources is to be measured by the estimated earned income of women and men (in PPP US dollars) (*income*).

Therefore, the aggregate GEM variable seeks to reflect the extent to which women and men are able to participate actively in economic and political life and take part in decision-making. A higher value of this aggregate measure and its constituent components are associated with lower gender inequality in political and economic life.

Table 3.5: GEM and exports – results for 2007-2008 (standard errors in parentheses)

	All countries	CEE with all countries	CEE only	All countries	CEE with all countries	CEE only
Main	1	2	3	4	5	6
rep_lnGDP	0.371***	-0.027	0.039	0.379***	-0.021	0.184
	(0.057)	(0.263)	(0.289)	(0.058)	(0.296)	(0.286)
part_lnGDP	0.808***	0.648***	0.406*	0.836***	0.643***	0.634**
	(0.060)	(0.185)	(0.216)	(0.055)	(0.198)	(0.257)
lrep_Land	-0.380***	0.038	-0.831*	-0.428***	0.068	-1.244***
	(0.142)	(0.343)	(0.487)	(0.133)	(0.378)	(0.421)
lpart_Land	0.299**	0.261	-1.428	0.283**	0.106	-2.296**
	(0.138)	(0.600)	(1.021)	(0.139)	(0.652)	(1.124)
EU	-0.026	0.024	-0.028	-0.455**	-0.366**	-0.409**
	(0.079)	(0.069)	(0.081)	(0.188)	(0.173)	(0.205)
GATT-WTO	0.137***	0.127		0.135***	0.150	
	(0.027)	(0.152)		(0.027)	(0.157)	
europe_agreement_eu	-0.024	0.016	-0.146*	-0.461**	-0.357**	-0.574**
	(0.080)	(0.071)	(0.084)	(0.190)	(0.175)	(0.233)
eu_europe_agreement	0.045	-0.051	-0.064	-0.422**	-0.460***	-0.515***
	(0.082)	(0.083)	(0.100)	(0.185)	(0.164)	(0.194)
rep_civil_liberties				0.099	0.088	-0.045
				(0.108)	(0.106)	(0.099)
part_civil_liberties				0.062	0.106	0.042
				(0.053)	(0.091)	(0.089)
lrep_gem	0.595***	2.363	-1.214	0.583***	2.371	-1.265
	(0.175)	(1.640)	(1.042)	(0.175)	(1.671)	(0.993)
lpart_gem	0.303	-0.161	0.007	0.318	-0.135	0.327
	(0.205)	(0.511)	(0.396)	(0.203)	(0.522)	(0.469)
N	16896	3724	826	16520	3484	746
N_g	8448	1862	413	8260	1742	373

- *** denotes statistical significance at the 1% level, - ** denotes statistical significance at the 5% level, * denotes statistical significance at the 10% level.

In column (1) of Table 3.5 we present the estimation results obtained for bilateral exports of all countries. The estimated parameter on the GEM variable is positive and statistically significant at the 1 per cent level only for the reporting country and not significant for the partner country. In columns (2) and

(3), we present the estimation results obtained for exports of CEE countries to all countries, and exports of CEE countries among themselves, respectively. However, it turns out that the estimated parameter on the GEM variable is not statistically significant. Therefore, there is no relationship between exports and gender inequalities in the CEE countries. This might be due to the relatively low level of gender discrimination in the Central and East European countries compared to the rest of the world or to the small number of observations available for this regression.

In columns (4)-(6) we check the robustness of these results by adding the civil liberties variable. It turns out that our results did not change as this variable was not statistically significant.

Table 3.6: GEM components and exports – results for 2007-2008 (standard errors in parentheses)

	All countries	CEE with all countries	CEE only	All countries	CEE with all countries	CEE only
	1	2	3	4	5	6
rep_lnGDP	0.389***	0.131	-0.073	0.394***	0.231	0.664*
	(0.051)	(0.193)	(0.400)	(0.051)	(0.302)	(0.344)
part_lnGDP	0.798***	0.579***	0.292	0.830***	0.581***	0.421
	(0.059)	(0.197)	(0.295)	(0.052)	(0.216)	(0.545)
lrep_Land	-0.332**	-0.020	-0.470	-0.381***	-0.076	-1.292***
	(0.143)	(0.385)	(0.577)	(0.134)	(0.410)	(0.473)
lpart_Land	0.384***	0.393	-2.039*	0.360***	0.212	-2.654**
	(0.136)	(0.575)	(1.084)	(0.137)	(0.619)	(1.321)
EU	-0.012	0.021	0.065	-0.461**	-0.391**	-0.401*
	(0.079)	(0.075)	(0.107)	(0.196)	(0.180)	(0.214)
GATT-WTO	0.134***	0.125		0.132***	0.147	
	(0.027)	(0.153)		(0.027)	(0.159)	
europe_agreement_eu	-0.019	0.012	-0.060	-0.462**	-0.371**	-0.534**
	(0.080)	(0.072)	(0.083)	(0.198)	(0.181)	(0.239)
eu_europe_agreement	0.051	-0.056	-0.085	-0.421**	-0.475***	-0.547***
	(0.082)	(0.085)	(0.105)	(0.193)	(0.171)	(0.199)
rep_civil_liberties				0.082	0.069	-0.120
				(0.110)	(0.111)	(0.111)
part_civil_liberties				0.073	0.130	0.071
				(0.053)	(0.091)	(0.088)

lrep_legis	0.157**	0.343*	-0.015	0.156**	0.341	-0.071
	(0.061)	(0.208)	(0.140)	(0.062)	(0.212)	(0.136)
lrep_seats	-0.120	0.267	0.871	-0.112	0.456	2.060**
	(0.121)	(0.516)	(0.817)	(0.123)	(0.652)	(0.851)
lrep_income	0.090**	-0.076	-0.182	0.092**	-0.029	0.116
	(0.042)	(0.163)	(0.226)	(0.042)	(0.155)	(0.222)
lrep_prof	-0.490***	0.223	2.033*	-0.503***	0.072	0.840
	(0.182)	(0.616)	(1.110)	(0.183)	(0.705)	(1.049)
lpart_legis	0.006	-0.028	0.035	0.002	-0.031	0.018
	(0.041)	(0.108)	(0.068)	(0.040)	(0.110)	(0.065)
lpart_seats	-0.282**	-0.375	-2.268***	-0.229*	-0.319	-2.094**
	(0.134)	(0.333)	(0.799)	(0.126)	(0.357)	(0.991)
lpart_income	0.025	-0.149	0.124	0.021	-0.165	0.158
	(0.042)	(0.107)	(0.166)	(0.042)	(0.112)	(0.196)
lpart_prof	-0.278**	-1.102***	0.453	-0.291**	-1.285***	-0.194
	(0.123)	(0.377)	(1.364)	(0.122)	(0.377)	(1.915)
N	16358	3660	826	15990	3424	746
N_g	8179	1830	413	7995	1712	373

- *** denotes statistical significance at the 1% level, - ** denotes statistical significance at the 5% level, * denotes statistical significance at the 10% level.

In Table 3.6, we disaggregate the GEM into its constituent components. The particular columns in Table 3.6 are the direct counterparts of the columns in Table 3.5. In column (1) of Table 3.6, we present the estimation results obtained for bilateral exports of all countries. It turns out that the majority of the estimated parameters on the GEM components are statistically significant although not all of them display the expected signs. In particular, the estimated coefficients on two variables: *legis* and *income* for the reporting country are positive and statistically significant which is in line with our expectations. However, the estimated signs of the parameters on *prof* for the reporting country and *seats* and *prof* for the partner country display unexpected negative signs.

In column (2), we report estimation results for exports of the CEE to all countries. Most gender inequality variables are not statistically significant. Only the *legis* variable is statistically significant at the 10 per cent level and displays a positive sign in the case of the reporting country while the *prof* variable is statistically significant at the 1 per cent level but displays a negative sign in the case of the partner country.

In column (3) we report the estimation results for exports of the CEE among themselves. The majority of gender inequality variables are not statistically significant. In the case of the reporting country, the only statistically significant variable at the 10 per cent level is the *prof* variable which displays a positive sign. While in the case of the partner country, the only statistically significant variable at the 1 percent level is the *seats* variable which displays a negative sign like in the case of the overall estimations for all countries reported in column (1).

In columns (4)-(6), we check the robustness of these results by adding the civil liberties variable. It turns out that this variable was not statistically significant. Hence, our results did not change much. In particular, no major changes were observed in the case of the estimation for all countries reported in column (4). In the case of estimates for exports of the CEE countries to all countries, the *legis* variable for the reporting country lost its previous statistical significance. In the case of estimates for the CEE exports among themselves, the *prof* variable lost its previous statistical significance while the *seats* variable for the reporting country became statistically significant at the 5 per cent level.

3.4 Summary and policy recommendations

In this chapter, we studied the role of human development and social inequalities in development of exports using the generalized gravity model by the Poisson estimator with fixed effects. Our empirical results for the period 1980-2010 show that there is a positive causal relationship between our most general measure of human development (HDI) and the level of bilateral trade for exports in the reporting countries with the exception of the CEE countries.

Looking at the disaggregated components of the HDI, we find that the income index displays a positive sign and is statistically significant for both the reporting and partner countries in the case of estimations for all countries. The income index for the reporting country remains statistically significant in the case of exports from the CEE countries to all countries but loses its statistical significance for the partner country. In the case of exports amongst the CEE countries, it is not statistically significant for any country. This might be due to the fact that country income disparities are relatively small among these countries.

The role of income disparities is limited only to the partner side. This means that a lower level of income inequality in the importing country is positively associated with a higher level of trade flows. This result should be treated with caution because the inclusion of the Gini variable greatly reduced the number of observations and probably affects the statistical significance of the HDI and the civil liberties variables which lose their statistical significance.

The results for the Gender Empowerment Measure (GEM) – another measure of social inequality - reveal that the GEM is positive and statistically significant only for the reporting countries in the full sample covering exports of all countries. Hence, a lower gender inequality in economic participation and decision-making power is associated with a higher level of exports. However, in the case of the CEE countries this variable is not statistically significant. This might result from the fact that the level of gender discrimination in the CEE countries is much lower compared to the whole world or it might be related to the small number of observations used in this regression.

We also disaggregated the GEM measure into its components. The more detailed results for the GEM in the regression for 2007-2008 led to mixed results. For example, the variable that measures the political participation of women (i.e. the percentage of seats held by women in national parliaments) displays a positive sign and is statistically significant for the reporter except specifically for the CEE countries. Thus, a higher participation of women in parliament is positively related to the bilateral level of exports. Similarly, a lower level of discrimination in terms of income is positively related to the level of exports for the whole sample. These unexpected results were obtained for reporting countries in which female participation in parliament and professional life was negatively associated with the level of trade.

Our empirical results demonstrated that human development variables are important in determining the level of exports. The majority of them are positively related to exports. The key variable measuring human development, the HDI, is positively related to exports, confirming that a positive relationship between human development and exports exists. However, the estimated impact of its components and other variables is rather differentiated. Nevertheless, economic policies oriented at increasing the level of human development may positively affect the level of exports.

The significance of the variable standing for Human Development is explained mainly by the quality of the education system and the level of per capita income. This suggests that investments in the education system result in increased human capital and consequently in a higher level of exports. Surprisingly, the role of healthcare measured by life expectancy is limited in our sample. However, this result may be due to data imperfections and should be treated with caution.

4 Export activity and human development in Central and Eastern European countries: A firm level analysis

Andrzej Cieślik, Jan Jakub Michałek, Anna Michałek

4.1 Introduction

In recent years, a new strand in the new trade theory literature emerged. In contrast to the previous literature, which assumed that firms are symmetric, this new literature focuses on firms' heterogeneity in terms of productivity and export performance. It turns out that only a small fraction of the most productive firms account for the majority of exports; most firms do not export and concentrate their activities on domestic markets only. The majority of empirical studies based on firm-level data are conducted for selected developed countries and for some developing countries, while the empirical evidence for the post-transition economies of Central and Eastern Europe is virtually non-existent. In particular, there are no studies, performed at firm level, linking human development with export performance.

In the latest strand of the new trade theory, Melitz (2003), relaxed the key assumption of firms' symmetry in Krugman's (1980) monopolistic competition model and introduced firms' heterogeneity in terms of labour productivity. In his model, productivity differences among firms are exogenously given and each firm has to pay a fixed cost when entering the domestic and foreign markets. The model predicts that the most productive firms with the lowest marginal costs can pay the fixed cost of entry and become an exporter. On the one hand, a fall in the importing costs will force the least productive firms to exit the domestic market and reallocate market shares from these firms to the more productive ones. As a result, the average level of productivity within the sector will increase. On the other hand, a reduction in the exporting costs will reduce the threshold level of productivity that firms need to achieve in order to export, and consequently the non-exporters with the highest productivity will be able to enter the foreign market.

The Melitz (2003) model can be used to study a whole range of various issues. In particular, it can be used to analyze the effects of human development on firms' export performance. The Melitz (2003) model assumes that the level of labour productivity is exogenous. However, as discussed in the previous chapter, productivity can be related to the level of human capital. It can be expected that a higher level of human capital is positively related with a higher level of firms' productivity and thus, it can positively affect the firm's export performance.

Therefore, the main goal of this chapter is to study the relationship between human development and firms' export performance, having taken into account firms' productivity and other firms' characteristics. The study is performed for firms residing in Central and East European (CEE) countries and Turkey. Our study is based on the BEEPS firm level data for the period starting in 2002 and ending in 2010. In the 1990s, these countries faced transition from non-market to market economies, and radically liberalized their multilateral and regional trade. We estimate probit regressions for the pooled data for all CEE countries and Turkey. Our hypothesis is that the probability of exporting increases with a higher level in the human development index and its components, having controlled for productivity, spending on research and development (R&D) activities, foreign ownership, and the firm's size.

The structure of this chapter is as follows. In Section 2,the relevant literature is reviewed. In Section 3, the empirical methodology and data are presented. In Section 4, our empirical results are discussed. Section 5 summarizes and concludes.

4.2 Literature Review

Firm heterogeneity has long been a major issue in economics. For example, according to the evolutionary theory, economic change occurs via interaction among heterogeneous agents in the presence of market selection (Winter 1971, Nelson and Winter 1982). In particular, Nelson (1991) made a strong case for the economic significance of discretionary differences among firms. Similarly, elements of firm heterogeneity can be found in the equilibrium models of industrial dynamics (Jovanovic 1982, Pakes and Ericsson 1998). Also some macroeconomic models rejected the standard assumption of a representative agent (Stoker 1993). However, firm heterogeneity has been introduced into the theoretical models of international trade only recently under growing pressure from empirical studies based on firm-level data (Bernard et al. 2003, Melitz 2003). The key prediction emerging from this new strand in international trade literature is that firms will resort to distinct international activities according to their productivity levels (Helpman et al. 2004). By now, empirical evidence on firm heterogeneity in economic literature has become extensive. According to Castellani and Zanfei (2006), intra-industry variance in productivity, wages and profitability exceeds inter-sectorial variance. For example, this has been demonstrated in the context of the US economy by Baily et al. (1992) for productivity, Davis and Haltiwanger (1991) for wages, and Mueller and Raunig (1999) for profitability. In the context of international trade, there has been a number of studies arguing that more productive firms tend to self-select into export markets. This has been demonstrated by Bernard and Wagner (1997) for Germany, Bernard and Jensen (1999) for the USA, Clerides et al. (1998) for Columbia, Mexico and Morocco, and Castellani (2002) for Italy.[19]

According to the EFIGE (2010) report on firm performance in seven European countries, labour productivity is an important determinant of export decisions. Unfortunately, these studies did not include the countries of Central and Eastern Europe with the exception of Hungary. Similar studies for the Visegrad countries (i.e. the Czech Republic, Slovakia, Hungary and Poland) and separately for Poland were conducted by Cieślik, Michałek and Michałek (2012 a, b). Their analysis showed that the productivity of the labour force is positively related to the probability of exporting. In addition, in their empirical studies, other factors that may affect export business decisions were examined. Their results showed that amongst others, a higher percentage of skilled workers, as well as a higher percentage of graduates amongst full-time workers, raised the propensity to export in all sectors of the economy. However, in all the aforementioned studies, the authors did not control for the level of human development.

4.3 Empirical methodology and data description

4.3.1 Empirical methodology

We use the probit model to study the relationship between exporting and human development, having controlled for firms' characteristics. Based on the previous theoretical literature, we develop an empirical model to investigate the effects of various firms' characteristics on their export performance. This probability is modeled as a linear function of firm, industry and country characteristics.

Let Y_i^* be our dependent variable indicating the export status of firm i. This variable is a latent variable. This means that instead of observing the volume of exports, we observe only a binary variable Y_i indicating the sign of Y_i^*. Our dependent variable follows a binary distribution and takes the value 1 when the firm exports and 0 otherwise:

---

19 The survey of early empirical evidence on firm heterogeneity and exporting has been provided by Tybout (2003).

$$Y_t = \begin{cases} 1 & if\ Y_i^* > 0 \\ 0 & if\ Y_i^* = 0 \end{cases}$$

Moreover, we assume that $Y_i^* = X_i\theta + \varepsilon_i$, where X_i is a vector of explanatory variables affecting exports, θ is the vector of parameters on these variables that needs to be estimated and ε_i is an error term which is assumed to be normally distributed with a zero mean. Hence, the probability that a firm exports can be written as:

$$Pr(Y_i = 1|X_i) = \Phi(\beta + X_i\theta)$$

4.3.2 Data description

Our analysis is based on the EBRD-World Bank Business Environment and Enterprise Performance Survey (BEEPS) data collected by the World Bank and the European Bank for Reconstruction and Development for the post-communist countries located in Europe and Central Asia (*ECA*) and Turkey. The main objective of the BEEPS survey was to obtain feedback from enterprises in the aforementioned countries on the state of the private sector. The survey examined the quality of the business environment as determined by a wide range of interactions between firms and the state. The surveys covered the manufacturing and services sectors and are representative of the variety of firms according to sector and location within each country. The data was collected for the years 2002, 2005, 2009 and 2010.

Our study focuses on the Central and Eastern European countries and Turkey. We assume that export activity occurs when at least one percent of sales revenue comes from sales made abroad. In Table 4.1, we present the export propensity of firms from the Central and Eastern European countries, treating Turkey as a benchmark – a market economy from the region free of a communist past.

Table 4.1: Comparison of the propensity to export amongst firms from post-communist countries as well as Turkey

Export (national sales less than or equal 99% of establishment's sales)		
Country	Mean	Freq.
Turkey	0.58	2465
Slovenia	0.55	685
Croatia	0.42	1148
Serbia	0.37	900

Slovakia	0.37	654
FYROM	0.36	736
Estonia	0.35	660
Lithuania	0.35	680
Hungary	0.35	1149
Bosnia	0.35	737
Czech Rep.	0.35	857
Bulgaria	0.32	1853
Latvia	0.29	651
Albania	0.27	732
Poland	0.27	2008
Belarus	0.26	848
Moldova	0.24	887
Ukraine	0.22	1902
Romania	0.21	1382
Armenia	0.19	895
Russia	0.17	2359
Kyrgyzstan	0.17	609
Georgia	0.17	746
Montenegro	0.13	153
Uzbekistan	0.13	921
Tajikistan	0.12	735
Azerbaijan	0.11	900
Kazakhstan	0.10	1378
Total	0.29	29630

Source: own calculations based on the BEEPS data.

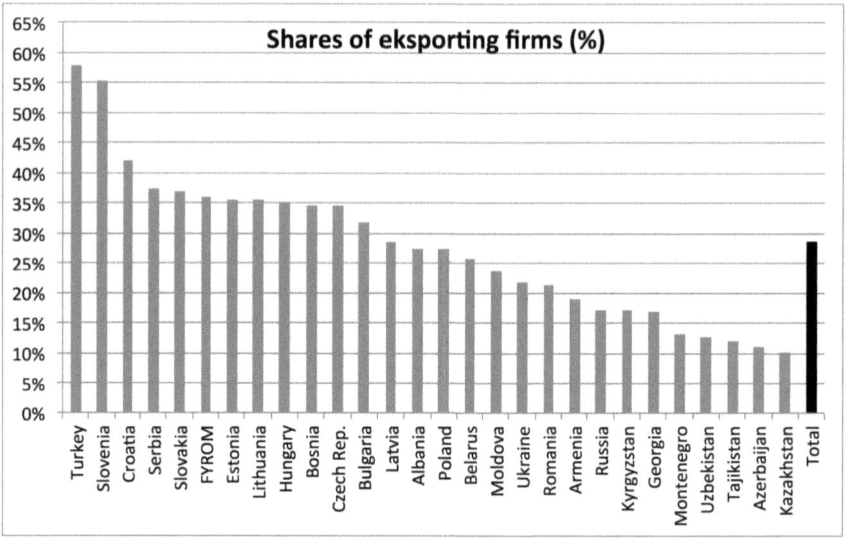

Fig. 4.1: *Share of exporting firms in CEE and Turkey; source: own calculations based on the BEEPS data*

Table 4.1 reveals a great degree of heterogeneity across firms located in different countries across the whole region. It can be noted that on average, firms residing in Turkey are the most export-oriented amongst the firms in the region. A high share of exporting firms is typical for the countries that emerged from the former Yugoslavia, which traditionally were more market-oriented and had more liberal trade regimes in the past compared to other communist countries. In contrast to the aforementioned countries, the share of exporters amongst all countries' firms is the lowest for firms residing in the former Soviet Union, with the exception of the Baltic states. This is in line with the phenomenon often observed, that firms from bigger countries usually sell their products on the domestic markets.

However, the great degree of heterogeneity in export performance, even among the CEE countries, cannot only be explained by the standard country characteristics that are usually stressed by the traditional trade theory. Therefore, it is also important to study the role of human development in determining export performance, together with firm characteristics, specifically for the new trade theory.

The probability of exporting for analyzed CEE firms is dependent on firm, sector and country characteristics. Firm and sector characteristics are based on survey questions regarding the individual characteristics of the firm, sector of activity, legal and economic status, characteristics of managers and the size of the firm, the infrastructure of services in the analyzed country, economic performance and key characteristics of the reviewed firms, as well as stakeholders, e.g. employers organizations, employees organizations, local government, central government, the ICT industry, SMEs, academics, etc. The country characteristic of our interest is the HDI which comes from the Human Development Report and has been described in the previous chapters. The sample used in our econometric analysis includes cross-section data for almost six thousand observations for firms located in the CEE countries in all analyzed years. In Table 4.2 we present the variables used in our study.

Table 4.2: Description of variables used in empirical study

Variable Name	BEEP input Name	Description
Dependent variable		
export	d3a	Binary variables that takes the value one if the establishment is exporting and zero if not.
Explanatory variables		
		Labour productivity
lprod	lprod=log(lprod) prod=exchange rate*(d2/l1)	Logarithm of productivity expressed as total amount of annual sales per full time employee. The annual sales are converted from local currencies to USD.
		Human capital
luniv	luniv=log(ECAq69)	Logarithm of % employees at end of fiscal year with a university degree.
lsk_prod	sk_prod=(l4a/l3a)*100 lsk_prod=log(sk_prod)	Logarithm of % of skilled production workers.
lunsk_prod	unsk_prod=(l4b/l3a)*100 lunsk_prod=log(unsk_prod)	Logarithm of % of unskilled production workers.
lRaD	RaD=(ECAo4/d2)*100 lRaD=log(RaD)	Logarithm of % of total annual sales spent on research and development.
		Internationalization of firm

foreign_tech	e6	Binary variable that takes the value one if the establishment uses technology licensed from a foreign-owned company and zero otherwise.
foreign_cap	b2b	Shares in capital of private foreign individuals, companies or organizations.
		Other firm characteristics
firm_size	firm_size=log(l1)	Logarithm of permanent, full-time employees of the firm.
age	age= 2010 - b5	Variable indicating how long the firm has been operating in the country (base year 2010).

4.4 Estimation results

In this section we present two sets of estimation results. First, we present results for the aggregated measure of human development – the HDI. Next, we show the results obtained for particular components of the HDI. We also check the robustness of our results by controlling the firm, country and time specific effects.

4.4.1 Results for the aggregated HDI

In columns (1)-(5) of Table 4.3, we present the estimation results for the model where export activity is explained by the aggregated measure of the HDI, the firm's productivity and by standard factors analyzed in other studies. Productivity is expressed as the total amount of annual sales per full time employee (*lprod*). Other factors that may affect export activity include the level of innovation proxied by the R&D spending (lRaD), the stock of human capital proxied by the percentage of employees with university degrees (*luniv*), and the proportion of skilled and unskilled workers among the production workers (*lsk_prod, lunsk_prod*). In addition, we control for the use of foreign technology (*foreign_tech*), foreign ownership (*foreign_cap*), the age (*age*) and the size of the firm (*firm_size*).

Table 4.3: Results for the aggregated HDI

	(1)	(2)	(3)	(4)	(5)
VARIABLES	base - lprod	log(HDI)	HDI	HDI	HDI
lprod	0.0101**	0.00983**	0.0114**	0.0222	0.0145***

	(0.00475)	(0.00467)	(0.00474)	(0.0154)	(0.00478)
luniv	0.0226***	0.0505***	0.0532***	0.0689***	0.0543***
	(0.00785)	(0.00755)	(0.00767)	(0.00816)	(0.00767)
lsk_prod	0.0120				
	(0.0106)				
lunsk_prod	-0.00272				
	(0.00449)				
lRaD	0.0698***	0.0737***	0.0558**	0.0788***	0.0698***
	(0.0217)	(0.0214)	(0.0219)	(0.0225)	(0.0218)
foreign_tech	0.642***	0.634***	0.136	0.239**	0.0745
	(0.0842)	(0.0832)	(0.0957)	(0.0967)	(0.0943)
foreign_cap	0.00771***	0.00739***	0.00822***	0.00789***	0.00830***
	(0.000766)	(0.000733)	(0.000743)	(0.000760)	(0.000742)
firm_size	0.285***	0.290***	0.253***	0.278***	0.252***
	(0.0157)	(0.0136)	(0.0140)	(0.0144)	(0.0140)
age	0.00372***	0.00256**	0.00354***	0.00134	0.00366***
	(0.00105)	(0.00105)	(0.00107)	(0.00111)	(0.00107)
l_hdi		3.012***	3.046***	21.47***	3.221***
		(0.210)	(0.215)	(2.948)	(0.218)
Constant	-1.911***	-0.925***	-0.944***	3.589***	-0.321**
	(0.0976)	(0.107)	(0.108)	(0.847)	(0.126)
Observations	5,295	5,932	5,931	5,932	5,932
Log likelihood	-2783	-2953	-2859	-2741	-2856
Pseudo R2	0.151	0.182	0.207	0.240	0.208
			Sectoral effects	Country effects	Time effects

Standard errors in parentheses; *** p<0.01, ** p<0.05, * p<0.1

Firstly, we will discuss the benchmark results presented in column (1) for the standard firm characteristics but without the measure of social development. Our estimation results reveal that almost all the variables are statistically significant at the 1 percent level with the exception of the productivity variable which is statistically significant at the 5 percent level, and the skilled and unskilled labour variables which are not statistically significant at all. The signs of the estimated parameters for our control variables are in line with expectations and results from other studies. Moreover, all measures of human capital; level of R&D spending and proportion of workers with university degrees are positively related to the probability of exporting. Finally, the probability of exporting increases with the firm's age, size, foreign ownership and the use of foreign technologies.

In column (2), we present the results obtained for the modified specification of our estimated equation that includes the HDI variable. The estimated parameter on the HDI variable displays a positive sign and is statistically significant at the 1 percent level. This means that the probability of exporting increases with the level of the HDI in the exporting country. The estimated signs of parameters on our control variables are in line with the benchmark estimation results.

In the remaining columns of Table 4.3, we control for sector specific effects, country effects and time effects. In all cases, the estimated parameter on the HDI variable remains positive and statistically significant at the 1 percent level. However, the inclusion of sector specific effects, country effects and time effects influences the statistical significance of other control variables. In particular, controlling for country specific effects makes labour productivity and firm age statistically not significant. In this case, the estimated parameter on the HDI variable increases very significantly. While controlling for sector specific and time specific effects makes the foreign technology variable statistically not significant.

4.4.2 The disaggregated results for HDI components

In columns (1)-(4) of Table 4.4 we present the results obtained for the particular components of the HDI.

Table 4.4: Disaggregated results for HDI components

	(1)	(2)	(3)	(4)
VARIABLES	components	components	components	components
lprod	0.0181***	0.0157***	0.0169	0.0185***
	(0.00508)	(0.00515)	(0.0169)	(0.00518)
luniv	0.0648***	0.0665***	0.0697***	0.0672***
	(0.00780)	(0.00790)	(0.00820)	(0.00789)
lRaD	0.0701***	0.0532**	0.0810***	0.0671***
	(0.0219)	(0.0223)	(0.0227)	(0.0221)
foreign_tech	0.550***	0.130	0.200**	0.0732
	(0.0855)	(0.0974)	(0.0977)	(0.0958)

foreign_cap	0.00768***	0.00822***	0.00797***	0.00822***
	(0.000746)	(0.000754)	(0.000762)	(0.000753)
firm_size	0.303***	0.274***	0.274***	0.273***
	(0.0140)	(0.0144)	(0.0145)	(0.0143)
Age	0.000450	0.00127	0.00137	0.00144
	(0.00107)	(0.00110)	(0.00111)	(0.00109)
l_life_expectancy	6.371***	7.029***	34.30***	7.092***
	(0.481)	(0.501)	(8.582)	(0.501)
l_mean_years_schooling	-0.934***	-0.505***	-0.113	-0.402**
	(0.163)	(0.169)	(3.169)	(0.171)
l_expected_years_schooling	0.771**	1.158***	-11.51***	1.370***
	(0.320)	(0.328)	(3.296)	(0.332)
l_gni_pc_2008	0.108*	-0.0172	3.250***	-0.0380
	(0.0590)	(0.0611)	(0.742)	(0.0615)
Constant	-30.14***	-33.79***	-149.5***	-34.09***
	(2.048)	(2.153)	(31.05)	(2.164)
Observations	5,932	5,931	5,932	5,932
Log likelihood	-2844	-2770	-2727	-2772
Pseudo R2	0.212	0.232	0.244	0.232
		Sectoral effects	Country effects	Time effects

Standard errors in parentheses; *** p<0.01, ** p<0.05, * p<0.1

In column (1), we present the results obtained for particular components of HDI, having controlled for the same set of firm and sector specific variables. Our analysis shows that not all HDI components are statistically significant. In particular, the estimated parameters on life expectancy, the expected years of schooling, and GNI per capita are positive and statistically significant although at various levels of statistical significance. Therefore, the positive relationship between exporting and the HDI is driven by life expectancy, the expected years of schooling and the level of income. These results are in line with our expectations.

However, in contrast to our expectations, the estimated parameter on the mean years of schooling displays a negative sign and is statistically significant at the 1 percent level. This surprising result might be due to the inclusion of human capital measures in the set of firm characteristics. In particular, the positive sign on the estimated parameter for the share of workers with a university degree and the R&D spending demonstrate that export orientation requires more intensive use of human capital.

In the remaining columns of Table 4.4, we control for sector specific effects, country effects and time effects. In all cases, the estimated parameter on the life expectancy variable remains positive and statistically significant at the 1 percent level. Nevertheless, the inclusion of sector specific effects, country effects and time effects influences the statistical significance of other HDI components and control variables. In particular, the change in the estimated parameter values and their statistical significance can be noticed in the case of the specification controlling for country specific effects reported in column (3). Those changes are especially visible for the estimated parameter on the expected years of schooling variable which becomes negative while in other specifications it displays a positive sign. In addition, the estimated parameter on the mean years of schooling variable loses its statistical significance. The estimated parameter on the GNI per capita variable is statistically significant at the 1 percent level only when the country specific effects are controlled for. Moreover, when the country specific effects are included in the model specification, the estimated parameter on the productivity variable loses its statistical significance.

4.5 Conclusions

In this chapter, we have investigated the determinants of export activity of firms in the Central and Eastern European countries and Turkey with a special focus on the role of human development. First, we started by estimating a probit regression for the pooled dataset that included all countries without a HDI variable. Our benchmark model estimation indicates that the probability of exporting increases with a higher level of productivity and measures of human capital, including the share of university graduates in productive employment and spending on R&D activities. Finally, the probability of exporting increases with the firm's age, size, foreign ownership and the use of foreign technologies.

Then, we extended the benchmark specification by including the HDI variable. The estimated parameter on the HDI variable displayed a positive sign and was statistically significant at the 1 percent level. This means that the probability of exporting increases with the level in the HDI in the exporting country. This result was robust and it did not change when we controlled for sector specific effects, country effects and time effects. In all cases, the estimated parameter on the HDI variable remained positive and statistically significant at the 1 percent level.

The results obtained for the separate components of the HDI revealed that only some HDI components were statistically significant. The estimated parameters on life expectancy, the expected years of schooling, and GNI per capita were positive and statistically significant. These results were in line with our expectations indicating that there is a positive relationship between exporting, life expectancy and GNI per capita.

The role of education in explaining the relationship between exporting and human development is less obvious. In the majority of cases, the estimated parameter on the expected years of schooling was positive and significant, while the estimated parameter on the mean years of schooling was negative and significant.

This surprising result might be due to controlling for the level of human capital at firm level. Both shares of workers with a university degree and R&D spending appeared to have a positive impact on the probability of exporting.

The estimations obtained for export performance using firm level data are generally in line with the results obtained using aggregated exports flows, however, a number of differences can be identified. In both cases, the aggregated measure of human development – the HDI, was positively related to export performance. Also the income index showed a positive correlation with the exporting firm's performance. However, the life expectancy index, which usually in the case of aggregated exports of CEE countries was not statistically significant, displayed a positive sign and was statistically significant in the analysis based on the firm level data. Also the role of education is not straightforward. The educational index was statistically significant in the analysis based on the aggregated exports of all countries, while in the firm level analysis, it was positive in the case of expected years of schooling and negative in the case of means years of schooling. Therefore, it seems that the level of human capital matters only for the exporting decisions of individual firms.

5 Human Development and FDI inflows at the macroeconomic level.

Michał Brzozowski

5.1 Introduction

In 2010 – for the first time – the developing and transition countries absorbed more than one-half, namely 52%, of global FDI inflows.[20] In Central and Eastern European countries, which are net importers of capital, the factors that influence the overall investment climate, such as the quality of infrastructure and institutions and skills of the labour force, are also important determinants of FDI inflows. This region is losing its competitive advantage stemming from low labour costs and it seems that stimulating human development is crucial for sustaining productivity growth and attracting foreign investors.

The purpose of this chapter is to analyze the determinants of long-term foreign inward investment with special attention paid to various aspects of human development. The methodological approach is outlined in the next section. In section 5.3, the total foreign capital inflow, aggregated from all source countries, in a wide sample of 150 countries is examined, including the 26 transition countries. The results suggest that the determinants of FDI inflows to the latter group are not different from the factors that shape foreign investors' decisions found in a worldwide sample. On the contrary, the analysis reveals a specificity of the determinants of FDI inflows to the group of 11 Central and Eastern European countries. In section 5.4, we therefore focus on bilateral inward FDI inflows from 34 European, Asian and American source countries, listed in the Appendix, into the 10 new member states of the EU and Croatia. Due to HDI data availability constraints, the period under investigation spans the years 1995 and 2000-2010.

5.2 Methodology

The determinants of total FDI inflows will be investigated with the aid of a dynamic panel regression analysis. The decision to invest abroad depends on numerous factors, which are sometimes difficult to measure, like in the case of

---

20 UNCTAD (2011).

an individual investor's perception of risk and development prospects of the host country. It can be conjectured, however, that at least some of these factors that are difficult to gauge, are relatively time-invariant and their influence can be traced back to the scale of past foreign capital inflows. The stock of FDI seems to do a good job as a proxy for the impact of time-invariant determinants of FDI flows. Moreover, the stock of accumulated foreign capital may trigger agglomeration effects, which reduce the costs of new foreign firms entering the host country market. Consequently the equation describing the magnitude of FDI flows (*fdiflows*) can be written as:

$$fdiflows_{it} = (1+\alpha) fdi_{it-1} + \boldsymbol{\beta}'\mathbf{X}_{it} + \varepsilon_{it}$$
$$\varepsilon_{it} = \mu_i + v_{it} \qquad (5.1)$$

where X_{it} is a matrix of explanatory variables, t is time index, i denotes a country in section 5.3 and a pair of countries (source and host country) in section 5.4 where bilateral flows are examined.

Taking into account the fact that FDI inflow is (approximately) equal to the change in the stock of foreign capital, ($fdiflows_t = fdi_t - fdi_{t-1}$), equation (5.1) can be rewritten in a form that will be the basis of the specification of the estimation equation:

$$fdi_{it} = \alpha\, fdi_{it-1} + \boldsymbol{\beta}'\mathbf{X}_{it} + \varepsilon_{it} \qquad (5.2)$$

The presence of foreign investors affects the economies of host countries and impacts on the variables that are considered to be the determinants of FDI. This reversed effect of FDI inflows on its own determinants and the fact that the lagged value of the dependent variable is included among the regressors in equation (5.2), require addressing the issue of endogeneity. One prominent way suggested by Arellano and Bond (1991) to deal with endogeneity in the dynamic panel model regression analysis was to take first differences of equation (5.2) and estimate it using the GMM. The estimated equation takes then the following form:

$$\Delta fdi_{it} = \alpha \Delta fdi_{it-1} + \boldsymbol{\beta}'\Delta\mathbf{X}_{it} + \Delta\varepsilon_{it} \qquad (5.3)$$

Blundell and Bond (1998) showed that the first-differencing eliminates the time-invariant variables and the GMM estimator is inefficient. They suggested supplementing the first-differenced equation with the levels equation and a joint estimation of this system of equations using the GMM. We follow this procedure in this chapter and use the heteroscedastic consistent, two-step estimation method with the small sample correction of Windmeijer (2005).

The first difference of the log of the stock of foreign capital (*fdi*) is the dependent variable. The stock of FDI is expressed in US dollars (total FDI inflow in section 5.3) and euros (bilateral FDI inflow in section 5.4) in constant prices. Taking the log eliminates the observations with no capital inflows. As a result, the regression model is designed to explain the magnitude of FDI inflows (intensive margin) and not the factors that affect the choice of the host country (extensive margin).

The emphasis is put on the various dimensions of human development and their influence on the foreign investors' decisions. The key variables included in the matrix X are thus the following indicators of human development:

- Human Development Index (HDI);
- The HDI components defined in the previous chapters: indices of income (incomex), life expectancy (lifex) and education (edux);
- Civil liberties index (from Freedom House);
- Gini index measuring income inequality;
- Gender Inequality Index (GII).

Besides the indicators of human development, the matrix X contains a set of control variables, distinct for total and bilateral FDI flows.

5.3 Determinants of total FDI inflows

The results of the regression analysis of the determinants of total FDI flows are reported in this section. By total FDI inflows, we mean the inflow to a host economy of foreign capital aggregated for all source countries. Data availability allowed estimating equation (5.3) for a maximum of 163 countries in the years 1995 and 2000-2010. Table 5.1 presents the results obtained for the entire sample.

The choice of control variables was guided by the determinants of location choices of multinationals and the predominant type of FDI observed since the 1990s.[21] The bulk of FDI flows between the developed countries are of a horizontal type with the cost reduction and exploitation of agglomeration effects in knowledge creation as the major motive for investing abroad. The market-seeking motive has been losing its importance in long-term capital flows to both developed and emerging market countries. The latter group attracts vertical investments from the industrial countries geared towards costs reduction and, to a lesser extent than in the past, towards the exploitation of natural resources.

The crucial role played by cost reduction as the motive for undertaking FDI, highlights the importance of labour, communication and transportation costs in the host country. The set of controls thus contains the labour income share,

---

21 See, e.g. Dunning (2003).

which measures the costs of labour, taking labour productivity into account. The transportation costs are proxied by a dummy, which is equal to 1 if a country is landlocked and 0 otherwise. Finally, the number of mobile phones per 100 inhabitants measures the communication costs. Only this last variable, denoted *mobile* turned out to be significant and it will be included as a covariate in the estimates of equation (5.3) presented in this section.

Although the market-seeking motive for undertaking FDI has seemed to fall in importance in recent years, the size of the host country market and its growth potential has been inserted among the regressands. Market size can be measured by either the GDP level or the population. The latter variable, denoted *popul*, turned out to be significant and the results obtained for this market size proxy are reported in this section. The rate of GDP growth proved to be a significant variable only if its lagged value, *L.gdpgr*, has been included in the set of control variables.

The risk of investing abroad depends on the macroeconomic conditions in the host country. Uncertainty about macroeconomic policy discourages foreign investors. High inflation generates risk and distorts efficient allocation of resources. To take into account the quality of monetary policy the index *monetqual* is defined as $\exp[-0.005\times(\text{inflation} - 2)^2]$. This measure of price stability rapidly deteriorates once inflation rises above 10 percent.[22] The sign accompanying the estimated coefficient of *monetqual* is a priori ambiguous. On the one hand, a higher quality of monetary policy and low inflation reduces the risk of investing and attracts FDI. On the other hand, restrictive monetary policy can be associated with high interest rates and low aggregate demand, thereby discouraging foreign investors.

As was mentioned above, FDI inflows to developed countries are mostly of a horizontal type, whereas vertical FDI flows to emerging market countries. To check whether the motives for investing in developed and developing countries are indeed different, a dummy variable *oecd* has been included which is equal to 1 for 25 countries that were OECD members before 1995. The significance of this variable would point to the specificity of the OECD countries that cannot be attributed to other covariates that determine the level of foreign long-term investment.

By the same token, the group of transition countries may be distinct with respect to the FDI determinants even compared with other emerging market host economies. The progress of the transition process can be quantified with the aid of transition indicators elaborated on by the European Bank for Reconstruction and Development (EBRD). The indicator gauges several aspects of transition to

---

22 See IMF (2007).

the market economy: price liberalization, financial sector liberalization, privatization, enterprise restructuring, infrastructure development and trade and forex reforms. None of the components of the transition indicator proved to be statistically significant. It can be conjectured that the other characteristics of transition countries, which are not included in the transition indicators, can affect FDI inflows. To test whether this is true or not, we have augmented the set of independent variables with the dummy *transition*, which is equal to 1 for the 26 formerly planned economies. The progress in transition has been most pronounced in the group of Central and Eastern European countries, which are now (or are about to become) members of the EU. For this reason, we also checked the statistical significance of the dummy variable *centeur* which is equal to 1 for the 11 countries in Central and Eastern Europe which are the New Member States.[23]

In all specifications, the set of independent variables comprises of the time dummies. Controlling for time effects allowed taking account of the global reduction of FDI flows during the financial crisis of 2007-2009. Moreover, the moment conditions imposed by the System GMM technique require no correlation across individuals in idiosyncratic disturbances. Time dummies make this assumption more likely to hold. They were significant in all specifications but the estimated coefficients are not displayed in the tables with the estimation result for the sake of concision.

Before testing the specificity of transition and developed countries, the benchmark model has been estimated, with a set of independent variables comprising population (*popul*), the number of mobile phone subscribers (*mobile*), the lagged rate of GDP growth (*L.gdpgr*), the Human Development Index (*hdi*), and the lagged value of the stock of foreign capital *L.fdi*. The results are reported in Table 5.1.

Table 5.1: Impact of the HDI on total FDI inflow. Dependent variable: Δfdi

VARIABLES	(1)	(2)	(3)	(4)	(5)
L.fdi	0.532***	0.615***	0.694***	0.686***	0.723***
	(0.157)	(0.146)	(0.108)	(0.0985)	(0.108)
popul	2.14e-09***	1.74e-09**	1.29e-09**	1.34e-09***	1.19e-09**
	(7.40e-10)	(7.28e-10)	(5.33e-10)	(4.77e-10)	(5.27e-10)
hdi	2.572**	1.953	0.466	0.505	0.158

23 This group consists of 8 countries that joined the EU in 2004, Romania, Bulgaria, and Croatia, that will become the member of the EU in 2013.

	(1.165)	(1.229)	(0.831)	(0.789)	(0.805)
mobile	0.00596***	0.00608***	0.00505***	0.00519***	0.00513***
	(0.00197)	(0.00199)	(0.00161)	(0.00161)	(0.00168)
L.gdpgr	0.00626	0.00997**	0.0152***	0.0147***	0.0156***
	(0.00408)	(0.00501)	(0.00523)	(0.00509)	(0.00509)
monetqual		-0.528***	-0.589***	-0.573***	-0.555***
		(0.148)	(0.158)	(0.159)	(0.167)
oecd			0.779***	0.794***	0.783***
			(0.222)	(0.212)	(0.250)
transition				0.0292	
				(0.0739)	
centeur					0.282***
					(0.0933)
Observations	1,603	1,539	1,539	1,539	1,539
Number of countries	163	158	158	158	158
AR1 test p-value	0.0603	0.0327	0.0108	0.0105	0.00990
AR2 test p-value	0.144	0.794	0.938	0.976	0.994
J-Hansen (p-value)	16.84 (0.465)	13.18 (0.724)	12.52 (0.767)	12.76 (0.752)	14.24 (0.650)

Standard errors in parentheses: *** $p<0.01$, ** $p<0.05$, * $p<0.1$. Instruments for the levels equation: *hdi, popul, monetqual, oecd, transition, centeur* and first differences of *L.fdi, mobile, L.gdpgr*; Instruments for the differenced equation: Δ*hdi*, Δ*popul*, Δ*monetqual* and lags 2 and up of *L.fdi, mobile, L.gdpgr*.

Before discussing the signs and significance of the estimated coefficients displayed in Table 5.1, it should be noted that the Arellano-Bond tests of the serial correlation of the error term and the Hansen J-test confirm the validity of instruments used in the estimation of equation (5.3). The error term is serially correlated of order 1 but the order-2 serial correlation was not found. The Hansen J-test does not allow rejecting the null that instruments are exogenous.

It stems from column (1) of Table 5.1 that the lagged value of foreign capital stock, the market size measured by population and the quality of communication infrastructure measured by the number of mobile phones attract foreign investors. The rate of GDP growth is statistically insignificant in column (1). The variable of interest – *hdi* – is statistically significant and is accompanied by the positive sign. Thus the benchmark regression shows that the overall level of human development measured by an index that combines level of income, education and health spurs the inflow of foreign long-term capital.

The coefficient of *hdi* loses its significance once the index of monetary policy quality *monetqual* is introduced in column (2) of Table 5.1. It may be conjectured that mature market economies usually feature a high level of human development and have established well performing institutions, including independent central banks that care about inflation. As a result, the significance of *hdi* in column (1) can be partly explained by the correlation of this variable with the quality of monetary policy. Interestingly, the sign of *monetqual* is negative meaning that tight monetary policy pursued in order to keep inflation low does not lure foreign investors.

The specificity of developed, transition and Central European countries has been analyzed by means of the three dummy variables *oecd, transition* and *centeur* and the results are reported in columns (3) – (5) of Table 5.1. Only the *oecd* and *centeur* dummies are statistically significant and the estimated coefficients are positive. These results allow concluding that the OECD and Central European countries have some unobserved characteristics that stimulate the inflow of foreign long-term capital. It is noteworthy that the dummy *transition* in column (4) is not statistically significant which suggests that 26 transition countries do not share common characteristics affecting the FDI inflow. By contrast, the group of Central European countries is distinct with respect to FDI determinants. To investigate deeper the factors that attract foreign investors in this region, the bilateral FDI inflows to 11 New Members of the EU will be scrutinized in the next section.

The Human Development Index is a composite measure that combines the level of income, education and health. It can be hypothesized that the components of the HDI have an offsetting impact on FDI and for this reason the variable *hdi* was insignificant in Table 5.1. To verify this hypothesis, equation (5.3) was re-estimated with the three indices that constitute the HDI in the set of independent variables. The *hdi* regressand was thus replaced with the income index *incomex*, life expectancy index *lifex*, and educational attainment index *edux*. The results are presented in Table 5.2.

Table 5.2: Impact of HDI components on total FDI inflow. Dependent variable: Δfdi

VARIABLES	(1)	(2)	(3)	(4)	(5)	(6)	(7)
L.fdi	0.689***	0.578***	0.746***	0.322	0.776***	0.329	0.714***
	(0.121)	(0.146)	(0.117)	(0.241)	(0.104)	(0.296)	(0.131)
popul	1.41e-09**	2.05e-09***	1.21e-09**	3.21e-09**	1.05e-09**	3.25e-09**	1.32e-09**
	(6.06e-10)	(7.46e-10)	(5.77e-10)	(1.25e-09)	(5.21e-10)	(1.46e-09)	(6.52e-10)

incomex	0.248	1.621**	0.449				
	(0.781)	(0.701)	(0.486)				
lifex	0.244			4.649**	0.653		
	(0.658)			(2.143)	(0.941)		
edux	0.978*					3.479*	0.417
	(0.534)					(1.959)	(0.583)
mobile	0.00429**	0.00615***	0.00379**	0.00723**	0.00282	0.00865***	0.00496**
	(0.00187)	(0.00180)	(0.00170)	(0.00283)	(0.00208)	(0.00311)	(0.00238)
L.gdpgr	0.00422	0.00258	0.00783***	0.00224	0.0125***	0.00167	0.00883*
	(0.00284)	(0.00265)	(0.00234)	(0.00392)	(0.00383)	(0.00387)	(0.00467)
monetqual	-0.261**	-0.349***	-0.371**	-0.141	-0.236	-0.148	-0.368**
	(0.131)	(0.125)	(0.142)	(0.191)	(0.163)	(0.225)	(0.178)
oecd			0.679**		0.631**		0.730**
			(0.290)		(0.296)		(0.319)
centeur			0.307***		0.310***		0.238***
			(0.0986)		(0.113)		(0.0891)
Observations	1,556	1,719	1,719	1,738	1,738	1,575	1,575
# of countries	158	167	167	168	168	159	159
AR1 test p-value	0.0265	0.0494	0.0127	0.403	0.00707	0.431	0.0224
AR2 test p-value	0.386	0.268	0.457	0.0394	0.473	0.0365	0.499
J-Hansen test	27.48	21.77	27.92	16.70	22.72	15.07	17.66
(p-value)	(0.438)	(0.749)	(0.415)	(0.475)	(0.159)	(0.590)	(0.411)

Standard errors in parentheses: *** $p<0.01$, ** $p<0.05$, * $p<0.1$. Instruments for the levels equation: *lifex, edux, popul, oecd, transition* and first differences of *L.fdi, mobile, L.gdpgr, incomex*; Instruments for the differenced equation: Δ*lifex*, Δ*edux*, Δ*popul*, Δ*monetqual* and lags 2 and up of *L.fdi, mobile, L.gdpgr, incomex.*

When all three constituent parts of the HDI are included in the set of independent variables in column (1) of Table 5.2, only the education index *edux* is statistically significant. It may be due to the fact that the three components of the HDI are correlated. To overcome this difficulty, their statistical significance was tested separately and the results are reported in columns (2) – (7). The results presented in columns (2), (4), and (6) suggest that all aspects of human development captured in the HDI have a positive impact on FDI. However, the *incomex*, *lifex* and *edux* become statistically insignificant once the *oecd* and *centeur* dummies are inserted among the covariates in columns (3), (5) and (7). It can be inferred from Table 5.2 that the OECD and Central European countries have some unobserved characteristics, correlated with the three components of the HDI, that attract foreign investors and have stronger influence on FDI than the various aspects of human development.

In all specifications of regression equations reported in Table 5.2, the dummy *transition* that distinguishes all 26 transition countries was statistically insignificant. To confirm that the group of all transition countries is not homogenous with respect to the determinants of FDI inflows, equation (5.3) was re-estimated using the data only for the 26 transition countries. The set of explanatory variables was extended to include the indicator of transition elaborated on by the EBRD. Only one of the components of the transition indicator, namely the indicator of enterprise restructuring, *restr*, has proved to be statistically significant but at the mere 10% significance level.

All the results obtained for the transition countries are reported in Table 5.3. In columns (1) and (2) the catchall *hdi* variable is included and it loses its significance when the *restr* index is added to the set of regressors. In the remaining columns of Table 5.3, the significance of the components of theHDI is tested, first jointly (in column 3) and then sequentially (columns 4 – 6). Only the education index is marginally significant in the last column of Table 5.3. Generally, the level of human development is not crucial for foreign investors contemplating establishing a subsidiary in one of the transition countries. There is only weak evidence that the level of education matters for attracting FDI.

Table 5.3: Impact of the HDI and its components on total FDI inflows to transition countries. Dependent variable: Δfdi

VARIABLES	(1)	(2)	(3)	(4)	(5)	(6)
L.fdi	0.291	0.282	0.447	0.334	0.0167	0.397*
	(0.227)		(0.578)	(0.233)	(0.299)	(0.221)
popul	2.37e-08**	2.23e-08***	2.78e-08	1.90e-08***	3.40e-08***	2.38e-08**
	(8.75e-09)	(4.71e-09)	(3.98e-08)	(6.80e-09)	(1.16e-08)	(9.66e-09)
incomex			-3.544	2.440		
			(12.08)	(2.114)		
lifex			0.811		7.472	
			(38.80)		(4.771)	
edux			11.15			6.941*
			(12.42)			(3.988)
mobile	0.00539**	0.00700**	0.00694	0.00772***	0.00921***	0.00510**
	(0.00208)	(0.00281)	(0.00643)	(0.00238)	(0.00177)	(0.00221)
L.gdpgr	0.000212	-0.00282	-0.00383	-0.00293	0.00617	-0.00184
	(0.00574)	(0.00864)	(0.0179)	(0.00708)	(0.00901)	(0.00525)

hdi	5.704*	-1.457				
	(3.069)	(5.947)				
restr		0.475*				
		(0.248)				
Observations	262	250	255	275	275	255
Number of countries	26	26	25	25	25	25
AR1 test p-value	0.229	0.143	0.375	0.240	0.813	0.182
AR2 test p-value	0.186	0.750	0.407	0.236	0.569	0.205
J-Hansen test	10.17	6.655	3.411	5.210	2.853	5.460
(p-value)	1.000	1.000	1	1	1.000	0.999

Standard errors in parentheses: *** p<0.01, ** p<0.05, * p<0.1. Instruments for the levels equation: *hdi, lifex, edux, popul, oecd, transition* and first differences of *L.fdi, mobile, L.gdpgr, incomex, restr*; Instruments for the differenced equation: Δ*lifex*, Δ*edux*, Δ*popul* and lags 2 and up of *L.fdi, mobile, L.gdpgr, incomex, restr.*

It can be concluded that the determinants of FDI inflows in the global sample and transition countries are alike. The size of the market and the number of mobile phones attract foreign investors and human development has no impact on FDI flows. Contrary to the results obtained for the global sample, the lagged value of the stock of foreign capital is not statistically significant in the transition countries. It seems that foreign investors are indifferent to the progress in transition, except for the enterprise restructuring reforms.

The similarity of results obtained for the global sample and transition countries allows abandoning the separate analysis of the latter group. Hence, the significance of the remaining measures of human development – civil liberties (*cl*) and income inequality (*gini*) – will be tested with the use of the data for all countries of the world. The results obtained for these two variables are displayed in the Table 5.4.

Table 5.4: Impact of civil liberties and income inequality on total FDI inflow. Dependent variable: Δfdi

VARIABLES	(1)	(2)	(3)
L.fdi	0.540***	0.648***	0.621***
	(0.149)	(0.127)	(0.138)
popul	2.25e-09***	1.62e-09***	2.29e-09
	(7.61e-10)	(6.03e-10)	(1.43e-09)
hdi	2.048	0.674	2.606
	(1.511)	(1.194)	(1.778)

mobile	0.00647***	0.00499***	0.00392
	(0.00181)	(0.00152)	(0.00567)
L.gdpgr	0.00824	0.0131**	0.0188
	(0.00548)	(0.00616)	(0.0196)
monetqual	-0.533***	-0.543***	-0.367
	(0.138)	(0.146)	(0.397)
oecd		0.726***	
		(0.258)	
cl	-0.111*	-0.0777	
	(0.0631)	(0.0657)	
gini			0.00364
			(0.0256)
Observations	1,524	1,524	263
Number of countries	156	156	113
AR1 test p-value	0.0518	0.0210	0.809
AR2 test p-value	0.959	0.918	0.407
J-Hansen test	11.22	12.79	9.425
(p-value)	0.845	0.750	0.666

Standard errors in parentheses; *** p<0.01, ** p<0.05, * p<0.1; Instruments for the levels equation: *hdi, popul, monetqual, oecd, cl, gini* and first differences of *L.fdi, mobile, L.gdpgr,*; Instruments for the differenced equation: *Δhdi, Δgini, Δcl, Δpopul, Δmonetqual* and lags 2 (1 in column 3) and up of *L.fdi, mobile, L.gdpgr*.

The first and second columns of Table 5.4 show the estimation results of a regression model with the HDI, and civil liberties and Gini indices in the set of explanatory variables. The *cl* variable is significant in column (1) at the 10% level and it enters with a negative sign, which means that a higher degree of civil liberties attracts foreign investors. This variable becomes insignificant once the OECD dummy is added to the set of regressors. It can be concluded that although the inhabitants of OECD countries have been granted a high degree of civil liberties (i.e. the value of *cl* is low in these countries), other unobserved characteristics of these economies are of greater importance for foreign investors.

The last column of Table 5.4 displays the estimation results of the regression equation with the Gini coefficient. The *gini* variable is not statistically significant. This result should be treated with caution as the time dimension of the sample is significantly reduced due to data availability. The number of observations drastically falls to 263 and the positive impact of income inequality on FDI inflows cannot be regarded as a robust result.

Generally, it can be inferred from the analysis of total FDI flows in the years 1995 and 2000-2010 that the size of the market, its rate of growth, the communication costs proxied by the number of mobile phones, and the accumulated stock of foreign capital are the most significant factors that spur FDI inflows. A high quality of monetary policy has been found to deter foreign investors. The real costs of labour did not prove to be significant.

The variables that measure the level of human development were found to exert a very fragile influence on foreign capital inflows. Although the HDI, the level of income, education, healthiness and civil liberties indices seem to have a positive impact on FDI inflows, the results obtained from the regression analysis are not robust to the inclusion of the monetary quality index or OECD membership dummy in the set of controls. The education index was the sole significant component of the HDI in transition countries.

The determinants of FDI in transition countries are not markedly different from those found in the global sample. By contrast, the 11 countries in Central and Eastern Europe, as well as the OECD countries, seem to have some unobserved characteristics that shape their investment attractiveness. To investigate deeper the factors affecting FDI inflows in the former group of countries, we turn in the next section to the analysis of bilateral FDI inflows.

5.4 The determinants of bilateral FDI inflows in Central and Eastern Europe

In this part of the chapter, we focus on the FDI inflows to 11 countries in Central and Eastern Europe, namely the 10 New Member states of the EU and Croatia, over the period 2000-2009.[24] FDI is decomposed into inflows from 34 sources countries.[25] The data on bilateral FDI inflows is from the Eurostat database. The set of control variables used in this section has been modified to include the characteristics of a pair of countries.

---

24 The host countries are: Bulgaria, Croatia, the Czech Republic, Estonia, Hungary, Latvia, Lithuania, Poland, Romania, Slovakia and Slovenia.

25 Those countries are: Austria, Belgium, Canada, Croatia, Cyprus, the Czech Republic, Dania, Estonia, Finland, France, Hungary, Germany, Greece, Ireland, Italy, Japan, Korea, Latvia, Lithuania, Luxemburg, Malta, the Netherlands, Norway, Poland, Portugal, Russia, Slovakia, Slovenia, Spain, Switzerland, Sweden, Turkey, the UK and the USA.

Bergstrand and Egger (2007) have extended the gravity model to provide the framework for the bilateral FDI inflows analysis. According to the gravity approach, very common in empirical studies of trade flows, the FDI inflow should be positively related to the size of the source and host economy and negatively to the transportation costs between them. In what follows, all variables pertaining to the source country will have the *part* ending (for *part*ner country), whereas the ending *rep* (for *rep*orting country) will be added to variables pertaining to the host country. The explanatory variables that come from the gravity model are the logarithms of the GDP level expressed in US PPP dollars in constant prices in the host (*gdprep*) and source (*gdppart*) economies and the logarithm of the distance between the two countries, (*dist*),which is a proxy for the transportation costs.[26]

Besides the three variables inherent in the gravity model, the set of independent variables comprises the degree of financial development in the source country (dcpart) proxied by the amount of credit to the private sector in percentage of GDP. Access for firms to external financing hinges on the degree of financial development and may affect the level of investment and therefore the productivity of firms. Some firms may face liquidity constraints and as a result be less productive and unable to operate abroad as shown in the heterogeneous firms' model of Helpman et al. (2004). Buch et al. (2009) and Li et al. (2011) indeed showed that firms from countries with well-developed financial markets invest more abroad than their counterparts from countries with less advanced financial intermediaries.

The importance of the costs reduction motive for undertaking both vertical and horizontal FDI will be tested by means of two variables. The number of mobile telephones per 100 inhabitants in the host country (mobilerep) is intended to measure the costs of communication. Labour costs will be measured by the income labour share, ulcrep, which takes into account not only the level of wages but also the level of productivity.

Monetary quality and the rate of growth of GDP, which were found to be significant in the previous section, are insignificant in the regression analysis of the bilateral FDI inflows. The same is true of the tariff and tax rate in the both the source and host country. The results of estimation with these variables are omitted.

The use of bilateral data allows distinguishing between vertical and horizontal FDI. According to Markusen and Maskus (2002) a positive (negative)

---

26 Distance is measured as the distance between the major cities of both countries and the data has been taken from the Centre d'études prospectives et d'informations internationales (CEPII) database.

coefficient of the variable that captures differences in countries' endowment in factors of production points to the vertical (horizontal) FDI. The level of per capita GDP is a viable proxy for the endowment in physical capital. Similarly, the level of human development can be interpreted in terms of the endowment in skills. The components of HDI thus reflect the endowment in physical capital (the income index, incomex), educational attainment (the education index, edux) and health (the index of life expectancy, lifex). The relative value of the HDI and its components in the source and host economies can be regarded as a measure of differences in factor endowments.

Following the interpretation of human development as a measure of factor endowment, the set of independent variables of the gravity model has been extended to include the relative value of the HDI and its components. The overall differences in factor endowment, *relhdi*, are quantified by the logarithm of the ratio between the HDI in the source and host country. The differences in physical capital endowment, *relincomex*, are measured by the logarithm of the ratio of the income index, incomex, in the source and host country. Finally, the differences in the human capital endowment are measured by the relative value of the education and life expectancy indices. Thus, *reledux* is the logarithm of the ratio of edux in the source and host economy, and *rellifex* is defined as the logarithm of the ratio of lifex in both countries.

The System GMM estimation method was used and the set of independent variables includes the time dummies. For the sake of brevity, the coefficients accompanying time dummies are not reported. The Arellano-Bond test for the serial correlation of the error term and the J-Hansen test for the exogeneity of instruments were applied. The estimation results of equation (5.3) using data for FDI inflows to 11 Central and Eastern European countries broken down by source countries are presented in Table 5.5.

Table 5.5: Impact of the HDI and its components on bilateral FDI inflows to 11 Central European countries. Dependent variable: Δfdi

VARIABLES	(1)	(2)	(3)	(4)	(5)
L.fdi	0.735***	0.761***	0.763***	0.790***	0.788***
	(0.0606)	(0.0694)	(0.0664)	(0.0684)	(0.0730)
dist	-0.414***	-0.347***	-0.340***	-0.416***	-0.379***
	(0.113)	(0.119)	(0.116)	(0.138)	(0.124)
gdprep	0.229***	0.241***	0.221***	0.217**	0.181**
	(0.0678)	(0.0838)	(0.0792)	(0.0877)	(0.0903)
gdppart	0.186**	0.0881	0.138*	0.212*	0.227*
	(0.0789)	(0.0543)	(0.0739)	(0.116)	(0.121)
dcpart	0.00532***	0.00387**	0.00445**	0.00543**	0.00552**
	(0.00192)	(0.00168)	(0.00179)	(0.00269)	(0.00255)
ulcrep	-1.304	-1.457	-2.009*	-1.523	-1.699*
	(1.042)	(0.908)	(1.036)	(0.943)	(0.935)
mobilerep	0.00246	0.00274	0.00275*	0.00248	0.00350*
	(0.00163)	(0.00167)	(0.00164)	(0.00154)	(0.00184)
relincomex		-1.190	-0.412		
		(0.997)	(0.674)		
rellifex		1.801		2.347*	
		(1.262)		(1.284)	
reledux		0.867*			1.487*
		(0.510)			(0.786)
relhdi	0.219				
	(1.016)				
Observations	2,103	1,826	1,858	1,858	1,826
AR1 test p-value	2.86e-07	7.17e-06	6.18e-06	9.21e-06	1.01e-05
AR2 test p-value	0.201	0.175	0.171	0.169	0.168
J-Hansen test	44.63	46.05	42.91	38.40	38.32
(p-value)	0.445	0.388	0.518	0.318	0.321

Standard errors in parentheses: *** $p<0.01$, ** $p<0.05$, * $p<0.1$. Instruments for the levels equation: *dist, gdppart, reledux, rellifex,* and first differences of *L.fdi, gdprep, mobilerep, dcpart, ulcrep, relhdi, relincomex*; Instruments for the differenced equation: Δ*dist*, Δ*gdppart*, Δ*reledux*, Δ*rellifex* and lags 1 and up of *L.fdi, mobilerep, dcpart, ulcrep, relhdi, relincomex.*

The first column of Table 5.5 shows the results for the relative value of the HDI index among the regressors. First of all, it should be noted that the key variables of the gravity model – the size of the countries and the distance between them – are significant and have the expected signs (i.e. positive for the size and negative or the distance). The labour (*ulcrep*) and communication (*mobilrep*) costs in the host economy are not significant. The level of financial development in the source country is a strong stimulant of FDI inflow. The relative value of the HDI is not significant, which suggests that neither vertical nor horizontal FDI have the lion's share of foreign capital flowing to the Central and Eastern European region.

In the remaining columns of Table 5.5, the significance of the relative value of the HDI components is tested. In column (2), the relative value of all three components of the HDI is added to the set of regressors. Only the relative value of the education index, *edux*, is statistically significant but at the mere 10% level. In the columns (3) – (5), the significance of the relative values of the HDI components is tested sequentially. The relative value of the life expectancy index and the education index is found to be significant but at a low level of significance.

Overall, the results reported in Table 5.5 do not allow for concluding that one type of FDI inflows – horizontal of vertical – dominates in Central and Eastern European countries. The variables reflecting differences in factor endowments are usually not statistically significant. There is only weak evidence that a higher value of education and life index boosts FDI inflows. A positive sign of the *reledux* and *rellifex* variables points to the vertical type of FDI flowing into the New Member States, with the caveat that the level of statistical significance is low.

In a wider sense, the concept of human development goes beyond educational attainment or life expectancy, and comprises civil liberties, which determine the functioning of an individual in the society. It may be instructive to test the hypothesis that the degree of civil liberties affects FDI inflows. Distribution of income is another feature of social and economic order that is related to human development and likely to influence foreign capital flows. For these reasons, we have inserted two novel variables into the set of regressors, namely *clrel* and *ginirel*, which are equal to the logarithms of the ratio of, respectively, civil liberties and the Gini indices in the source and host countries. The estimation results are presented in Table 5.6.

Table 5.6: Impact of civil liberties and income inequality on bilateral FDI inflows to 11 Central European countries. Dependent variable: Δfdi

VARIABLES	(1)	(2)
L.fdi	0.736***	0.609***
	(0.0607)	(0.0933)
dist	-0.421***	-0.482**
	(0.107)	(0.202)
gdprep	0.232***	0.352***
	(0.0772)	(0.126)
gdppart	0.224**	0.0458
	(0.0880)	(0.135)
dcpart	0.00600***	0.00188
	(0.00206)	(0.00162)
ulcrep	-1.973*	-1.314
	(1.069)	(1.139)
mobilerep	0.00341**	0.00185
	(0.00171)	(0.00209)
relcl	-0.0228	
	(0.0774)	
relgini		0.0470
		(0.293)
Observations	2103	1174
AR1 test p-value	5.05e-07	3.89e-05
AR2 test p-value	0.205	0.545
J-Hansen test	32.45	58.83
(p-value)	(0.592)	(0.0667)

Standard errors in parentheses: *** p<0.01, ** p<0.05, * p<0.1. Instruments for the levels equation: *dist, gdppart, relcl, relgini* and first differences of *L.fdi, gdprep, mobilerep, dcpart, ulcrep*; Instruments for the differenced equation: Δ*dist*, Δ*gdppart*, Δ*relcl*, Δ*relgini,* and lags 1 and up of *L.fdi, mobilerep, dcpart, ulcrep.*

The relative value of civil liberties and the Gini indices in Table 5.6 turned out to be insignificant. Thus, the differences in the endowment in human capital that originates in a higher degree of civil liberties and income equality do not affect FDI inflow in the Central and Eastern European countries. It should be noted, however, that all investigated countries (source, as well as host) have achieved a high degree of civil liberties and the variability of the *relcl* variable was low, which could impinge on the results. When interpreting the insignificance of the *ginirel* in the second column of Table 5.6, one should be aware that data availability reduced drastically the number of observations so that drawing definitive and firm conclusions would be hazardous.

Gender inequality is the last aspect of human development that could potentially influence FDI flows and can be analyzed quantitatively. The GII has been calculated only for 2008, which precludes the use of dynamic panel regression analysis. We relied on static panel regression analysis because the inflows of FDI to 11 countries allowed for a cluster sample, where each host country is a cluster. Since the FDI inflow to one of the host economies from various source countries is likely to be correlated, allowing for an unobserved cluster effect is important. The Hausman test favoured the random effects model and the estimation results are reported in Table 5.7.

The FDI inflow has been replaced by the stock of foreign capital in Table 5.7 for two reasons. Firstly, the degree of gender equality does not change a lot within the span of several years, and the value of the index in 2008 reflects the situation in the preceding period as well. Secondly, the value of FDI inflow in 2008 has been distorted by the financial crisis that led to an abrupt fall in capital flows across borders. The stock of foreign capital is less vulnerable to this shock. Taking into account the persistence of the GII and the specificity of the year 2008 from the perspective of capital flows, it seems justified to use the stock of foreign capital instead of its change as the dependent variable in Table 5.7.

Table 5.7: Impact of gender inequality on bilateral FDI inflows to 11 Central European countries. Dependent variable: fdi

VARIABLES	(1)	(2)	(3)	(4)
L.fdi	-0.145**	-0.0915*	-0.0950*	-0.102**
	(0.0568)	(0.0489)	(0.0485)	(0.0484)
dist	-1.489***	-1.613***	-1.523***	-1.471***
	(0.169)	(0.151)	(0.154)	(0.150)
gdprep	1.312***	1.185***	1.132***	1.124***
	(0.150)	(0.133)	(0.134)	(0.134)
gdppart	0.499***	0.535***	0.533***	0.542***
	(0.0830)	(0.0705)	(0.0699)	(0.0697)

dcpart	0.0194***	0.0168***	0.0159***	0.0164***
	(0.00213)	(0.00196)	(0.00197)	(0.00195)
ulcrep	1.342			
	(1.893)			
mobilerep	0.0117**	0.0146***	0.0115**	0.0103**
	(0.00487)	(0.00472)	(0.00486)	(0.00480)
relhdi		5.744***	2.823	
		(1.630)	(2.034)	
relgii			-1.188**	-1.612***
			(0.503)	(0.400)
Constant	-35.03***	-31.63***	-30.40***	-30.61***
	(4.698)	(4.008)	(4.005)	(4.010)
Observations	197	259	259	259
Wald test χ^2	200.6	254.5	264.7	261.8
(p-value)	(0)	(0)	(0)	(0)

Standard errors in parentheses. *** p<0.01, ** p<0.05, * p<0.1

The first column in Table 5.7 displays the estimation results of the benchmark gravity model. In the year 2008, the size of the partner courtiers stimulated FDI inflow and the distance between them was a significant obstacle to foreign investors. Better communication infrastructure attracted foreign investors and the labour costs did not exert a significant influence. The development of financial market in the source country facilitated investment abroad. There is one important difference between the results in Table 5.7 and those discussed before: the lagged value of the stock of foreign capital has a negative sign. This result can be interpreted in light of the worldwide retrenchment of companies hit by the financial crisis of 2008. It seems that capital withdrawal was proportional to the magnitude of the accumulated stock of FDI.

In the second column of Table 5.7, the relative value of the HDI index, *relhdi*, is added to the set of regressors. The estimated coefficient is positive and statistically significant, meaning that larger differences in human capital endowment increased FDI inflows in 2008. The results support the hypothesis that FDI inflows in Central and Eastern Europe are mostly of a vertical type.

Finally, in columns (3) and (4) the significance of *relgii*, the logarithm of the ratio of the GII indices in the source and host country, is tested. It stems from

Table 5.7 that greater gender inequality in the source country relative to the host economy puts a break on FDI inflows. This result is robust to the inclusion of the overall index of human development among the covariates in column (3). Gender inequality seems to be more important than other aspects of human development because *relhdi* becomes insignificant in column (3). It should be noted, however, that the results in Table 5.7 can be contaminated by the problem of reverse causation, as for instance, the situation of women in the labour market may depend on the presence of foreign investors.

The results presented in this section speak in favour of the gravity model as the methodological framework for an analysis of FDI inflows to 11 Central and Eastern European countries broken down by source countries. The key variables of the gravity model, the size of partner economies and the distance between them, are significant and have the predicted sign. Moreover, there is also evidence that a higher degree of financial development in the source country and a larger number of mobile phones in the host country were associated over the period 2000-2009 with a larger FDI inflow.

The relative endowment in human capital exerts a weak and fragile influence of FDI flows. Only the two components of the HDI, namely the relative values of education and life expectancy indices, were found to be positively associated with the FDI inflow but at the mere 10% significance level. The degrees of civil liberties and income inequality have no impact on foreign investment. By contrast, the discrepancy in the degree of gender equality in the source and host countries significantly deters foreign investment. This conclusion needs, however, to be confirmed when longer time series of the GII will be available for researchers. Generally, the analysis of FDI inflows, both total and broken down by source country, has revealed that the role of human development as a determinant of FDI flows is very limited in the global sample, as well as in the countries in Central and Eastern Europe.

6 Firm Level Analysis of FDI and Human Development

Łukasz Goczek

6.1 Introduction

The growth of foreign direct investment (FDI) flows outgrows the rate of growth of other international transactions, particularly trade flows between countries. Currently almost half of trade flows are intrafirm (Bloningen 2005). At the same time, the growing dependence of emerging economies on FDI is usually seen as a highly desirable aspect of development of these markets, since this type of investment is attributed with a number of positive effects for the hosting economy. In this context, most literature on the effects of FDI points to the transfer of improved management techniques, technology spillovers, and easier access to international financial markets, associated with investment made by companies with foreign capital. The literature also indicates that FDI is the most stable long-term commitment that these countries can make on the international capital markets in order to finance their deficits on current accounts (World Bank, 2007; Próchniak and Witkowski, 2013).

These positive effects have drawn the attention of many economic researchers, who aim to investigate the factors that are likely determinants of the location and magnitude of FDI. These determinants range from taxes, GDP, and other "classic" to this literature macroeconomic variables, to factors that are likely more endogenous within the FDI activity, such as trade protection and trade flows. These latter determinants of FDI open up the larger issue of varying microeconomic motivations for FDI that are to a large degree ignored, by the, mostly macroeconomic in scope, partial equilibrium literature. This approach does not take into account many factors relating to business environment in the host country. However, it is straightforward to argue that FDI should flow into countries with relatively stable economic conditions and strong institutions, and that investors should be concerned about political instability, inflexible regulations, and poor social development indicators among prospective workers. Still, there is extraordinarily little evidence to support these arguments (Walsh and Yu, 2010). This lack of evidence is probably caused by firm-level data shortage, although this has changed with the recent advent of large international datasets for firms.

The purpose of this chapter is to explore, with the use of quantitative methods, the relationship between FDI and social development at a firm level.

The study focused on obstacles to businesses associated with social development as perceived by companies with foreign capital in Central and Eastern Europe. The second part of the chapter contains a brief literature review; the third part describes the data and the methodology of estimating the empirical model, the fourth part presents the results obtained using the econometrically estimated model. The last part of the chapter presents our conclusions.

6.2 Literature review

A favourable business environment is important for both the decision about the involvement of foreign investors in a given FDI host country and the decision on the scale of the commitment of foreign capital. Before making an investment, investors look at certain major economic policy issues particularly relating to trade, labour, governance, regulatory quality, and the availability of physical and social infrastructure. Factors describing the business environment analyzed in this respect are very important for foreign investors, since companies with foreign capital may have a different profile of activity to domestic companies and thus they may react differently to the country's current difficulties and obstacles to doing business. These difficulties can be particularly severe in the area of social development, in particular related to deficiencies in appropriate education and training of local staff. This is because qualified human capital increases business productivity by making better use of current technologies and to enable the introduction of new ones (Acemoglu, and Shimer, 1999).

By looking at a firm level, researchers have asked why companies would want to service foreign markets through affiliate production rather than through exporting or licensing arrangements. Dunning (1993) outlines four motives for a firm to engage in this type of investment: access to resources, access to markets, efficiency gains and acquisition of strategic assets. Wei (2000) finds that corruption significantly adds to firm costs and impedes FDI inflows. Javorcik-Smarzynska and Spatareanu (2005) show that regulation matters for foreign investors. Wei and Smarzyńska (2000) present evidence that corruption reduces inward FDI and shifts the ownership structure towards joint ventures. Habib and Zurawicki (2001, 2002) also provide evidence in the line of an unfavourable business environment deterring foreign direct investments. They find the impact of bad governance on FDI to be larger than that on local investment. They conclude that foreign investors are more sensitive to these traits of the host economy than their local counterparts are.

Skilled human capital increases the productivity of the company, which allows companies to make better use of current technologies and enable them to benefit from new ones (Acemoglu and Shimer, 1999, Bresnahan, Brynjolfsson and Hitt, 2002). In addition, a number of other factors that determine the share of foreign investment could be pointed out. For example, financial development is an important aspect of the business environment. It increases business efficiency by stimulating profitable investment and better selection and allocation of resources to the most profitable projects (Levine, 1997). Johnson et al. (2000) show that companies with foreign capital may have weaker ties with local authorities. This often puts them at a disadvantage relative to their local competition, which can resort to informal ways of influence when competing for a place in the market by bribing officials in order to obtain benefits in the application of laws and regulations to reduce business efficiency when it is not possible to reach the relevant intermediaries. Foreign companies may also be less effective than local companies because they may face difficulties in understanding the characteristics of local markets. Problems associated with inadequate transport and telecommunications, or uncertainty of electricity supply, etc. add to the cost of reaching customers and increase the cost of doing business (World Bank, 1994).

A relatively large part of the research on FDI firm-level determinants has been done focusing on the region of Central and Eastern Europe. This is naturally caused by funding of large surveys by international firms, Javorcik-Smarzynska (2004), using a firm-level data set from Eastern Europe and the former Soviet Union, that finds empirical evidence for the fact that the strength of the patent laws and the overall level of intellectual property rights protection affect FDI inflows in several high-technology sectors. Anghel (2006) shows using Amadeus data on an international set of firms, that the FDI stock is higher in countries that have higher growth rates of GDP, are more open to trade, enjoy a better control of the degree of corruption and have achieved substantial progress in the transition process. Benacek, Gronicki, and Holland (2000) suggest that market seeking has been the primary motive of investors, national and regional market access was the primary factor that influenced potential investors. Factor cost advantages were not considered an important motive for locating in Central Europe by most investors. Bellak, Leibrecht, and Stehrer (2000) show that for four CEE countries not much can be gained (against other EU countries) in terms of FDI from a further lowering of taxes. This is because the largest gaps arise from deficiencies in research and development in general. Instead, policies should strive to increase the share of higher educated workers as this is relatively low compared to that of the US-plus-EU-6 economies. Goczek (2013) finds that companies with foreign capital often encounter difficulties with inadequate education of the workforce in relation to companies with domestic capital, both private and public.

6.3 Methodology

The empirical model is aimed at analyzing the firm-level determinants of the inflow of foreign capital with particular emphasis on the degree of social development. The data used in the model is derived from an empirical study, the "Business Environment and Enterprise Performance Survey" of the World Bank and the European Bank for Reconstruction and Development. This survey provided data on the business operating environment of firms in Central and Eastern Europe, such as their relationship with the state, methods of financing, difficulties in recruiting staff, infrastructure shortages, informal payments and corruption. The survey was conducted in 29 countries of Central and Eastern Europe every three years. Subsequent editions of the study took place in the years 1999, 2002, 2005 and 2008. The results of the first study were not used in the investigation, because they are not comparable with later because of another questionnaire and a different group of countries analyzed. The other three editions of the survey covered about 25,000 companies that employ five or more people. These companies are either in private or state hands and are foreign, have different sizes, reach different levels of income and have different types of core business. There are variables of interest in foreign ownership in these companies, and in the difficulties encountered in the conduct of business, as well as in a number of their characteristics.[27]

The following main hypothesis is verified in the study of determinants of the share of foreign ownership at the firm level: social development factors have a positive impact on the level of foreign direct investment. Moreover, during the investigation, several control hypotheses were also tested:

- Firms with foreign capital are more likely to encounter problems with infrastructure.
- Firms with foreign capital have an easier access to financing
- Firms with foreign capital often encounter problems of an informal nature, especially in contacts with the state.
- A quick and impartial judicial system is relatively more important to companies with foreign capital.
- Firms with foreign capital are generally bigger than domestic companies.

---

27 Percentage of denied responses differed depending on the question. Enterprises willing to respond to questions about property (91 replies do not know the 25,000 firms), are less likely when it comes to the difficulties they encounter, especially the difficulties that arise at the interface with the state.

- The scope of the difficulties in doing business faced by a given company may vary from country to country.

The empirical investigations were carried out on a sample of 25,000 companies from Central and Eastern Europe starting from 2002 and ending in 2008. The study was based on regression analysis in which the variables of interest – related to social development - were used. These were mainly variables corresponding to education and women's inequality. The adopted methodology was to select a small model and test the obtained results for robustness (bottom-up or specific-to-general – Lutkepohl, 2007).

The investigation follows Smarzynska and Spatareanu (2004) and Aitken and Harrison (1999) in constructing the dependent variable. These authors proposed the percentage of capital owned by the foreign company in the domestic company as a measure of the FDI stock. Therefore, the equation of the empirical model aimed at assessing the impact of social development factors on the level of foreign direct investment at the firm level is as follows:

$$y = x\beta + \varepsilon \qquad (6.1)$$

where x is the vector of explanatory variables (both of interest and control), $x\beta$ is a vector of coefficients, ε is the random error component. The dependent variable y is the share of foreign ownership in the capital of a company.

It may be noted that the empirical verification of hypothesized relationships cannot be fully identified in terms of causality using the model defined by (6.1). This means that the proposed estimation and hypotheses need to be merely understood as postulated correlations. What's more, it can also be argued that the estimates carried out on microeconomic data using the share of foreign ownership in the capital of sampled firms may not easily translate to conclusions and recommendations at a macroeconomic level. It should also be noted that the dependent variable is censored because it ranges, depending on the adopted method of estimation, between zero and one, or zero and one hundred. Some of these problems have been tackled by selecting a relevant estimation technique. These choices are described below.

A statistically correct estimation using simple linear regression methods is not possible when using a variable representing foreign ownership in the capital of the companies as an indicator of the level of foreign direct investment. This is due to the problem of sample censoring - the model should describe the level of foreign investment at the firm level, but this value is observable only if the foreign investment actually has been made. These are the situations where the marginal benefit exceeds the marginal cost to foreign investors – meaning that a foreign company or a person is willing to invest in a given firm in the country. However, the opposite case is unobservable, in which the costs were higher than the benefits, meaning that some unknown difficulties have prevented investment in a company from a given country. In other words, the costs and difficulties of a prohibitively high value are not observed. For this reason, it can be concluded that the variable describing the amount of foreign investment is censored.

Three methods of dealing with the phenomenon of non-random sample censoring were considered. The first is a double-sided truncated Tobit, the second is complementary logistic regression (sometimes called Complementary Log-Log Regression), which approximates ordered categories to observations; the third is the Fractional Logit. The Tobin correction (1979) used with censoring on both sides at the level of 0 and 100 can correct the results for the impact of non-random (systematic in determinants) unobservable heterogeneity in the sample. This model assumes that the variable of interest, y^* is not fully observed in the whole range between minus and plus infinity. Instead, the variable y is observed, which is defined as follows: $y = 0$, if $y^* \leq 0$, $y = y^*$, where $0 < y^* < 1$ and $y = 1$ if $y^* \geq 1$. It is also assumed that there is a linear relationship between the unobserved variable and the explanatory variables:

$$E(y^*|x) = x\beta \qquad (6.2)$$

This method, however, can be challenged on theoretical grounds by raising doubts about the nature of censoring of the sample. It can be argued that the mechanism causing the truncation of the sample is not non-random, but rather is caused by the very nature of the variable - by definition the share of foreign capital in the capital of a given company is always limited by 0 and 100 (or 0 and 1). Thus, the phenomenon of failing to invest in a given company and the maximum possible involvement of foreign capital in a given company does not affect the results.

A common solution to the problem of censoring the sample "by definition" whenever the observations are fractions is the logistic regression method, but this also faces a number of problems due to the nature of the data on the share of foreign ownership in the capital of companies. The estimated logistic regression equation takes the form:

$$E(log[y/(1-y)]|x = x\beta \qquad (6.3)$$

It can be noted however that the logistic transformation is possible only when the variable y is from the open interval between 0 and 1 but the data collected on the share of foreign ownership is dominated by the values 0 and 1, which prevent this transformation. Dependent variable transformation methods that can be found in the literature are usually based on changing its range (for example by adding a scalar value to all observations). These methods, however, are always arbitrary and more importantly they may affect the results in a nontrivial and unexpected way.

One of the ways of addressing the latter phenomenon is fitting a logistic regression using a logit transformation under the assumption that the variables are discrete and ordered. This method is called a complementary logistic regression. In this case, the equation describing the investigated phenomenon is expressed by the following formula:

$$Pr(y \neq 0 | x) = G(x\beta) = 1 - exp\{-exp(x\beta)\}, \quad (6.4)$$

where the value 0 is interpreted as a negative outcome (lack of foreign investment). At the same time all other values of the dependent variable are treated (with the exception of missing values) as a positive result (the existence of foreign investments). The described model can be estimated by the quasi-maximum likelihood estimator of the variance robust to heteroscedascity.

The obvious drawback of this method is that it gives greater weight to observations taking values from the range (0.1), which under these assumptions are all treated as the existence of foreign investment. Thus it simplifies the decision of the foreign investing entity to one level - to invest or not, ignoring the decision about the scale of the involvement at the selection stage. Therefore, a third method was proposed, which is the Fractional Logit by Papke and Wooldridge (1996). The equation for estimating the model of interest is:

$$E(y | x) = G(x\beta) = \frac{\exp(x\beta)}{1 + \exp(x\beta)} \quad (6.5)$$

In this model, one can estimate the vector of parameters β using the following Bernoulli log-likelihood function:

$$I(\beta) = y \log[G(x\beta)] + (1 - y)\log[1 - G(x\beta)]. \quad (6.6)$$

Assuming a logit function for $G(z)$ gives the following variance:

$$Var(y|x) = \sigma^2 \cdot G(x\beta)[1 - G(x\beta)]. \quad (6.7)$$

This method has several advantages. It is quite easy to compute using quasi log-likelihood methods. The advantage of this approach compared to ordinary logistic regression and Tobin's correction is not leaving behind observations in which the share of foreign capital is exactly equal to zero or unity.

The problems of the potential endogeneity of some of the variables and the self-selection in the sample were considered during robustness tests. Results obtained with a two-stage estimation method do not indicate the presence of any of these statistical problems. In the first case, it was probably due to the fact that companies are willing to disclose information about their property structure and therefore there is no potential for the self-selection phenomenon in this regard. As for the endogeneity problem, the opposite direction of the impact of the investigated variable on the explanatory variables (FDI inflow increases the level of education in the country) appear to be very unlikely from a theoretical viewpoint.

6.4 Estimation results

Tables 6.1 - 6.4 present the regression results that explain the percentage of foreign capital in firm capital with the percentage of employees with higher education, the proportion of skilled workers and a number of control variables. These estimates were obtained using the two-limit Tobit method (censored on both sides). The fractional logit method gave very similar results (they are in Tables 6A.1-6A.4 in the Appendix). Furthermore, very similar results were obtained with the use of complementary logistic regression (not shown). The tables do not report the results for dummy variables for countries and sectors as the Wald test has shown their joint insignificance and, therefore, they were dropped altogether from the models.

Both variables reflecting the recruitment of educated workers by companies with foreign capital were statistically significant. The percentage of employees with university education was significant at the 0.01 level; the significance of the percentage of skilled workers was generally lower, while the coefficient was generally higher. This result proved to be unaffected by the selection of variables in the model.

There were only three cases in which the education variables were no longer significant and they were all associated with a significant reduction in the number of observations in the sample. The first case was a model specification in which the variable "Is the Top Manager female?" was included. This variable proved to be insignificant, but it reduced the significance of the educational variables. This result can easily be called into question - a very small percentage of firms responded to this question, and therefore the sample size, which in other models amounts to about 13-17 thousand companies, was only 3670 in this case. A similar result, in the second case, can be seen in the first column of Table 6.2 – a drop in the number of observations by three-quarters (up to 3000 observations) probably caused by the insignificance of the variables of the basic model. In the third case, the variable "% of people using computers at work" was added to the model. This variable was significant, but this was associated with a significant reduction in the number of observations.[28]

---

28 It should be noted that this variable is similar to the variables describing education - computers are typically used for activities requiring higher levels of education. It is therefore considered that this result, although expected and plausible, does not play a particularly important role in confirming the main hypothesis in this part of the study.

Table 6.1: Tobit estimation results

	(1)	(2)	(3)	(4)
% of employees at the end of the fiscal year with a university degree	1.2307***	-0.3690	1.2162***	1.1708***
	(0.0978)	(0.2197)	(0.0992)	(0.1107)
% of skilled employees at the end of the fiscal year	25.4719**	24.1902	25.6037**	41.6691***
	(9.5911)	(22.8909)	(9.7400)	(11.0080)
Is the Top Manager female?		15.2373		
		(8.9434)		
Did you experience insufficient water supply for production in last fiscal year?			2.5233	
			(4.2479)	
Over the 2006 fiscal year, did this establishment experience power outages?			-6.6903	
			(3.9606)	
In the last fiscal year, what were this establishment's total annual sales?				-0.0000
				(0.0000)
Constant	-279.2456***	-243.7084***	-273.1576***	-284.0878***
	(10.8910)	(27.7680)	(13.6180)	(12.4444)
Observations	17205	3670	16721	13654

Source: own calculations. Standard errors in parentheses, * p<.05, ** p<.01, *** p<.001.

Table 6.2 Tobit estimation results - cont.

	(1)	(2)	(3)	(4)	(5)
% of employees at the end of the fiscal year with a university degree	-0.3636	0.9395***	1.4956***	1.5125***	1.4923***
	(0.2476)	(0.1422)	(0.1218)	(0.1166)	(0.1166)
% of skilled employees at end of the fiscal year	20.2200	39.0218**	45.1689***	33.1394**	37.5547***
	(26.4161)	(13.9918)	(11.8257)	(11.2282)	(11.3005)
Total cost of inspections - official and unofficial payments	0.0000				
	(0.0000)				
Number of working days spent by staff dealing with inspections procedures		0.1868*			
		(0.0792)			

Percentage of total annual sales paid for security in the last fiscal year			-1.1264		
			(1.0527)		
Losses due to theft, robbery, vandalism or arson in the last fiscal year (% of sales)				-6.2465***	
				(1.3497)	
Percentage of total annual sales paid in informal payments					-4.2340***
					(1.0696)
Constant	-209.1730***	-304.1093***	-298.2319***	-302.6070***	-295.3646***
	(24.7582)	(15.8559)	(13.7458)	(13.0992)	(13.1409)
Observations	3000	10511	11534	13549	12697

Source: own calculations. Standard errors in parentheses, * p<.05, ** p<.01, *** p<.001.

Table 6.3: Tobit estimation results - cont.

	(1)	(2)	(3)	(4)	(5)
% of employees at end of the fiscal year with a university degree	1.1801***	1.1321***	1.1457***	1.0983***	1.2311***
	(0.0975)	(0.0996)	(0.0999)	(0.1004)	(0.0993)
% of skilled employees at end of the fiscal year	27.4528**	22.2974*	21.0206*	18.7115*	26.8639**
	(9.5889)	(9.8350)	(9.8107)	(9.8825)	(9.7551)
How much of an obstacle is: Access to finance	-18.3447***				
	(1.7067)				
The court system is fair, impartial and uncorrupted		1.0550			
		(1.1776)			
"The court system is quick"			-1.8380		
			(1.2402)		
"The court system is able to enforce its decisions"				-1.6629	
				(1.1303)	
What % of senior management time was spent in dealing with government regulations?					0.3380
					(0.1872)
Constant	- 249.5947***	- 272.3223***	- 265.8642***	- 262.0646***	- 283.1606***
	(10.6388)	(11.4482)	(11.2241)	(11.3484)	(11.1840)
Observations	16528	16070	15968	15772	16721

Source: own calculations. Standard errors in parentheses, * p<.05, ** p<.01, *** p<.001.

Table 6.4: Tobit estimation results - cont.

	(1)	(2)	(3)	(4)
% of employees at end of the fiscal year with a university degree	1.2279***	0.9777***	-0.6111**	0.8689***
	(0.0979)	(0.1268)	(0.2349)	(0.1356)
% of skilled employees at end of the fiscal year	23.3916*	26.4911*	38.9955	37.2681**
	(9.6039)	(12.3402)	(24.5572)	(13.3536)
How much of an obstacle is: transportation of goods, supplies and inputs?	5.5815*			
	(2.1817)			
Do you use technology licensed from a foreign-owned company?		14.6289***		
		(3.0366)		
% of establishment's workforce that regularly use computers in their jobs			0.6288**	
			(0.1980)	
Total number of inspections in the last fiscal year				0.7450***
				(0.1903)
Constant	-280.3546***	-273.5188***	-237.1002***	-304.6454***
	(10.9926)	(14.7491)	(24.3362)	(15.3628)
Observations	17034	12517	3670	11248

Source: own calculations. Standard errors in parentheses, * p<.05, ** p<.01, *** p<.001.

Based on the above results it can therefore be concluded that companies with foreign capital employ higher-skilled and better educated workers.[29] This result is robust to the addition of other variables in the model. Moreover, the estimated coefficient is always the same size irrespective of control variables – this enables us to argue that the study is carried out correctly in statistical terms.

The results concerning control variables were diverse. Interestingly, the hypothesis that companies with foreign capital have particular difficulties with informal relationships in contact with the state in the economy has not been confirmed. As a rule, these difficulties were lower for these firms relative to domestic firms. The variables pertaining to different types of informal payments were not statistically significant. Nevertheless, some of the results may

29 This result may be due to the fact that foreign firms in the sample are more advanced and more export oriented. It is difficult, however, to determine whether this finding also indicates that increasing human capital attracts foreign direct investment. The results presented in Goczek (2013) can put this result in perspective - according to the author, the biggest obstacle to business for companies with foreign capital is an insufficiently educated workforce. These two results when combined allow us to reach the conclusions presented in the conclusions section of the chapter.

indirectly provide some backing to the control hypotheses. Enterprises with foreign capital were controlled during state inspections relatively more often and their managers spend significantly more time in contact with the state authorities. Perhaps the lack of contact of foreign capital firms with local intermediaries dealing with the state officials has no effect on the experience of corruption, but harassment with long-running state inspections is in fact more common amongst these firms (Table 6.4 column 4).

The importance of control variables relating to the inadequacy of technical infrastructure is ambiguous. Companies with foreign capital are not more likely to be troubled by problems with water supply or electricity than domestic firms; however these results depend on the method of estimation. The foreign owned companies complained significantly more often about the shortcomings of the transport infrastructure, but perhaps they simply dealt with this problem more often – almost by definition, they are faced with the necessity of transporting people and goods over long distances. Thus, only this kind of infrastructure could have an impact on the size of the involvement of foreign capital in a given economy, however, this result was also not robust to changes in the methods of estimation.

As the results shown in the first column of Table 6.3 indicate, development of the local financial market did not matter for enterprises with foreign capital, which confirms the main thesis of empirical studies on external financing difficulties by Goczek (2012). The author points out that companies with foreign capital face relatively fewer difficulties in getting external financing, as these companies are able to transfer some of the capital from parent companies.

During the next stage of research, the scale effects hypothesis (whether a large scale of a given company influences the results) was tested by adding the number of employees and the value of sales of the company to the model. While the number of employees was significant, the value of sales was not. The addition of these variables did not affect the variables relating to the main hypothesis of this section. The results of these estimations are reported in Tables 6.5-6.8.

Table 6.5: Fractional Logit results – scale effects

	(1)	(2)	(3)	(4)
% of employees at the end of the fiscal year with a university degree	0.0280***	0.0108	0.0324***	0.0282***
	(0.0007)	(0.0061)	(0.0011)	(0.0063)
% of skilled employees at the end of the fiscal year	-0.0630	5.5611***	0.4404***	-0.1169
	(0.0827)	(1.2272)	(0.1219)	(0.7136)

Number of employees at the end of the fiscal year	0.6480***	0.0969*	0.7195***	0.6724***
	(0.0137)	(0.0429)	(0.0206)	(0.1199)
Is the Top Manager female?		-0.2347		
		(0.2426)		
Did you experience insufficient water supply for production in the last fiscal year?			-0.4398***	
			(0.0805)	
Over the fiscal year 2006, did this establishment experience power outages?			0.4194***	
			(0.0647)	
In the last fiscal year, what were this establishment's total annual sales?				-0.0000
				(0.0000)
Constant	-11.3162***	-8.3545***	-13.0056***	-11.6292***
	(0.1930)	(1.2566)	(0.3192)	(1.6925)
Observations	16164	558	11344	16164

Source: own calculations. Standard errors in parentheses, * p<.05, ** p<.01, *** p<.001.

Table 6.6: Fractional Logit results – scale effects - cont.

	(1)	(2)	(3)	(4)	(5)
% of employees at end of the fiscal year with a university degree	0.0276***	0.0283***	0.0094	0.0110	0.0290***
	(0.0037)	(0.0078)	(0.0063)	(0.0069)	(0.0007)
% of skilled employees at the end of fiscal year	1.0853**	-0.1406	5.3690***	5.6638***	-0.0339
	(0.4207)	(0.8910)	(1.2679)	(1.2808)	(0.0834)
Number of employees at the end of the fiscal year	0.8052***	0.6759***	0.0853	0.0993*	0.5888***
	(0.0728)	(0.1509)	(0.0442)	(0.0460)	(0.0139)
How much of an obstacle is: transportation of goods, supplies and inputs?	1.0927***				
	(0.2871)				
Do you use technology licensed from a foreign-owned company?		1.2408			
		(3.6338)			
Does this establishment compete against unregistered or informal firms?					
How much of an obstacle are			-0.0765		

the informal sector competitors to your operations?			(0.0575)		
How much of an obstacle are the formal sector competitors to your operations?			0.0283		
			(0.0895)		
% of the establishment's workforce that regularly use computers in their jobs				0.0002	
				(0.0073)	
Total number of inspections in last fiscal year					-0.0004
					(0.0006)
Constant	-12.9715***	-14.1607	-8.3938***	-8.9052***	-10.4748***
	(1.0002)	(7.6845)	(1.2573)	(1.1955)	(0.1937)
Observations	15873	15537	558	5580	13844

Source: own calculations. Standard errors in parentheses, * p<.05, ** p<.01, *** p<.001.

Table 6.7: Fractional Logit results – scale effects - cont.

	(1)	(2)	(3)	(4)	(5)
% of employees at the end of fiscal year with a university degree	0.0163**	0.0289***	0.0267***	0.0128***	0.0502***
	(0.0063)	(0.0007)	(0.0007)	(0.0003)	(0.0014)
% of skilled employees at the end of fiscal year	5.4677***	-0.0577	0.0330	-0.3733***	0.2238
	(1.2994)	(0.0833)	(0.0845)	(0.0328)	(0.1349)
Number of employees at the end of the fiscal year	0.0943*	0.6060***	0.7065***	0.5029***	0.9797***
	(0.0480)	(0.0146)	(0.0144)	(0.0051)	(0.0228)
Total cost of inspections - official and unofficial payments	0.0000				
	(0.0000)				
Number of working days spent by staff dealing with inspections procedures		-0.0034**			
		(0.0013)			
% of sales from products/services subject to compulsory certificates					
% of total annual sales paid for security in the last fiscal year			-0.1276***		
			(0.0095)		
Losses due to theft, robbery,				0.0039*	

vandalism or arson in the last fiscal year (% of sales)				(0.0018)	
Percentage of total annual sales paid in informal payments					-0.1411***
					(0.0107)
Constant	-8.7814***	-10.6624***	-11.9221***	-8.1220***	-16.9843***
	(1.2694)	(0.1988)	(0.2019)	(0.0601)	(0.3475)
Observations	492	13769	15010	15559	12197

Source: own calculations. Standard errors in parentheses, * p<.05, ** p<.01, *** p<.001.

Table 6.8: Fractional Logit results – scale effects – cont.

	(1)	(2)	(3)	(4)	(5)
% of employees at the end of the fiscal year with a university degree	0.0264***	0.0283***	0.0280***	0.0271***	0.0304***
	(0.0007)	(0.0009)	(0.0008)	(0.0009)	(0.0009)
% of skilled employees at the end of the fiscal year	0.1481	0.0793	0.0769	-0.0825	0.3683***
	(0.0807)	(0.1030)	(0.0871)	(0.0968)	(0.0968)
Number of employees at the end of the fiscal year	0.6060***	0.6611***	0.6603***	0.6058***	0.5960***
	(0.0134)	(0.0173)	(0.0145)	(0.0169)	(0.0147)
How much of an obstacle is: Access to finance	-0.1048***				
	(0.0160)				
The court system is fair, impartial and uncorrupted		-0.2668***			
		(0.0193)			
"The court system is quick"			-0.0535**		
			(0.0195)		
"The court system is able to enforce its decisions"				-0.1983***	
				(0.0166)	
What % of senior management time was spent in dealing with government regulations?					-0.0488***
					(0.0026)
Constant	-10.4657***	-11.0044***	-11.4925***	-10.2132***	-10.4964***
	(0.1924)	(0.2437)	(0.2130)	(0.2410)	(0.2120)
Observations	14715	15799	15786	15491	13910

Source: own calculations. Standard errors in parentheses, * p<.05, ** p<.01, *** p<.001.

Lastly, variables previously tested on the country-level (country characteristics that are the same for each firm in a given country) were added to the analysis. As already mentioned, dummy variables were jointly insignificant, however, in almost all cases, three of them turned out to be significant (they were Hungary and Kazakhstan with a negative sign, Estonia with a positive sign). Therefore, at the outset of the investigation, variables at the macroeconomic level were expected to be insignificant. The following measures of social development were examined:

- The Human Development Index (HDI);
- The individual components of the HDI: logarithm of income per capita and life expectancy. For some of the countries, the variables "average number of years of education" or "the expected number of years of education" were not available;
- The Freedom House Index of civil liberties;
- Income inequality measured by the Gini index.

Results for the HDI variable are shown in Tables 6.9-6.12. The HDI index was significant in all specifications. The adding of this variable did not affect the strength of the relationship between education and FDI, despite the fact that they both contain a similar component of education. This relationship was significant and positive. Then, the HDI variable was disaggregated and its components were then added to the regression alongside the index of civil liberties and the Gini index. The results of the addition of these variables to the model are shown in Tables 6.A5-6.A8 in the Appendix. As already mentioned, for some of the countries, the variables "average number of years of education" or "the expected number of years of education" were not available. None of the tested components of the HDI were significant, i.e. neither the logarithm of the level of income per capita nor life expectancy. This result could be caused by the fact that these variables are themselves correlated. Nevertheless, significant and of the assumed sign were both indices – the Civil Liberties index and Gini coefficient.

Table 6.9: Fractional Logit estimation results - HDI

	(1)	(2)	(3)	(4)	(5)
% of employees at the end of the fiscal year with a university degree	0.0097***	-0.0038	0.0097***	0.0087***	0.0111***
	(0.0008)	(0.0024)	(0.0008)	(0.0009)	(0.0009)
% of skilled employees at the end of fiscal year	-0.1271	-0.0079	-0.0905	-0.0813	-0.0903
	(0.0742)	(0.1460)	(0.0763)	(0.0844)	(0.0950)

HDI	1.9248***	2.0491*	1.9543***	1.7212***	1.4484***
	(0.3637)	(0.8484)	(0.3684)	(0.4031)	(0.4155)
Is the Top Manager female?		0.2049			
		(0.1199)			
Did you experience insufficient water supply for production in the last fiscal year?			0.0086		
			(0.0382)		
Over the fiscal year 2006, did this establishment experience power outages?			-0.0726*		
			(0.0339)		
In the last fiscal year, what were this establishment's total annual sales?				-0.0000	
				(0.0000)	
% of total annual sales paid in informal payments					-0.0351***
					(0.0102)
Constant	-3.8479***	-4.0443***	-3.7934***	-3.7134***	-3.5496***
	(0.2856)	(0.6993)	(0.2916)	(0.3171)	(0.3277)
Observations	17203	3670	16719	13652	12695

Source: own calculations. Standard errors in parentheses, * p<.05, ** p<.01, *** p<.001.

Table 6.10: Fractional Logit estimation results – HDI – cont.

	(1)	(2)	(3)	(4)	(5)
% of employees at the end of the fiscal year with a university degree	0.0098***	0.0071***	-0.0037	-0.0037	0.0065***
	(0.0008)	(0.0010)	(0.0023)	(0.0024)	(0.0011)
% of skilled employees at the end of the fiscal year	-0.1340	-0.1744*	-0.0162	-0.0033	-0.1472
	(0.0744)	(0.0864)	(0.1426)	(0.1380)	(0.0917)
How much of an obstacle is: transportation of goods, supplies and inputs?	0.0441*				
	(0.0203)				
HDI	1.9874***	1.1241*	2.0440*	1.8114*	1.9956***
	(0.3658)	(0.4632)	(0.8459)	(0.8567)	(0.4982)
Do you use technology licensed from a foreign-owned company?		-0.0990***			
		(0.0233)			
Does this establishment			0.0362*		

compete against unregistered or informal firms?			(0.0183)		
How much of an obstacle are the informal sector competitors to your operations?				-0.0490**	
				(0.0166)	
How much of an obstacle are the formal sector competitors to your operations?				-0.0005	
				(0.0231)	
Total number of inspections in the last fiscal year					0.0064***
					(0.0016)
Constant	-3.9212***	-3.0818***	-3.6942***	-3.4759***	-3.9501***
	(0.2882)	(0.3627)	(0.6590)	(0.6666)	(0.3906)
Observations	17032	12517	3670	3670	11248

Source: own calculations. Standard errors in parentheses, * p<.05, ** p<.01, *** p<.001.

Table 6.11: Fractional Logit estimation results – HDI – cont.

	(1)	(2)	(3)	(4)	(5)
% of employees at the end of the fiscal year with a university degree	-0.0030	0.0070***	-0.0013	0.0108***	0.0111***
	(0.0026)	(0.0011)	(0.0029)	(0.0009)	(0.0009)
% of skilled employees at the end of the fiscal year	0.0463	-0.1550	-0.0635	-0.1475	-0.1589
	(0.1823)	(0.1053)	(0.1597)	(0.0896)	(0.0923)
Total cost of inspections - official and unofficial payments	0.0000				
	(0.0000)				
HDI	3.3169***	2.3275***	1.1170	1.5329***	1.9858***
	(0.9353)	(0.5123)	(1.0169)	(0.4499)	(0.4091)
Number of working days spent by staff dealing with inspections procedures		0.0016**			
		(0.0006)			
% of total annual sales paid in informal payments			-0.0008		
			(0.0018)		
% of total annual sales paid for security in the last fiscal year				-0.0064	
				(0.0097)	

Losses due to theft, robbery, vandalism or arson in the last fiscal year (% of sales)					-0.0576***
					(0.0138)
Constant	-4.6161***	-4.1561***	-2.7424***	-3.6044***	-3.9362***
	(0.7332)	(0.4017)	(0.8047)	(0.3543)	(0.3224)
Observations	3000	10511	1957	11532	13548

Source: own calculations. Standard errors in parentheses, * p<.05, ** p<.01, *** p<.001.

Table 6.12: Fractional Logit estimation results – HDI – cont.

	(1)	(2)	(3)	(4)	(5)
% of employees at the end of the fiscal year with a university degree	0.0094***	0.0091***	0.0092***	0.0089***	0.0097***
	(0.0008)	(0.0008)	(0.0008)	(0.0008)	(0.0008)
% of skilled employees at the end of the fiscal year	-0.1103	-0.1372	-0.1346	-0.1570*	-0.1233
	(0.0748)	(0.0764)	(0.0758)	(0.0761)	(0.0748)
How much of an obstacle is: Access to finance	-0.1653***				
	(0.0143)				
HDI	1.8675***	1.8833***	1.8972***	1.9040***	1.9884***
	(0.3666)	(0.3762)	(0.3770)	(0.3796)	(0.3694)
The court system is fair, impartial and uncorrupted		0.0073			
		(0.0115)			
"The court system is quick"			-0.0165		
			(0.0116)		
"The court system is able to enforce its decisions"				-0.0169	
				(0.0106)	
What % of senior management time was spent in dealing with goverment regulations?					0.0032
					(0.0017)
Constant	-3.5978***	-3.8044***	-3.7732***	-3.7444***	-3.9270***
	(0.2884)	(0.2939)	(0.2966)	(0.2974)	(0.2909)
Observations	16526	16068	15966	15770	16719

Source: own calculations. Standard errors in parentheses, * p<.05, ** p<.01, *** p<.001.

The analysis carried out in this part of the study was motivated by the need of a more thorough examination of the hypothesis that companies with foreign capital employ workers with higher education and skilled workers more often than similar nationally owned firms do. The results of the econometric investigation confirmed this hypothesis. This was robust both to the choice of estimation methods and to the choice of different sets of control variables in the model. Robustness was established regarding not only the variables' statistical significance, but also regarding the strength of the impact, as shown by a small variation of the estimated coefficient of the variable proxying the level of education. Thus, the main research hypothesis assuming a positive relationship between foreign direct investment and the level of education was confirmed in the data.

On this basis, it can be concluded that the level of education, both higher, and vocational (as shown by the variable "% of skilled workers") is a social development factor, which significantly and positively affects the share of foreign capital in the surveyed companies. This suggests that raising the level of education, should increase the amount of incoming foreign direct investment.

6.5 Summary

The subject of the study was to examine the determinants of foreign direct investment at the enterprise level. In this context, these determinants were analyzed in the empirical model as obstacles to doing business. The study focused on social development determinants of FDI as perceived by companies with foreign capital. The investigated factors mostly dealt with education and skills of workers in Central and Eastern Europe. For this purpose, an empirical study was conducted with a sample of 25,000 companies in the region of Central and Eastern Europe during 2002-2008.

As mentioned earlier, the surveyed companies had a representative character of the whole economy; therefore it is possible to draw more general conclusions, including those drawn from the whole group of companies in the region. This study revealed that companies with foreign capital more often encounter difficulties associated with an insufficiently educated labour force in relation to the companies with the participation of private capital. This analysis was developed to demonstrate that these companies employ workers with higher education and skilled workers more often than similar firms with ownership that is national, private or public. This result was robust to the selection of statistical methods for estimating and was robust to the addition of different control variables to the model. Robustness concerned not only the significance, but also the strength of the impact of the investigated, as demonstrated by the small variation in the estimated coefficients.

This analysis complementing the study indicates that firms with foreign capital often employ workers with higher education and skilled workers than similar firms with a national property, private or public. This conclusion confirms earlier findings from the study of foreign direct investment at the macroeconomic level (Brzozowski, Goczek, 2013). Moreover, the study results are in line with the results in Goczek (2013) that showed that companies with foreign capital encounter difficulties with inadequate education of the workforce more often than companies with domestic capital, both private and public. On this basis, it can be concluded that the level of education, both higher and vocational, is a factor of social development which significantly and positively affects the share of foreign capital in the surveyed companies. This suggests that raising the level of education, which, according to the surveyed companies with foreign capital in the analyzed countries is too low, should increase the scale of incoming foreign direct investment. The influence of the other factors of social development, such as the inequality of women was insignificant or impossible to estimate based on the collected data and, therefore, was not investigated at the firm level.

Appendix to Chapter 6

Table 6.A1: Fractional Logit estimation results

	(1)	(2)	(3)	(4)
% of employees at the end of the fiscal year with a university degree	0.0178***	0.0153*	0.0210***	0.0263***
	(0.0006)	(0.0076)	(0.0008)	(0.0006)
% of skilled employees at the end of the fiscal year	1.7353***	3.5579*	3.0576***	1.9394***
	(0.0608)	(1.6661)	(0.0880)	(0.0652)
Is the Top Manager female?		-0.1866		
		(0.3202)		
Did you experience insufficient water supply for production in the last fiscal year?			0.2134***	
			(0.0616)	
Over the fiscal year 2006, did this establishment experience power outages?			0.7647***	
			(0.0465)	
In the last fiscal year, what were this establishment's total annual sales?				0.0000
				(0.0000)
Constant	-3.1473***	-5.4222***	-5.8946***	-3.4397***
	(0.0577)	(1.3369)	(0.1448)	(0.0629)
Observations	21922	6280	16231	16234

Source: own calculations. Standard errors in parentheses, * p<.05, ** p<.01, *** p<.001.

Table 6.A2: Fractional Logit estimation results

	(1)	(2)	(3)	(4)	(5)
% of employees at the end of the fiscal year with a university degree	0.0213***	0.0178***	0.0147*	0.0131*	0.0182***
	(0.0006)	(0.0006)	(0.0059)	(0.0051)	(0.0006)
% of skilled employees at the end of the fiscal year	1.4957***	1.7620***	3.4296**	3.1813**	1.4963***
	(0.0626)	(0.0617)	(1.2877)	(1.0690)	(0.0606)
How much of an obstacle is: transportation of goods, supplies and inputs?	+0.1112***				
	(0.0241)				
Do you use technology licensed from a foreign-owned company?		0.1232			
		(0.1140)			
Does this establishment compete			-0.0803		

against unregistered or informal firms?			(0.0505)		
How much of an obstacle are the informal sector competitors to your operations?				-0.1592**	
				(0.0496)	
How much of an obstacle are the formal sector competitors to your operations?				0.1342	
				(0.0800)	
Total number of inspections in last fiscal year					0.0014**
					(0.0005)
Constant	-3.3275***	- 3.3972***	- 5.6057***	- 5.5076***	- 2.8948***
	(0.0615)	(0.2353)	(0.9690)	(0.8180)	(0.0573)
Observations	21347	21147	6280	6280	18613

Source: own calculations. Standard errors in parentheses, * p<.05, ** p<.01, *** p<.001.

Table 6.A3: Fractional Logit estimation results

	(1)	(2)	(3)	(4)	(5)
% of employees at the end of the fiscal year with a university degree	0.0199**	0.0183***	0.0177***	0.0113***	0.0228***
	(0.0074)	(0.0006)	(0.0006)	(0.0002)	(0.0007)
% of skilled employees at the end of the fiscal year	3.3259*	1.5128***	1.9777***	1.2435***	2.2380***
	(1.6376)	(0.0605)	(0.0619)	(0.0249)	(0.0739)
Total cost of inspections - official and unofficial payments	0.0000				- 0.1361***
	(0.0000)				(0.0077)
Number of working days spent by staff dealing with inspections procedures		0.0023*			
		(0.0009)			
Percentage of total annual sales paid for security in the last fiscal year			- 0.1301***		
			(0.0094)		
Losses due to theft, robbery, vandalism or arson in the last fiscal year (% of sales)				- 0.0466***	
				(0.0017)	
% of total annual sales paid in informal payments					- 0.1361***
					(0.0077)

Constant	-5.6399***	-2.8960***	-3.0545***	-2.4762***	
	(1.2124)	(0.0573)	(0.0574)	(0.0217)	
Observations	539	18511	19792	21235	16150

Source: own calculations. Standard errors in parentheses, * p<.05, ** p<.01, *** p<.001.

Table 6.A4: Fractional Logit estimation results

	(1)	(2)	(3)	(4)	(5)
% of employees at the end of the fiscal year with a university degree	0.0165***	0.0169***	0.0182***	0.0164***	0.0166***
	(0.0006)	(0.0006)	(0.0006)	(0.0006)	(0.0006)
% of skilled employees at the end of the fiscal year	1.6405***	1.7918***	1.8944***	1.3444***	1.9185***
	(0.0603)	(0.0617)	(0.0646)	(0.0631)	(0.0672)
How much of an obstacle is: Access to finance	-0.0938***				
	(0.0133)				
The court system is fair, impartial and uncorrupted		-0.1247***			
		(0.0117)			
"The court system is quick"			-0.0892***		
			(0.0134)		
"The court system is able to enforce its decisions"				-0.1540***	
				(0.0112)	
What % of senior management time was spent in dealing with government regulations?					-0.0412***
					(0.0017)
Constant	-2.7830***	-2.8291***	-3.1542***	-2.5190***	-2.8461***
	(0.0627)	(0.0629)	(0.0668)	(0.0660)	(0.0662)
Observations	20171	21522	21229	20925	19650

Source: own calculations. Standard errors in parentheses, * p<.05, ** p<.01, *** p<.001.

Table 6.A5: Fractional Logit estimation results– other macroeconomic-level variables

	(1)	(2)	(3)	(4)	(5)
% of employees at the end of fiscal year with a university degree	0.0102***	-0.0010	0.0102***	0.0093***	0.0113***
	(0.0008)	(0.0024)	(0.0008)	(0.0009)	(0.0009)
% of skilled employees at the end of the fiscal year	-0.1368	0.0019	-0.1029	-0.0857	-0.1232
	(0.0736)	(0.1433)	(0.0756)	(0.0837)	(0.0951)
GDP	-0.0000	-0.0000	-0.0000	-0.0000	-0.0000
	(0.0000)	(0.0000)	(0.0000)	(0.0000)	(0.0000)
Civil Liberties	-0.0716***	-0.0925*	-0.0705***	-0.0732***	-0.0737***
	(0.0188)	(0.0440)	(0.0192)	(0.0212)	(0.0218)
Life	0.0114	0.0483*	0.0098	0.0135	-0.0059
	(0.0091)	(0.0193)	(0.0094)	(0.0103)	(0.0109)
Gini	-0.0150**	0.0071	-0.0164**	-0.0121*	-0.0214***
	(0.0052)	(0.0113)	(0.0053)	(0.0060)	(0.0062)
Is the Top Manager female?		0.1914			
		(0.1167)			
Did you experience insufficient water supply for production in the last fiscal year?			0.0076		
			(0.0379)		
Over the fiscal year 2006, did this establishment experience power outages?			-0.0706*		
			(0.0340)		
In the last fiscal year, what were this establishment's total annual sales?				-0.0000	
				(0.0000)	
% of total annual sales paid in informal payments					-0.0374***
					(0.0102)
Constant	-2.4747***	-5.8324***	-2.2489**	-2.7046***	-1.0215
	(0.7094)	(1.4605)	(0.7366)	(0.7970)	(0.8572)
Observations	17203	3670	16719	13652	12695

Source: own calculations. Standard errors in parentheses, * p<.05, ** p<.01, *** p<.001.

Table 6.A6: Fractional Logit estimation results – other macroeconomic-level variables

	(1)	(2)	(3)	(4)	(5)
% of employees at end of the fiscal year with a university degree	0.0103***	0.0076***	-0.0009	-0.0031	0.0073***
	(0.0008)	(0.0010)	(0.0024)	(0.0026)	(0.0011)
% of skilled employees at the end of the fiscal year	-0.1427	-0.1732*	-0.0039	0.0098	-0.1421
	(0.0738)	(0.0860)	(0.1407)	(0.1435)	(0.0914)
How much of an obstacle is: transportation of goods, supplies and inputs?	0.0458*				
	(0.0205)				
GDP	-0.0000	-0.0000	-0.0000	-0.0000	0.0000
	(0.0000)	(0.0000)	(0.0000)	(0.0000)	(0.0000)
Civil Liberties	-0.0703***	-0.0517*	-0.0910*	-0.0907*	-0.0640**
	(0.0189)	(0.0236)	(0.0440)	(0.0440)	(0.0248)
Life	0.0116	0.0139	0.0481*	0.0465*	0.0178
	(0.0091)	(0.0113)	(0.0193)	(0.0193)	(0.0117)
Gini	-0.0156**	-0.0072	0.0057	0.0072	-0.0072
	(0.0052)	(0.0066)	(0.0113)	(0.0113)	(0.0068)
Do you use technology licensed from a foreign-owned company?		-0.0993***			
		(0.0233)			
Does this establishment compete against unregistered or informal firms?			0.0350		
			(0.0183)		
% of establishment's workforce that regularly use computers in their jobs				0.0042*	
				(0.0020)	
Total number of inspections in last fiscal year					0.0063***
					(0.0016)
Constant	-2.5048***	-2.8058**	-5.4608***	-5.3880***	-3.3462***
	(0.7122)	(0.8679)	(1.4569)	(1.4607)	(0.9010)
Observations	17032	12517	3670	3670	11248

Source: own calculations. Standard errors in parentheses, * p<.05, ** p<.01, *** p<.001.

Table 6.A7: Fractional Logit estimation results – other macroeconomic-level variables

	(1)	(2)	(3)	(4)	(5)
% of employees at the end of the fiscal year with a university degree	0.0009	0.0078***	0.0032	0.0112***	0.0114***
	(0.0027)	(0.0011)	(0.0030)	(0.0009)	(0.0009)
% of skilled employees at the end of the fiscal year	0.0451	-0.1535	-0.0363	-0.1586	-0.1755
	(0.1790)	(0.1052)	(0.1606)	(0.0887)	(0.0924)
Total cost of inspections - official and unofficial payments	0.0000				
	(0.0000)				
GDP	-0.0000	0.0000	-0.0000*	-0.0000	0.0000
	(0.0000)	(0.0000)	(0.0000)	(0.0000)	(0.0000)
Civil Liberties	-0.1476**	-0.0789**	0.0231	-0.0667**	-0.0448*
	(0.0487)	(0.0256)	(0.0518)	(0.0229)	(0.0213)
Life	0.0499*	0.0167	0.1218***	0.0078	0.0112
	(0.0209)	(0.0121)	(0.0255)	(0.0113)	(0.0106)
Gini	0.0156	-0.0055	-0.0092	-0.0145*	-0.0159**
	(0.0122)	(0.0071)	(0.0142)	(0.0065)	(0.0059)
Number of working days spent by staff dealing with inspections procedures		0.0018**			
		(0.0006)			
% of total annual sales paid in informal payments			0.0009		
			(0.0018)		
% of total annual sales paid for security in the last fiscal year				-0.0048	
				(0.0096)	
Losses due to theft, robbery, vandalism or arson in the last fiscal year (% of sales)					-0.0565***
					(0.0137)
Constant	-5.7704***	-3.2395***	-10.1912***	-2.2643**	-2.6107**
	(1.5814)	(0.9304)	(1.9851)	(0.8756)	(0.8391)
Observations	3000	10511	1957	11532	13548

Source: own calculations. Standard errors in parentheses, * p<.05, ** p<.01, *** p<.001.

Table 6.A8: Fractional Logit estimation results – other macroeconomic-level variables

	(1)	(2)	(3)	(4)	(5)
% of employees at the end of the fiscal year with a university degree	0.0100***	0.0096***	0.0098***	0.0094***	0.0102***
	(0.0008)	(0.0008)	(0.0008)	(0.0008)	(0.0008)
% of skilled employees at the end of the fiscal year	-0.1198	-0.1468	-0.1417	-0.1653*	-0.1326
	(0.0742)	(0.0757)	(0.0753)	(0.0756)	(0.0742)
How much of an obstacle is: Access to finance	-0.1683***				
	(0.0143)				
GDP	-0.0000	-0.0000	-0.0000	-0.0000	-0.0000
	(0.0000)	(0.0000)	(0.0000)	(0.0000)	(0.0000)
Civil Liberties	-0.0737***	-0.0719***	-0.0750***	-0.0717***	-0.0752***
	(0.0190)	(0.0195)	(0.0197)	(0.0198)	(0.0191)
Life	0.0143	0.0132	0.0143	0.0148	0.0103
	(0.0093)	(0.0094)	(0.0094)	(0.0094)	(0.0093)
Gini	-0.0149**	-0.0135*	-0.0113*	-0.0133*	-0.0156**
	(0.0053)	(0.0054)	(0.0054)	(0.0054)	(0.0053)
The court system is fair, impartial and uncorrupted		0.0058			
		(0.0115)			
"The court system is quick"			-0.0160		
			(0.0117)		
"The court system is able to enforce its decisions"				-0.0169	
				(0.0106)	
What % of senior management time was spent in dealing with government regulations?					0.0038*
					(0.0017)
Constant	-2.4473***	-2.6213***	-2.7293***	-2.6769***	-2.3952***
	(0.7201)	(0.7268)	(0.7281)	(0.7323)	(0.7216)
Observations	16526	16068	15966	15770	16719

Source: own calculations. Standard errors in parentheses, * p<.05, ** p<.01, *** p<.001.

Summary and conclusions

In our book, we have analyzed the relationship between human development and international trade and inflow of foreign direct investments. We studied the role of social inequalities in development of exports using both aggregate and firm-level data. Our empirical results demonstrated that human development variables are important in determining the level of exports. Estimation results obtained from the generalized gravity model estimated by the Poisson estimator with fixed effects for the period 1980-2010 showed that there was a positive causal relationship between our most general measure of human development (the HDI) and the level of exports for all countries. Our estimation results, obtained by estimating probit regression for the CEE countries on the firm-level dataset, confirmed the positive role of the HDI. The estimated parameter on the HDI variable displayed a positive sign and was statistically significant. This result was robust and it did not change when we controlled for sector specific effects, country effects and time effects. This means that the probability of exporting increases with the level of HDI in the exporting country.

Looking at the disaggregated components of the HDI, we found that in regressions based on aggregate data, the income index displayed a positive sign and was statistically significant for both the reporting and partner countries in the case of estimations for all countries. The income index for the reporting country remains statistically significant in the case of exports from the CEE countries to all countries but loses its statistical significance for the partner country. In the case of exports amongst the CEE countries, it is not statistically significant for any country. This might be due to the fact that country income disparities are relatively small among these countries.

The results obtained using firm level data for the separate components of the HDI revealed that only some HDI sub-indices were statistically significant. The estimated parameters on life expectancy, the expected years of schooling, and GNI per capita were positive and statistically significant. The role of education in explaining the relationship between exporting and human development is less obvious. In the majority of cases, the estimated parameter on the expected years of schooling was positive, while the parameter on the mean years of schooling was negative. This surprising result might be due to controlling for the level of human capital at the firm level.

The role of other human development measures was analyzed only at the aggregate level, for a limited sample and time span. The significance of income disparities was studied using the Gini index. It turned out that its role was limited only to the partner side. This means that the lower level of income inequality in the importing country was positively associated with a higher level of trade flows.

The results for the Gender Empowerment Measure (GEM) revealed that the GEM was positive and statistically significant only for the reporting countries in the full sample covering the exports of all countries. Hence, a lower gender inequality in economic participation and decision-making power was associated with a higher level of exports. However, in the case of the CEE countries this variable was not statistically significant as the level of gender discrimination in the CEE countries was much lower compared to the whole world.

We also disaggregated the GEM measure into its components. However, the results were rather ambiguous. For example, a higher participation of women in parliament was positively related to a bilateral level of exports. Similarly, the lower level of discrimination in terms of income was positively related to the level of exports for the whole sample. These unexpected results were obtained for reporting countries in which female participation in parliament and professional life was negatively associated with the level of trade.

The last analyzed indicator of human development was the level of civil liberties. It turned out that a higher level of civil liberties has a positive impact on trade flows. This conclusion is true both in terms of global trade as well as trade in the countries of Central and Eastern Europe with the rest of the world. However, trade in goods between countries of the region does not seem to depend on the extent of civil liberties. This might be due to the fact that all those countries were undergoing the transition process in about the same period.

Openness to international capital flows has been another vital ingredient in a successful transition process. We investigated the role played by human development in attracting FDI in the CEE countries during the last decade. The analysis was conducted at firm as well as macroeconomic levels.

The estimation results obtained using firm-level data and tobit and fractional logit methodology showed that human capital is significantly correlated with the share of foreign capital. This conclusion is valid for two measures of human capital, namely the percentage of employees with university education and the percentage of skilled workers. The analysis also revealed that a higher share of foreign capital is positively associated with the percentage of people using computers at work, which can be interpreted as another measure of the level of skills of the workforce.

The share of foreign capital ownership is also positively linked to the overall level of human development in the country hosting FDI. The value of the HDI, civil liberties and the Gini indices was found to be statistically significant variables. However, the components of the HDI were not statistically significant, probably owing to the strong correlation between them. It should be stressed that all of the estimation results obtained at the firm level were robust to the choice of the control variables and estimation method.

It was difficult to assess the role of gender equality in attracting foreign capital because of the lack of an adequate measure of women's nondiscrimination at a firm level. An imperfect proxy that was used was a dummy that is equal to 1 if the top manager is female and 0 otherwise. This variable turned out to be insignificant.

The analysis of the FDI determinants at a country level was pursued using two approaches. In the first stage, the total FDI inflows, without distinguishing the source countries, have been analyzed in a global sample of countries by means of the System GMM estimation method. The significance of the HDI was found to critically depend on the inclusion amongst the regressors of the monetary policy quality index and OECD membership dummy variables. The results thus suggest that the quality of macroeconomic policy and the unobserved characteristics of the OECD countries have a stronger impact on FDI inflows than the level of human development. This conclusion also holds for the components of the HDI, that is the income, education and life expectancy indices.

The two other dimensions of human development, namely the degree of civil liberties and income inequality seem to be unrelated to FDI flows at a macroeconomic level. In the latter case, the conclusion is undermined by a sizeable reduction in the number of observations resulting from the unavailability of data on the Gini index.

The analysis of total FDI inflows revealed that FDI determinants in the global and transition countries sample are alike. By contrast, the 10 New Member States of the EU and Croatia seem to be distinct with respect to the factors that attract and deter foreign investors. To examine the FDI inflows into this group of countries in greater detail, the gravity model and the bilateral FDI inflows data has been employed in the second stage of the analysis at a macroeconomic level. It was found that the relative difference of the life expectancy and education indices between the source and the host country is weakly and positively associated with the FDI inflow. This result is indicative of the predominantly vertical type of FDI in Central European countries, but it should be treated with caution as it was obtained at the very low significance level.

The gap in the degree of civil liberties and income inequality between the host and the source country was found to be insignificant too. By contrast, a large discrepancy between the degree of gender equality in both countries engaged in FDI is strongly and negatively related to the magnitude of capital inflow. The availability of the Gender Inequality Index for only one year, namely 2008, marked by the global financial crisis, is an important caveat for this conclusion.

Our results demonstrated that there is a significant and positive relationship between the level of human development and international trade and capital flows. Therefore, human development can be treated as an important goal for economic policy but it can also contribute to a higher level of internationalization of the economy. We hope that this book will be a contribution to the discussion on the role of social factors in an open economy.

References

Acemoglu, D., Shimer R. (1999), *Efficient Unemployment Insurance*, Journal of Political Economy 107(5), pp. 893-28.

Agosin, M.R., Machado R. (2006), *Openness and the International Allocation of Foreign Direct Investment*, Working Paper RE2-06-004, Inter-American Development Bank.

Aitken B. J., Harrison A. E. (1999), *Do Domestic Firms Benefit from Direct Foreign Investment? Evidence from Venezuela*, American Economic Review 89(3), pp. 605-618.

Akin, M.S., Vlad V. (2011), *The Relationship Between Education and Foreign Direct Investment: Testing the Inverse U Shape*, European Journal of Economic and Political Studies 4(1), pp. 27-46.

Alsan, M., Bloom D.E., Canning D. (2006), *The Effect of Population Health on Foreign Direct Investment Inflows to Low- and Middle-Income Countries*, World Development 34(4), pp. 613-630.

Anderson, J. (1979), *A Theoretical Foundation for the Gravity Equation*, The American Economic Review 69(1), pp. 106-116.

Anderson, J. E., van Wincoop E. (2003), *Gravity with Gravitas: A Solution to the Border Puzzle,* The American Economic Review 93(1), pp. 170-192.

Anderson, J. E., van Wincoop E. (2004), *Trade Costs*, Journal of Economic Literature 42(3), pp. 691-751.

Anghel, B. (2006), *Foreign Direct Investment in the Transition Countries: A Dynamic Analysis at Firm and Sector Level*, mimeo.

Arellano, M., Bond S. (1991), *Some test of specification for panel data: Monte Carlo evidence and an application to employment equations*, Review of Economic Studies 58(2), pp. 277-297.

Baily, M., Hulten C., Campbell D. (1992), *Productivity Dynamics in Manufacturing Plants*, Brooking Papers on Economic Activity, Microeconomics, pp. 187-249.

Barro, R. J., Lee J. W. (2000), *International Data on Educational Attainment: Updates and Implications,* CID Working Paper No. 42, Harvard University.

Barro, R. J., Lee J. W. (2010), *A New Data Set of Educational Attainment in the World, 1950-2010*, NBER Working Papers No. 15902.

BEEPS (2010), *The Business Environment and Enterprise Performance Survey 2008-2009. A Report on methodology and observations*, World Bank.

Bellak C., Leibrecht M., Stehrer R. (2008), *The Role of Public Policy in Closing Foreign Direct Investment Gaps: An Empirical Analysis*, wiiw Working Papers 48, The Vienna Institute for International Economic Studies.

Benacek, V., Gronicki M., Holland D. (2000), *The Determinants and Impact of Foreign Direct Investment in Central and Eastern Europe*, mimeo.

Bergstrand, J. H. (1989), *The Generalized Gravity Equation, Monopolistic Competition, and the Factor-Proportions Theory in International Trade*, The Review of Economics and Statistics 71(1), pp. 143-153.

Bergstrand, J. H. (1990), *The Heckscher-Ohlin-Samuelson Model, The Linder Hypothesis and the Determinants of Bilateral Intra-Industry Trade,* The Economic Journal 100(403), pp. 1216-1229.

Bergstrand, J. H., Egger P. (2007), *A Knowledge-and-Physical-Capital Model of International Trade Flows, Foreign Direct Investment, and Multinational Enterprises*, Journal of International Economics 73(2), pp. 278-308.

Bernard, A, Eaton J., Jensen J., Kortum S. (2003), *Plants and Productivity in International Trade,* American Economic Review 93(4), pp. 1268-90.

Bernard, A., Jensen J. B. (1999), *Exceptional exporter performance: cause, effect, or both?*, Journal of International Economics 47(1), pp.1-26.

Bernard, A., Wagner J. (1997), *Exports and success in German manufacturing*, Weltwirtschaftliches Archiv 133(1), pp.134-57.

Blanton, S. L., Blanton R. G. (2007), *What Attracts Foreign Investors? An Examination of Human Rights and Foreign Direct Investment*, Journal of Politics 69(1), pp. 143-155.

Bloningen, B. A. (2005), *A Review of the Empirical Literature on FDI Determinants*, Atlantic Economic Journal 33(4), pp. 383-403.

Blundell, R., Bond S. (1998), *Initial Conditions and Moment Restrictions in Dynamic Panel Data Models*, Journal of Econometrics 87(1), pp. 115-143.

Bresnahan, T, Brynjolfsson E., Lorin E. (2002), *Information, Technology, Workplace Organization and the Demand for Skilled Labor, Firm-level Evidence,* Quarterly Journal of Economics 117(1), pp. 339-76.

Brzozowski M, Goczek Ł. (2013), *Rozwój społeczny a napływ BIZ*, in: J. Michałek, M. Brzozowski, A. Cieślik (eds.) *Wpływ rozwoju społecznego na handel i inwestycje zagraniczne*, PWE.

Buch, C.M., Kesternich I., Lipponer A., Schnitzer M. (2009), *Financial Constraints and the Margins of FDI*, Deutsche Bundesbank Discussion Paper, Series 1: Economic Studies No. 29/2009.

Busse, M., Nunnenkamp P. (2009), *Gender Disparity in Education and the International Competition for Foreign Direct Investment*, Feminist Economics 15(3), pp. 61-90.

Carstensen, K., Toubal F. (2004), *Foreign Direct Investment in Central and Eastern European Countries: A Dynamic Panel Analysis*, Journal of Comparative Economics 32(1), pp. 3-22.

Castellani D. (2002), *Export Behavior and Productivity Growth: Evidence from Italian Manufacturing Firms,* Review of World Economics 138(4), pp. 605-628.

Castellani, D., Zanfei A. (2006), *Multinational Firms, Innovations and Productivity*, Edward Elgar, Cheltenham.

Cheng, L.K., Kwan Y. K. (2000), *What Are the Determinants of the Location of Foreign Direct Investment? The Chinese Experience*, Journal of International Economics 51(2), pp.379-400.

Cieślik A., Michałek J. J., Michałek A. (2012a), *Export activity in Visegrad-4 countries: A Firm-level investigation*, Ekonomia, forthcoming.

Cieślik A., Michałek J. J., Michałek A. (2012b), *Determinanty działalności eksportowej polskich przedsiębiorstw*, Gospodarka Narodowa LXXX/XXI, pp. 67-84.

Cieślik A., Michałek J. J., Mycielski J. (2012), *Social Development and International Trade in Central Europe*, Equilibrium, Quarterly Journal of Economics and Economic Policy 7(2), pp.7-20.

Clerides S.K., Lach S., Tybout J. R. (1998), *Is learning by Exporting Important? Micro-dynamic Evidence from Colombia, Mexico and Morocco*, Quarterly Journal of Economics 113(3), pp. 903-48.

Davis S., Haltiwanger J. (1991), *Wage Dispersion between and within US Manufacturing Plants 1963-86*, Brooking Papers on Economic Activity, Microeconomics, pp. 115-80.

Decanq, K., Lugo M. A. (2010), *Weights in Multidimensional Indices of Well-Being: an overview*, Center for Economic Studies Discussion Papers, nr ces10.06, Katholieke Universiteit Leuven.

Dunning, J. H. (1993), *Multinational Enterprises and the Global Economy*, Harlow: Addison-Wesley.

Dunning, J.H. (2003), *Determinants of Foreign Direct Investment: Globalization-Induced Changes and the Role of Policies*, in. B. Tungodden, N. Stern, I. Kolstad (eds.) *Toward Pro-Poor Policies. Aid, Institutions, and Globalization.* 5-th Annual World Bank Conference on Development Economics-Europe 2003, World Bank and Oxford University Press, Washington D.C. and New York, pp. 279-290.

EFIGE, (2010), *European Firms in a Global Economy: The Global Operations of European Firms. The second EFIGR Policy Report,* Bruegel.

Fujita, M. (2010), *The Evolution of Spatial Economics: From Thünen to the New Economic Geography*, The Japanese Economic Review 61(1), pp. 1-32.

Goczek, Ł (2013), *Bezpośrednie inwestycje zagraniczne i niewystarczająco wykształcona siła robocza - badanie empiryczne przedsiębiorstw*, Studia Ekonomiczne (forthcoming).

Goczek, Ł. (2012), *Empiryczne determinanty ograniczonego dostępu do finansowania przedsiębiorstw*, Bank i Kredyt No. 2/2012.

Granger, C.W.J. (1969), *Investigating causal relations by econometric models and cross-spectral methods*, Econometrica 37(3), pp. 424–438.

Grossfeld, I., Senik C. (2010), *The emerging aversion to inequality. Evidence from subjective data*, Economics of Transition 18(1), pp. 1 –26.

Habib, M., Zurawicki L. (2002), *Corruption and Foreign Direct Investment,* Journal of International Business Studies 33(2), pp. 291-307.

Hausman, J. A., Hall B. H., Griliches Z. (1984), *Econometric models for count data with an application to the patents–R & D relationship*. Econometrica 52(4), pp. 909–938.

HDI, (2008), *Human Development Indices: A statistical update 2008*, United Nations Development Program.

HDR, *Human Development Report*, United Nations Development Program, different issues.

Helpman, E., Melitz M., Yeaple S. (2004), *Export versus FDI with Heterogeneous Firms*, American Economic Review 94(1), pp. 300-316.

ILO, (2008), *World of Work Report 2008: Income Inequalities in the Age of Financial Globalization*, International Institute for Labour Studies, Geneva.

IMF, (2007), *World Economic Outlook*, October 2007, Chapter 5, International Monetary Fund, Washington D.C.

Ismail, N.W. (2009), *The Determinants of Foreign Direct Investment in ASEAN: A Semi-Gravity Approach*, Transition Studies Review 16(3), pp. 710-722.

Johnson, S, Kaufmann D., McMillan J., Woodruff C. (2000), *Why do firms hide? Bribes and unofficial activity after communism*, Journal of Public Economics, 76(3), pp. 495-520.

Jovanovic, B. (1982), *Selection and the Evolution of Industry*, Econometrica 50(3), 649-70.

Klasen, S. (2006), *Special Issue: Revisiting the Gender-Related Development Index and Gender Empowerment Measure*, Journal of Human Development and Capabilities 7(2), pp. 243-274.

Krugman, P. (1980), *Scale Economies, Product Differentiation, and the Pattern of Trade*, American Economic Review 70(5), pp. 950-959.

Levine, R. (1997), *Financial Development and Economic Growth: Views and Agenda*, Journal of Economic Literature 35(2), pp. 688-726.

Li, J., Hou L., Zhang J. (2011), *Capital Endowment, Credit Constraints and FDI: Analysis Based on Heterogeneous Firms*, Frontiers of Economics in China 6(1), pp. 55-75.

Liang, K.-Y., Zeger S. L. (1986), *Longitudinal data analysis using generalized linear models.* Biometrika 73(1), pp. 13–22.

Lucas, R.E. (1990), *Why Doesn't Capital Flow from Rich to Poor Countries?*, American Economic Review 80(2), pp. 92-96.

Lutkepohl, H. (2007), *General-to-specific or specific-to-general modelling? An opinion on current econometric terminology*, Journal of Econometrics 136(1), pp. 319-324.

Lutz, W., Goujon A., K.C. S., Sanderson W. (2007), *Reconstruction of population by age, sex and level of educational attainment of 120 countries for 1970-2000,* Vienna Yearbook of Population Research, pp. 193-235.

Maddison, A. (2010), *Historical Statistics of World Economy: 1-2008 AD*, Organization for Economic Cooperation and Development, Paris.

Majeed, M.T., Ahmad E. (2008), *Human Capital Development and FDI in Developing Countries*, Journal of Economic Cooperation 29(3), pp. 79-104.

Markusen, J.R. (1986), *Explaining the Volume of Trade: An Eclectic Approach*, American Economic Review 76(5), pp. 1002-1011.

Markusen, J.R., Maskus K. E. (2002), *Discriminating Among Alternative Theories of the Multinational Enterprise*, Review of International Economics 10(4), pp. 694-707.

Melitz, M. J. (2003), *The Impact of Trade on Intra-Industry Reallocations and Aggregate Industry Productivity*, Econometrica 71(6), pp. 1695-1725.

Miyamoto, K. (2003), *Human Capital Formation and Foreign Direct Investment in Developing Countries.* OECD Development Center Working Paper No. 211.

Mueller D., Raunig B. (1999), *Heterogeneities within Industries and Structure-Performance Models*, Review of Industrial Organization 15(4), pp. 303-320.

Nelson R., Winter, S. (1982), *An Evolutionary Theory of Economic Change*, Cambridge M.A., Harvard University Press.

Nelson, R. (1991), *Why do firms differ and how does it matter?*, Strategic Management Journal vol. 12, pp. 61-74.

Noorbakhsh, F., Paloni, A., Youssef, A. (2001), *Human Capital and FDI Inflows to Developing Countries: New Empirical Evidence*, World Development 29(9), pp. 1593-1610.

Noorkbakhsh, F. (1998), *The Human Development Index: Some Technical Issues and Alternative Indices*, Journal of International Development vol. 10(5), pp. 589-605.

Nunnenkamp, P., Spatz, J. (2003), *Intellectual Property Rights and Foreign Direct Investment: The Role of Industry and Host-Country Characteristics*, Kiel Working Paper No. 1167, Kiel Institute for World Economics.

Pakes A., Ericson R. (1998), *Empirical Implications of Alternative Models of Firm Dynamics*, Journal of Economic Theory 71(1), pp. 1-46.

Papke, L., Wooldridge J. (1996), *Econometric Methods for Fractional Response Variables with an Application to 401(k) Plan Participation Rates*, Journal of Applied Econometrics 11(6), pp. 619–632.

Próchniak M., Witkowski B. (2013), *Time stability of the beta convergence among EU countries: Bayesian model averaging perspective*, Economic Modelling vol. 30, pp. 322-333.

Ranis, G., Stewart F. (2005), *Dynamic Links between the Economy and Human Development*, DESA Working Paper No. 8 ST/ESA/2005/DWP/8.

Ranis, G., Stewart F., Ramirez A. (2000), *Economic Growth and Human Development*, World Development 28(2), pp. 197-219.

Razin, A., Sadka E., Tong H. (2008), *Bilateral FDI Flows: Threshold Barriers and Productivity Shocks*, CESifo Economic Studies 54(3), pp. 451-470.

Riley, J.C. (2005), *Poverty and Life Expectancy*. Cambridge University Press, Cambridge.

Santos Silva, J.M.C, Tenreyro S. (2006), *The Log of Gravity,* Review of Economics and Statistics 88(4), pp. 641-658.

Sen, A.K. (1976), *Real National Income*, Review of Economic Studies 43(1), pp. 19-39.

Smarzynska Javorcik, B., Spatareanu M. (2005), *Do Foreign Investors Care about Labor Market Regulations?*, Review of World Economics (Weltwirtschaftliches Archiv) 141(3), pp. 375-403.

Stoker, T. (1993), *Empirical Approaches to the Problem of Aggregation over Individuals*, Journal of Economic Literature 31(4), pp. 1827-1874.

Tobin, J. (1958), *Estimation of relationships for limited dependent variables*, Econometrica 26(1), pp. 24–36.

Tsen, W.H. (2005), *The Determinants of Foreign Direct Investment in Manufacturing Industry of Malaysia*, Journal of Economic Cooperation 26(2), pp. 91-110.

Tybout, J.R. (2003), *Plant and Firm Level Evidence on "New" Trade Theories*, in: Choi E. Kwon, J. Harrigan (eds.) *Handbook of International Trade*, Oxford, Basil Blackwell.

UNCTAD ,(2011), *World Investment Report 2011. Non-Equity Modes of International Production and Development*, United Nations, New York and Geneva.

UNDESA, (2009), *World Population Prospects: The 2008 Revision*, United Nations Department of Economic and Social Affairs, New York.

UNU-WIDER, (2008), *World Income Inequality Database 2008*, United Nations University – World Institute for Development Economics Research, Helsinki.

Vernon, R. (1966), *International Investment and International Trade in the Product Cycle*, Quarterly Journal of Economics 80(2), pp. 190-207.

Walsh, J., Yu J. (2010), *Determinants of Foreign Direct Investment: A Sectoral and Institutional Approach*, IMF Working Paper WP-10/187.

Windmeijer, F. (2005), *A finite sample correction for the variance of linear efficient two-step GMM estimators*, Journal of Econometrics 126(1), pp. 25-51.

Winter, S. (1971), *Satisficing, Selection and Innovative Remnant*, The Quarterly Journal of Economics 85(2), pp. 237-261.

World Bank, (1994), *World Development Report 1994: Infrastructure for Development*, The World Bank, Washington DC.

Zhang K.H., Markusen J. R. (1999), *Vertical Multinationals and Host-Country Characteristics*, Journal of Development Economics 59(2), pp. 233-252.

Polish Studies in Economics

Edited by Ryszard Kokoszczyński

Volume 1 Wojciech Grabowski: Employee Stock Options, Payout Policy, and Stock Returns. Shareholders and Option Holders in Large U.S. Technology Corporations. 2012.

Volume 2 Jan Jakub Michałek / Michał Brzozowski / Andrzej Cieślik (eds.): The Relationship between Human Development, Exports and Foreign Direct Investments in Emerging Europe. 2013.

www.peterlang.de

Management of Stochastic Demand
in Make-to-Stock Manufacturing

Forschungsergebnisse der Wirtschaftsuniversität Wien

Band 37

PETER LANG
Frankfurt am Main · Berlin · Bern · Bruxelles · New York · Oxford · Wien

Rainer Quante

Management of Stochastic Demand in Make-to-Stock Manufacturing

PETER LANG
Internationaler Verlag der Wissenschaften

Bibliographic Information published by the Deutsche Nationalbibliothek
The Deutsche Nationalbibliothek lists this publication in the Deutsche Nationalbibliografie; detailed bibliographic data is available in the internet at <http://www.d-nb.de>.

Cover design:
Atelier Platen according to a design of the advertising agency Publique.

University logo of the Vienna University of Economics and Business Administration.
Printed with kindly permission of the University.

Sponsored by the Vienna University of Economics an Business Administration.

ISSN 1613-3056
ISBN 978-3-631-59409-4

www.peterlang.de

Für meine Eltern

Contents

List of Figures

List of Tables

Nomenclature

aATP	Allocated Available-to-Promise
AP	Allocation Planning
APS	Advanced Planning Systems
ATO	Assemble-to-Order
ATP	Available-to-Promise
BOP	Batch Order Processing
CDF	Cummulative Distribution Function
cf.	confer, compare
CODP	Customer Order Decoupling Point
CPU	Central Processing Unit
CTP	Capable-to-Promise
CV	Coefficient of Variation
DLP	Deterministic Linear Programming
DM	Demand Management
EPO	Enterprise Profit Optimization
ERP	Enterprise Resource Planning
FCFS	First-Come-First-Served
GHz	Gigahertz
GLPK	GNU Linear Programming Kit
GOP	Global Order Processing
GSL	GNU Scientific Library
IP	Integrated Pricing
IR	Inventory Rationing
KPI	Key Performance Indicator
LP	Linear Programming

MB	Megabyte
MRP	Material Resource Planning
MTO	Make-to-Order
NB	Negative Binomial Distribution
ODF	Origin-Destination-Fare
PC	Personal Computer
PTP	Profitable-to-Promise
RLP	Randomized Linear Programming
RM	Revenue Management
SIC	Stochastic Inventory Control
SOPA	Single Order Processing After Allocation Planning
SOPA_A	Aggregated SOPA
SOPA_D	Disaggregated SOPA
TRM	Traditional Revenue Management
uATP	Unallocated Available-to-Promise

Chapter 1

Introduction

1.1 Research Topic and Motivation

"The theory of inventory control tells us how much safety stock is necessary for fulfilling 99% of the orders in time, but not how to select the 1%, maybe some tens of orders per day, which are postponed or cancelled." (Fleischmann and Meyr, 2004, p. 14)

Although not explicitly stated, the authors indicate that there is more to demand management than just achieving a high service level. Rejection or postponement of orders are decisions that should be properly considered, since they play a critical role for any enterprise. Hill (2000) concisely sums it up when stating that "the most important orders are the ones that you turn down".

A number of concepts and methods emerged in the past decades addressing this issue by trying to more actively manage demand. One prominent example for successful demand management is the emergence of revenue management, which was first applied in the pricing strategies of airline tickets.

In the late 1970s, deregulation of the American airline market allowed new airlines to enter the market. Specialized only on the most profitable routes, the new airlines were highly successful and gained substantial market shares, so that the established airlines had to react to the increased competition. As most of them operated a large network with manifold destinations, they could not compete in a conventional manner against the highly-specialized new-comers able to offer much lower prices: due to specialization, the new airlines had less infrastructure costs, less maintenance costs and by focusing on the most popular destinations they reached a high seat utilization. In contrast, on many flights of the established airlines, seats were not completely sold—especially on the less popular routes and on weekends.

American Airlines was the first player to react to the new market conditions by an innovative pricing strategy. Instead of a cost-covering pricing of seats, they set the prices for some tickets on the less-utilized flights on the basis of marginal costs. Since marginal costs of an additional passenger are close to zero, American Airlines realized that it is better to sell the seat for a very low price, instead of leaving it empty.

Looking back, the new ticket pricing strategy developed by American Airlines sounds intuitive, but at that time it was an innovative way of thinking.

It was a simple idea that enabled American Airlines to offer competitive and even lower prices than the competing low-cost airlines. The only problem was to identify which seats could be sold for normal prices and which seats to sell for low prices because they would stay empty otherwise. American Airlines tied the availability of low-price tickets to conditions which were fulfilled only by leisure customers usually not willing to pay the normal prices. For example, low-price tickets had to be bought 30 days in advance, preventing business travelers from buying these tickets. Thus, the introduction of specialized tickets designed for a specific customer class enabled American Airlines to skim much more revenues from the total possible market potential.

In the last decades, revenue management (RM) has become a very popular method of managing demand to increase profitability. This is not astonishing given the high revenue increasing potentials of RM. Boyd (1998, p. 29) for instance states that "revenue improvements from implementing a revenue management system can range from 2–8 percent (or more) depending on the carrier". The German airline Lufthansa AG reported an increase in revenues of €715 Mio. in 1997 (Klophaus, 1998, p. 150)—approximately equal to the result of normal operations in this year (Kimms and Klein, 2005, p. 2). As seen in the case of American Airlines, the success of RM essentially relies on identifying and exploiting differences in the customers' willingness to pay.

However, RM is mainly deployed in service industries—as for example airlines, car rentals, or hotels. It has not (yet) proven to be as successful in other domains of application as, e.g., in manufacturing. In those industries, different demand management concepts evolved in the past (for an overview see Fleischmann and Meyr, 2004). Demand management in manufacturing is often handled by a demand fulfillment module of the so-called advanced planning systems (APS). This module takes into account production quantities determined by a mid-term master planning module and short-term production planning. Based on these quantities, the demand fulfillment module decides on the basis of simple rules which customer to fulfill at which time, e.g. rules such as the first-come-first-served (FCFS) principle. As these rules are rather simple and created with a focus on general applicability, the results of demand fulfillment in APS leave space for improvements. Therefore, demand management in manufacturing might learn from the experiences gained in the service industries during the last decades.

Accordingly, practitioners as well as researchers put more and more effort in exploring ways to adapt RM concepts to the specific needs of manufacturing (Harris and Pinder, 1995, Swann, 1999, Arslan et al., 2007, Gupta and Wang, 2007). The core idea is that customer differentiation is beneficial also in a manufacturing environment. Additionally, the building block of RM in the service industries—perishable assets—corresponds to perishable capacity in manufacturing industries. For instance, an empty seat in an airplane can be compared to a machine standing still due to an insufficient number of orders.

However, the majority of scientific research focuses on adapting RM concepts to make-to-order environments because of the mentioned correspondence of perishable assets and perishable capacities in make-to-order manufacturing. In make-to-stock manufacturing environments, this correspondence does not apply as the machines schedules are based on forecasts instead of specific customer orders. The aim of this thesis is thus to analyze the current state-of-the-art in demand management (irrespective of a specific industry), and then relating the ideas found in the literature to make-to-stock manufacturing environments.

Our starting point is the current process of demand fulfillment in APS for make-to-stock manufacturing. In the case of make-to-stock, production planning is done on the basis of demand forecasts: when a customer order arrives, it can be either fulfilled from on-hand inventory or postponed to later arriving supply. The basic question to be answered in this thesis is to decide if it pays off to refuse a low margin customer order in expectancy of future more profitable orders.

The analysis relies on a number of assumptions as summarized in the following:

- Make-to-stock manufacturing environment with scarce capacities
- Deterministic future incoming supply
- Customers with different priorities
- Immediate order confirmation required
- Customers are willing to accept a late delivery under a price discount

In the short-term, it is assumed that the later arriving supply quantities are known and can be promised to arriving customers. Additionally, we assume a setting of scarce capacities, because the case of oversupply in make-to-stock manufacturing reduces to simply accepting and fulfilling all arriving customers orders. A further assumption in this work is that customers can be segmented according to their different willingness to pay, different costs of fulfillment, or different strategic importance. The first case typically applies to airlines when they charge different prices according to the remaining booking time and other factors like remaining capacity. In the second case, the costs of serving a customer order can be used as a differentiator. Note that only those costs which can still be influenced when accepting the order are relevant here. This includes, for example, transportation costs, taxes, and any variable costs of downstream production. The third case, the discrimination according to the strategic importance of customers may go beyond immediate costs and revenues. For example, loyal customers may be extremely important and should be given more favorable terms than occasional customers (see Quante et al. (2009b, Sect. 3.1.5) for a further discussion). In addition, customers are assumed to require an immediate response to their order, but are willing to accept a late delivery under a price discount. Note that these assumptions are equivalent to those in the work of Meyr (2009).

1.2 Organization, Objectives and Contributions

The idea of this thesis originates from the current state of the art of demand fulfillment in make-to-stock manufacturing. where in general APS are used as supporting tools. Therefore, this work starts in Chapter 2 with a description of the current state-of-the-art in demand fulfillment and introduces the required terms and definitions.

In order to search the literature for alternative approaches and concepts suitable for make-to-stock manufacturing, we decided to systematically classify the literature dealing with demand management. The focus was explicitly also beyond manufacturing when reviewing the literature, since we want to search in other disciplines for further ideas. We start introducing a framework for demand management (DM) in Chapter 3 and identify generic model types. In addition, a classification of commercial software solutions is presented in order to get an idea of how these solutions work.

Subsequently, based on the framework of Chapter 3, the general types are aligned to the specific requirements of make-to-stock manufacturing at the beginning of Chapter 4 and shortcomings of the respective model types are identified. A detailed analysis of specific models follows with a focus on manufacturing environments, but without concentrating on make-to-stock systems at this point.

Based on the literature review, Chapter 5 presents new models that reflect important characteristics of order fulfillment in make-to-stock production environments, namely customer heterogeneity, limited short-term supply flexibility, and short-term allocation flexibility. Previous literature has not addressed the interplay between these factors. The presented models are primarily based on the ideas of revenue management. We prove structural properties of the models and derive an optimal demand fulfillment policy. The result links order fulfillment in make-to-stock manufacturing to revenue management concepts. By this, we provide a way to unite the currently distinct concepts.

As these models of Chapter 5 explicitly take into account stochastic demand, we compare the developed models with existing deterministic ones described in Section 4.3. Before we conduct an extensive numerical study assessing the performance of various models in Chapter 7, we introduce the used simulation environment in Chapter 6. We show the superiority of the developed approaches in stochastic environments over the simple FCFS policy and the deterministic models of Section 4.3. Additionally, we identify which key influence factors drive the potential benefits.

This work concludes in Chapter 8 with a discussion of the results and issues for future research.

Chapter 2

Demand Fulfillment in Make-to-Stock Manufacturing

In this chapter, we provide a description of the current state of demand fulfillment in make-to-stock manufacturing. In order to do this, we start with an introduction of basic concepts as the customer order decoupling point. Subsequently, we discuss the structure of advanced planning systems and show the activities involved in an exemplary demand fulfillment process in make-to-stock manufacturing. Additionally, we explain the notion of available-to-promise.

2.1 Make-to-Stock and the Customer Order Decoupling Point

In the work of Fleischmann and Meyr (2004) it is shown that demand fulfillment is strongly related to the position of the customer order decoupling point (CODP). Therefore—before we explain demand fulfillment and advanced planning systems in more detail—we give a short explanation of the CODP. As seen in Fig. 2.1, the CODP divides the supply chain into forecast-driven and order-driven processes (Sharman, 1984, Hoekstra and Romme, 1992).

The CODP holds the inventory that is needed to hedge against forecast errors and replenishment uncertainty. The CODP plays a pivotal role in our analysis since many decisions upstream of the CODP are dependent on the available inventory and on future replenishment orders. For a more detailed discussion of the CODP concept and its impact in different production environments (including make-to-order (MTO), assemble-to-order (ATO) and

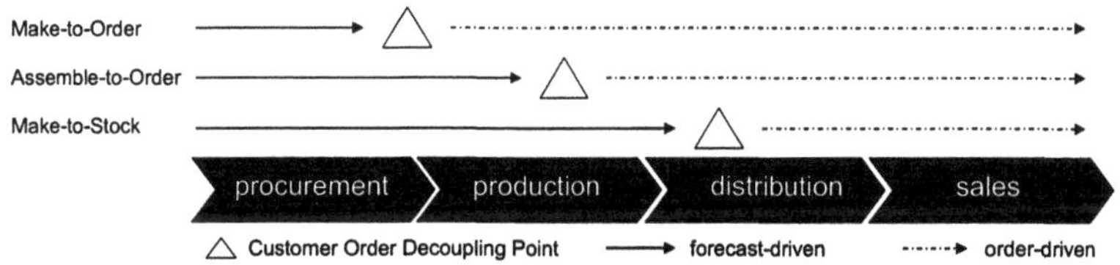

Figure 2.1: Customer Order Decoupling Point

make-to-stock (MTS)) we refer to Fleischmann and Meyr (2004). Note that the supply chain may contain additional production processes downstream of the CODP, but this is not the case for MTS production, since the CODP holds already the final product.

2.2 Structure of Advanced Planning Systems

Tasks of demand management are well-established in make-to-stock manufacturing companies and are usually supported by modern information systems, in particular advanced planning systems. These systems provide support for the entire planning tasks along the supply chain, from long-term strategic decision making to short-term operational decisions. Rohde et al. (2000) classify the supply chain decisions in a two-dimensional matrix (Fig. 2.2). This matrix is vertically structured according to the planning horizon and horizontally structured according to the sequence of planning tasks—from upstream to downstream in the supply chain.

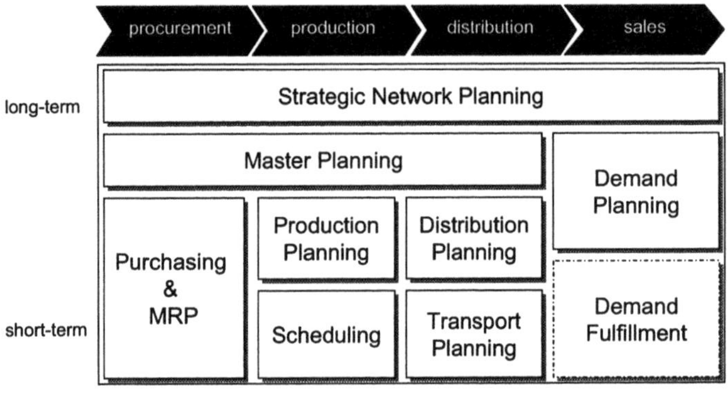

Figure 2.2: Structure of Advanced Planning Systems (Rohde et al., 2000)

The planning tasks in the supply chain extend from procurement of raw materials over production and distribution towards selling of final products. Since all these tasks are interrelated, a consecutive processing will not lead to optimal plans. For instance, selling of products can only be done with information about production and distribution in order to generate reliable due dates. On the other hand, the production task requires reliable demand forecasts in order to decide about lot-sizes and working times. To be able to support all these tasks, APS usually have several modules structured according to planning horizon and forecast accuracy. In order to cope with the interdependencies, the modules are organized in a hierarchical order. Long-term decisions based on low forecast accuracy provide the limits of the lower tasks which are done on the basis of better information. In order to do so, the upper tasks anticipate decision making in lower levels (Schneeweiß, 2003, Sect. 2.1). From top to down, the decisions become more accurate. Fig. 2.2 illustrates that on the top level, the *strategic network planning* is responsible for coordinating the entire supply chain. One the levels below, the tasks become more specialized.

The planning tasks associated with this thesis are located in the lower-right corner and are supported from the so-called *demand fulfillment* module. In order to illustrate how demand fulfillment for make-to-stock manufacturing is supported by advanced planning systems, Fig. 2.3 illustrates the involved supply chain activities and information flow in an exemplary consumer goods MTS supply chain.

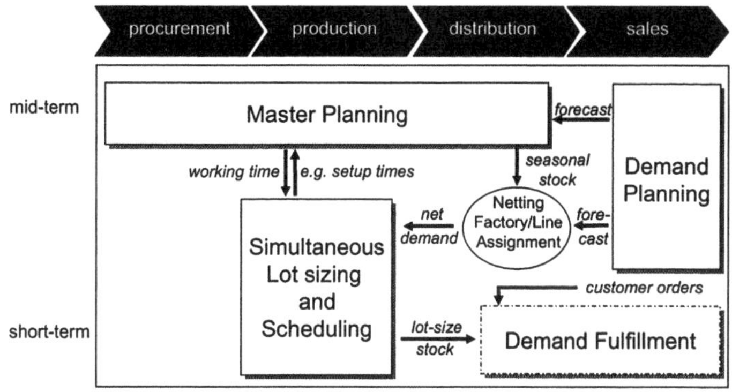

Figure 2.3: Exemplary Structure of an Advanced Planning System for Make-to-Stock Manufacturing (Fleischmann et al., 2008, p. 97)

In the mid-term, the *demand planning* activity is responsible for generating aggregate demand forecasts which are handed over to the *master planning* activity. It receives deterministic demand forecasts and prices as inputs from the demand planning (Kilger and Wagner, 2008) and then determines the best combinations of sales, production and replenishment quantities and the corresponding inventories under given capacity constraints. The planning horizon usually ranges from a few weeks up to several months. Therefore, data accuracy is low and the planning can only be done on the basis of aggregated data, i.e., products and customers are aggregated to groups or classes, respectively. In order to be able to balance supply with demand, the master planning activity basically determines the extent of seasonal stocks and possible changes of working times. A detailed description of the master planning activity can be found in the work of Rohde and Wagner (2008).

The generated master plan is handed over to the short-term activities. As demand forecasts usually become more accurate on the short-term, the planned stocks (from the master plan) and the current inventory are matched with the short-term demand forecasts. The result of this planning step is the *net demand*, which serves as input for the *lot-sizing and scheduling* task. This step additionally considers the working time restrictions from the master plan and computes the lot-sizes of the anticipated production quantities. Note, as this is a make-to-stock environment, all planning tasks up to here are performed on the basis of forecasts.

The last activity—which is the essential one in the scope of this work—is *demand fulfillment*. This activity takes into account the planned production quantities and quotes incoming customer orders according to their desired delivery date. This activity is the only one considered so far that is not based on forecasts but on the actual customer orders. In traditional material resource planning systems (MRP), order quotes are generated on the basis of available inventory. If there is no stock on-hand, the orders are quoted against the production lead-time. Kilger and Meyr (2008, p. 182) give a simple example that illustrates the weakness of such an order promising mechanism: it is not guaranteed that capacity constraints are not violated and a feasible plan is generated. Therefore, modern APS make use of more sophisticated methods. The inner logic of these methods is based on the notion of available-to-promise (ATP). In the following section, we introduce this key functionality of modern APS demand fulfillment solutions.

2.3 Available-to-Promise

2.3.1 Definition

The notion of available-to-promise is strongly related to advanced planning systems, and, with the success of APS solutions in the past years, is facing increasing attention. Nevertheless, it is not a very new concept. Fischer (2001) and Kilger and Meyr (2008) mention the work of Schwendinger (1979) as the earliest reference to available-to-promise. Since there is already a detailed analysis and literature review of ATP (see Fischer, 2001), we will not cite any references before the year 2001 and put an emphasis on the years thereafter.

Kilger and Meyr (2008) define ATP as "... the current and future availability of supply and capacity that can be used to accept new customer orders". A different definition of ATP is provided in the work of Ball et al. (2004), in which ATP is defined as "... a business function [...] directly linking customer orders with enterprise resources". The commercial software vendor SAP defines ATP quantity as the "... quantity available to MRP for new sales orders" and

ATP check as a "...function used to check [...] if a product can be confirmed" (SAP Help Portal, 2008).

Throughout this work, we follow the definition of Kilger and Meyr (2008) when referring to the term ATP and see it as a quantity rather than a functionality. It is important to note that a positive ATP quantity does not mean that there is stock on-hand, because ATP takes also future available quantities into account that are still to be produced. In the work of Fischer (2001), four different functions associated with the notion of ATP are identified:

- Availability check of products and evaluation of alternative solutions
- Order confirmation and due date assignment
- Steps taken in case of temporary inability to deliver
- Due date monitoring and order repromising

In the first step, the ATP quantities are used to check the availability of products. In cases when the product is currently not available, the next time the product will be available can directly be derived from the ATP quantities (as future supplies are considered). The availability check allows for a direct confirmation of customer orders including the determination of due dates. These two functions are essential for this work. The other two functions involve more activities as demand fulfillment and are beyond the scope of this work. For example, in case of temporary inability to deliver, a re-planning of the production (lot-sizing and scheduling) has to be done.

2.3.2 Dimensions of ATP

As seen before, the master planning activity calculates aggregated plans structured according to certain categories, e.g., product or customer groups. As the master plan is generally the basis for calculating ATP quantities, ATP exhibits a similar structure. Kilger and Meyr (2008, p. 184) mention several alternative possibilities to structure ATP quantities, e.g., location, sourcing type, region, market etc. but refer to *product, time* and *customer* as the most important ones. In the following, we give a short description of these three dimensions.

The level of detail of the ATP quantities in the ***product dimension*** corresponds to the location of the CODP. In case of MTO/ATO, products are customer specific and production/assembly is driven by incoming customer orders. The current and future supply and capacity that is taken into account to accept new customer orders is represented by the production capacity after the CODP and the inventory of semi-finished goods stored at the CODP. In the case of MTS manufacturing, the production is entirely based on forecasts. The current and future supply taken into account when the customer order arrives is hence represented by finished goods.

The master plan is generally created for a few weeks up to a few months. Accordingly, the granularity of the ***time dimension*** ranges from days to months, mostly depending on the forecast accuracy. The ATP quantities are therefore also structured according to certain time buckets, from which the customer orders are fulfilled.

The third important dimension is the ***customer dimension***. Kilger and Meyr (2008) distinguish this dimension according to a supply- or demand constraint mode. Since the motivation of this thesis is driven by the problem to decide which customer to fulfill first when capacity is scarce, the supply constraint mode is the important one in this thesis. In this mode, not all orders can be fulfilled and the ATP functionality has to provide means to decide about customer priorities. Thus, APS assign customers to certain classes in order to have a customer hierarchy.

The allocation of the quantities from the master plan to customer hierarchies is usually done in APS on the basis of simple rules. Kilger and Meyr (2008, Sect. 9.4.3) distinguishes three important rules:

- *Rank based*: Allocation of quantities according to predefined ranks. The customer with the highest rank gets the forecasted quantities, the lower ranks the remaining quantities.
- *Per committed*: The quantities are allocated proportionally to the forecasts of the different customers. If customer A has forecasted 100, and B 200, then B gets twice as much as A irrespective of the actual available quantities.
- *Fixed split*: This rule is independent of the demand forecasts. Quantities are allocated according to a predefined fixed ratio, e.g., customer A gets 60%, B gets 40%.

The process of determining the available quantities is called *allocation planning* (AP).

To find a reliable due date for a customer order, it is searched through demand fulfillment alternatives in the mentioned dimensions. This means, e.g., to search in the time dimension, checking for ATP back- or forwards in time, in the product dimension, checking for substitute products, and in the customer dimension, checking for availability in other priority classes (Kilger and Meyr, 2008). This process is called *order promising*. Usually, simple rules are defined as search strategies for the different dimensions (Meyr et al., 2008a, Sect. 18.3.1). Profitability of different fulfillment alternatives is generally not taken into account during this search. However, recent software systems do not only consider *available-to-promise* (ATP) quantities (available inventory) or *capable-to-promise* (CTP) quantities (available capacity), but also follow a *profitable-to-promise* (PTP) logic that enables them to compare customer orders and fulfillment alternatives according to their priority. CTP quantities are defined as "... the remaining capacity of the assembly lines, if this capacity is a potential bottleneck" (Fleischmann and Meyr, 2004). As they are only applicable in MTO and ATO production systems, CTP is not relevant here.

Chapter 3

A Framework for Demand Management

In this chapter, we propose a classification framework for demand management. This framework is subsequently used to identify general types of models and software in relation to the most important key-decision variables in supply chain management. To demonstrate the correspondence of the identified general types of models with current scientific research, we present and discuss important review papers for each of the identified types. In contrast to the subsequent Chapter 4, we will not discuss single research papers in this chapter.

We start this chapter with a definition of demand management as it is understood in this work, following by a detailed description of the framework. Once the framework is introduced, we discuss the identified model types supplemented by references to important review papers.

3.1 Demand Management Defined

Demand management as it is understood in this work is closely related to the previously described demand fulfillment in APS. As we have seen, the notion of demand fulfillment is common in manufacturing, but similar concepts exist in other industries, e.g., the earlier mentioned revenue management in the service industries. Therefore—as we do not solely build on the notion of demand fulfillment—we refer to the concepts developed in this work as *demand management* concepts.

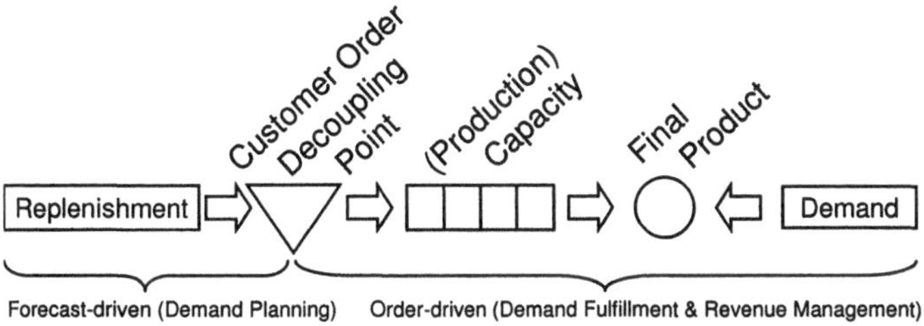

Figure 3.1: Supply Chain Elements (Quante et al., 2009b)

In order to define demand management in the following, we adopt the supply chain framework of Quante et al. (2009b) as shown in Fig. 3.1. Relevant in this work are the processes in the supply chain downstream of the CODP (order-driven processes). The framework shows the analogy between demand fulfillment and revenue management as it extends elements like the CODP (which is important for demand fulfillment) with elements representing revenue management concepts. For instance, pricing decisions can be linked to the item *final product* and capacity allocation decisions are linked to the item *demand*.

Demand management is closely tied to decisions in the depicted supply chain and therefore depends on its specific characteristics. For example, the current inventory at the CODP or the remaining production capacity may influence pricing decisions or promised due dates. By capturing these characteristics, the depicted elements of the supply chain framework provide a systematic basis for identifying demand management models and software.

3.2 General Model Types for Demand Management

3.2.1 Classifying Demand Management Models

This section introduces a framework for generic demand management types developed to classify different literature streams. The structure of the framework follows the work of Quante et al. (2009b). The authors distinguish demand management models according to demand or price decisions, and control over the replenishment quantity (as shown in Fig. 3.2). With these two dimensions, distinct model types corresponding to common research streams are identified. Quante et al. (2009b) note that these two dimensions are the "key decision variables regarding demand and supply". Before reviewing each model type in detail, the two dimensions are described in the following. Models in the first row of Fig. 3.2 take demand as entirely exogenous. They satisfy demand first-come-first-served (FCFS) at a given price. In particular, these models do not consider a segmentation of customers. The middle and bottom row of Fig. 3.2 represent a more active management of demand. The models in the second row influence the demand by adjusting prices. Like in the first row, the customers are not segmented into specific classes and treated all equal just distinguished according to their willingness to pay. The bottom row entails models that explicitly consider heterogeneous customers. In response to a customer request, these models face a trade-off between accepting a current, low-priority customer now versus reserving the resources for high-priority customers expected in the future. The distinction between the middle and bottom row in Fig. 3.2 corresponds with the classification of RM models of Talluri and van Ryzin

Demand / Price consideration	Replenishment consideration: None	Replenishment consideration: Data	Replenishment consideration: Decision variable
Data	-	Order Promising	Stochastic Inventory Control
Price-based	Markdown / Pricing / Auctions	Trade Promotions	Integrated Pricing
Quantity-based	Traditional RM	aATP	Inventory Rationing

Figure 3.2: Types of Demand Management Models (Quante et al., 2009b)

(2004). In order to follow their terminology, models are labeled as *price-based* or *quantity-based.*

The columns in Fig. 3.2 reflect the way models decide about inventory replenishment at the CODP. In the first column, models do not consider replenishments. As for example, in airline revenue management, the seats in an airplane can not be replenished when sold out. In the middle column, inventory replenishments are considered but not actively influenced. The right column entails models that actively decide about the quantities they want to replenish.

In the following, we briefly discuss each of the aforementioned model types. We will refer to available review papers for each of the model types. A detailed discussion of individual articles relevant in this work is following in Chapter 4.

3.2.2 Single-Class Exogenous Demand Models

No models were found fitting in the upper left cell of Fig. 3.2. This is not surprising since models with a given price and no consideration of replenishment or inventory, respectively, have nothing to decide on, neither on the demand nor on the replenishment side of the supply chain.

In the next cell to the right, the so-called ***order promising*** models consider price (i.e. demand), current inventory, and future replenishment quantities as given. This results in information about product availability and delivery times. For each incoming customer order the model decides real-time on the due date. The decision is made in a greedy fashion, based on availability of goods. As an example, the basic order promising model of Sect. 4.3.1 falls in this category. An introduction and overview of this so-called "real-time mode" or "single-order-processing" models is given in Ball et al. (2004), Chen et al. (2001), and Fleischmann and Meyr (2004). Additionally, a broad overview of due date management models with an emphasis on stochastic models is included in the work of Keskinocak and Tayur (2004).

The upper right cell of Fig. 3.2 holds the vast class of ***stochastic inventory control*** (SIC) models, which focus on optimal inventory replenishment. Some of these models primarily address the structure of optimal replenishment policies, as for example the famous (s, S)-policy proven by Scarf (1960). Other models seek to determine optimal control parameters of such policies, such as the optimal ordering time, order quantity and inventory review intervals. Many SIC models build on the classical *newsvendor* model, which seeks to determine the optimal order quantity for a perishable product under stochastic demand. An overview of single-period newsvendor problems is given by Khouja (1999). Silver (1981) provides an overview and typology of many standard inventory problems, such as the ones mentioned above. General up-to-date overviews of inventory models can be found in the textbooks by Silver et al. (1998), Porteus (2002) and Tempelmeier (2006).

3.2.3 Price-Based Demand Models

The model types in the middle row of Fig. 3.2 treat price as a decision, which influences the demand. Pure ***pricing*** models aim to determine an optimal selling price, without considering replenishments. For example, given a price-demand relation, the goal is to find the price which maximizes total revenues. Mild et al. (2006) review factors influencing demand and show how to find optimal prices.

Markdown models determine the right price path for inventory clearance for a given amount of inventory, which cannot be replenished during the planning horizon. Elmaghraby and Keskinocak (2003) classify several dynamic pricing models with and without replenishment decisions, the latter ones including markdown models.

Auctions, as discussed for example by Talluri and van Ryzin (2004, Sect. 6), take a fundamentally different approach to pricing. They provide a price-discovery mechanism and thereby an alternative to posting fixed prices. This approach is particularly valuable if little demand information is available. The aforementioned authors discuss the close connection between auctions and dynamic pricing.

Trade promotion models represent a type of pricing models that consider replenishments as an exogenous input and therefore fit in the second column of Fig. 3.2. Neslin (2002) provides an overview and discusses the reasons for promotions.

Research in ***integrated pricing*** (IP) models dates back to Whitin (1955) who extends the EOQ-formula as well as the classical newsvendor model with price decisions. This field has seen extensive research in the last decades, which is summarized, for example, by Petruzzi and Dada (1999). Recent research focuses on multiple period models, which are discussed in the well-known literature reviews of Chan et al. (2004), Elmaghraby and Keskinocak (2003) and Yano and Gilbert (2003). Few models exist for environments in which replenishment, prices and due dates are set simultaneously. Some models of this type and other models dealing with due date setting can be found, for example, in the previously mentioned review paper by Keskinocak and Tayur (2004).

From an application-oriented perspective it is worthwhile comparing IP and a successive application of pricing & SIC models. While IP models recognize the interdependence between pricing and replenishment and therefore determine decisions simultaneously, they do so at the cost of a more simplified demand and supply representation. Pure pricing models may include sophisticated demand functions, including reference price effects, promotion effects, and competition (Mild et al., 2006). Similarly, SIC models consider factors such as multiple suppliers and quantity-discounts. IP models typically cannot deal with these factors due to tractability (Elmaghraby and Keskinocak, 2003, Sect. 4).

3.2.4 Quantity-Based Demand Models

Models in the bottom row of Fig. 3.2 take prices as exogenous but manage demand by means of rationing strategies. In contrast to the models of the top and middle row, the models distinguish multiple customer classes and prioritize them rather than fulfilling orders in an FCFS manner.

The type ***traditional revenue management*** (TRM) in the first cell of the third row refers to models that are common in airline applications. In these models, given units of a perishable product (e.g., seats on a flight on a specific day) are allocated to customers with different priorities or different willingness to pay. The basic question is whether to accept a given order or to reserve capacity in anticipation of more profitable future orders. McGill and van Ryzin (1999) and Pak and Piersma (2002) provide an overview and a short history of research in traditional revenue management with a focus on airline applications. Boyd and Bilegan (2003) discuss models focusing on e-commerce applications. The recent review by Chiang et al. (2007) includes an overview of RM practices in different industries.

Models of the type *Allocated available-to-promise* (***aATP***) are similar to the order promising type of the top row except for differentiating between multiple customer classes. Scarce resources (inventory on hand, planned stock at the CODP or capacity downstream of the DP) are allocated to these classes according to customer profitability or other priority measures. Within each class, customer requests are usually handled FCFS, just as in traditional order promising. Examples of these type have been discussed before in Sect. 4.3.2. Guerrero and Kern (1988) introduce the general problem of accepting and refusing orders and discuss the requirements and implications of order promising mechanisms. For reviews of the mostly deterministic models of this type the reader is referred to Kilger and Meyr (2008) and Pibernik (2005).

If customer requests do not have to be answered instantaneously, several customer orders can be collected and jointly promised in a *batch*, thereby creating higher degrees of freedom for selecting the most important or profitable orders within a simultaneous optimization process. Overviews of these so-called "batch order promising models" can again be found in the work of Ball et al. (2004), Chen et al. (2001) or Fleischmann and Meyr (2004).

A review of integrated due-date management and job-scheduling models with deterministic orders is provided by Gordon et al. (2002). The article considers batch-models in which due dates are determined according to current capacity and the desired delivery date. Keskinocak and Tayur (2004) give a general overview of due-date setting models.

aATP and TRM models are similar in that they decide about demand fulfillment with respect to different customer classes. The most significant difference concerns the perishability of resources. TRM considers "perishable" products, e.g., empty seats on a specific flight, which are lost after the departure date, whereas the ATP quantities managed in aATP models are generally storable. Another difference concerns the time horizon. TRM models typically consider a fixed day of capacity availability, e.g., the departure date of a flight. In contrast, aATP models consider multiple periods linked through the storability of excess inventory. Furthermore, aATP models usually assume deterministic demand whereas demand in TRM models is stochastic.

The last model type within the grid concerns ***inventory rationing*** (IR) models. Similar to the relationship between aATP and order promising, IR models extend SIC models by distinguishing and prioritizing multiple customer classes. For an early review refer to Kleijn and Dekker (1998). As traditional SIC models, IR models may consider deterministic or stochastic replenishment lead times. A further distinction within this class of models concerns the number of demand classes considered, which may be general or limited to two classes.

IR and aATP models differ in terms of exogenous versus endogenous replenishment. Specifically, IR models consider replenishment decisions with stationary deterministic or stochastic lead times. In contrast, aATP typically considers capacitated, dynamic and deterministic arrivals of push-based production (=replenishment) quantities. To this end, aATP usually assumes deterministic and dynamic demand forecasts whereas IR models assume stochastic demand.

In addition to the model types captured in Fig. 3.2, a few recent research streams aim to combine several types by simultaneously considering multiple attributes. For example, Kocabıyıkoğlu and Popescu (2005) jointly analyze price and allocation decisions with two customer classes. Since most quantity-based models assume exogenous prices, this seems to be a promising direction for future research. Bitran and Caldentey (2003) formulate a general model of this problem and review the current state of research. Another approach is pursued in Ding et al. (2006) in which trade promotion models are combined with inventory rationing models. The authors denote the resulting new problem type by ADP, referring to the **a**llocation of available stock, **d**iscounting and **p**rioritization of customers.

3.3 General Software Types for Demand Management

3.3.1 Classifying Demand Management Software

The software market for demand and supply chain solutions has changed in recent years. For many years the focus was on the supply side. The interest is now, however, turning to end-to-end solutions including the demand side. Big supply chain solution providers like Oracle and SAP are investing large amounts in the acquisition of demand-related know-how. For example, in 2005 SAP took over Khimetrics, a leading vendor of markdown, price, and promotion-optimization solutions. Oracle—after taking over one of its largest competitors in supply chain solutions, Peoplesoft, in 2005—simultaneously invested in the demand solutions of Demantra (2006), ProfitLogic (2005) and Retek (2005), all of them leading vendors of retail revenue management software. Another big consolidation occurred in 2006 when JDA Software—a provider of specialized retail solutions—took over Manugistics, a supply chain solution provider focusing on profit optimization in the consumer goods industry.

The scope of our current analysis is restricted to software supporting short-term decision making in DM. These solutions draw data from other software systems, such as Customer Relationship Management systems on the demand side (Buttle, 2004) and Enterprise Resource Planning systems (Stadtler and

Kilger, 2008) on the supply side. Since these systems themselves do not focus on decision making we do not include them in our analysis.

As discussed in the previous section, scientific optimization models are fairly well described in the literature. One can easily identify data, decision variables, restrictions and solution strategies. Moreover, the solution quality is often analyzed in detailed numerical studies. This is different for commercial software solutions. Usually, available information is scarce and reveals little of the underlying technology. Software users can only assess the supported input data, available options, and the resulting output that is automatically calculated. The solution quality can hardly be evaluated objectively and is usually judged by user experience.

Our analysis of software modules reflects this limited availability of objective information. We build our characterization of software types and functionalities primarily on available software reviews and whitepapers. As a starting point we use essentially the same dimensions as for the scientific models. Model data and decisions roughly correspond with software input and output, respectively.

Fig. 3.3 structures software types along the same axes as the model types of Section 3.2. We choose names according to the functionality of commercial software modules on the market. The remainder of this section briefly reviews each of these software types.

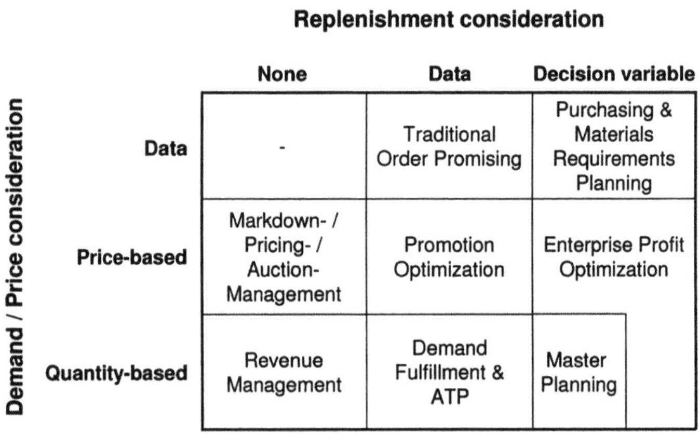

Figure 3.3: Types of Demand Management Software (Quante et al., 2009b)

3.3.2 Single-Class Exogenous Demand Solutions

The mid upper cell of Fig. 3.3 denoted by ***traditional order promising*** contains traditional software modules for short-term order promising under known inventory availability. When a customer order arrives, the software simply determines whether the order can be satisfied out of available inventory. If not, the order is backlogged according to a standard lead time without considering future capacity or additional incoming supply. It is easy to see that this approach can lead to an order peak after the standard lead time and thus to severe capacity problems in the future. Kilger and Meyr (2008) illustrate this situation in a simple example.

Refilling of inventory is usually left to ***purchasing & materials requirements planning*** modules, which are part of enterprise resource planning (ERP) systems. Essentially, these systems support refilling of non-bottleneck material and components from a single vendor. An overview of these classical systems can be found, for example, in the textbook of Vollmann et al. (2005). Since these classical systems provide sufficient solution quality only for very simple settings, specialized inventory modules consider extensions such as capacitated replenishment, stochastic demand, and multiple suppliers (Stadtler, 2008). Such modules usually are part of larger advanced planning and supply chain planning software suites. Additionally, there are specialized vendors of supply-chain wide inventory optimization tools, such as Optiant (Optiant, 2007) with its inventory suite Powerchain and Smartops (Smartops, 2007).

3.3.3 Price-Based Solutions

Markdown management systems are mainly used in retail, for example for end-of-season stock clearance. An example of markdown management systems is B_Line, described by Mantrala and Rao (2001) under the name MARK. The system takes possible prices and corresponding demand probability distributions for each period as inputs and can find both markdown and markup price paths. The output consists of a specific price in each period. Furthermore, MARK is capable of finding a suitable amount of initial inventory by iterating through a discrete set of possible inventory levels. Elmaghraby and Keskinocak (2003, Sect. 3.2) describe the capability of markdown solutions.

Software systems of the type ***pricing management*** are relatively new. This is due to improvements in computing power and increased availability of past sales data. The rise of data warehouses and cheap computing power has recently allowed the use of automated pricing systems for many applications. Pricing management systems are based on complex price-demand functions for which suitable parameters have to be estimated, a process requiring vast amounts of past sales data. For example, to estimate price elasticity, the sales data must include a certain degree of diversity, corresponding with at least a few past price changes. Capacity or inventory restrictions are usually not considered in these types of software (see for example Mild et al., 2006).

The quick expansion of e-commerce applications has boosted the use of ***auction systems***. The large number of different systems merits a review in its own right and exceeds the scope of our analysis. We refer to Kambil and van Heck (2002) for a systematic introduction to this field. Vakali et al. (2001) discuss the characteristics of internet-based auction systems and present a short survey of popular applications.

Similar to the previously described markdown systems, ***promotion optimization*** is also used in retail environments, as described by Elmaghraby and Keskinocak (2003, Sect. 3.2). Very detailed information about the capability of such systems can be found on-line, for example from the vendors mentioned at the beginning of this section.

The term ***enterprise profit optimization*** (EPO) was coined by the software company Manugistics, who claims to be the first vendor offering an integrated pricing and supply solution (Manugistics, 2002). Furthermore, Manugistics software is meant to be able to allocate scarce resources to the most profitable customers, thus simultaneously applying ideas of quantity-based DM. Demand and supply planning is realized in many solutions, but not in an integrated way and not including price decisions. Most APS forecast demand for different price levels and then successively analyze—within the context of mid-term planning—several what-if scenarios and their effects on the total supply chain.

3.3.4 Quantity-Based Solutions

APS software modules that support mid-term, aggregated supply and demand decisions are known as ***master planning*** modules (Meyr et al., 2008b) as previously mentioned in Sect. 2.2. They receive deterministic demand forecasts and prices as inputs from the demand planning module of APS (Kilger and Wagner, 2008) and then determine the best combinations of sales, production and replenishment quantities and the corresponding inventories under given capacity constraints. Quantities can be allocated to different customer classes. In terms of the supply chain framework in Fig. 3.1, master planning modules deal with forecast-driven planning activities (e.g., push-based replenishment of the CODP) and therefore fall outside the scope of our definition of DM. However, we feel that they deserve mention since their resulting allocations serve as the primary input for the short-term, capacity-checked order promising, executed by the Demand Fulfillment and ATP modules of APS. A detailed list of options considered in master planning modules can be found in the work of Rohde and Wagner (2008).

The type in the lower middle cell takes capacity and inventory replenishments into account and corresponds to the ***demand fulfillment & ATP*** modules of APS previously described in Chapter 2. These modules extend the aforementioned traditional order promising and determine due dates for incoming customer orders, which promise to be more reliable than simple standard lead times. In addition, if ATP quantities are allocated to customer priority classes—in the usually implemented aggregated way—order promising differentiates with respect to customer importance, based on customer profitability or strategic impact.

Revenue management software is widely used by airlines, hotel chains, and car rental agencies. RM software systems basically take the given capacity and offered tariffs as input and decide on acceptance or rejection of customer orders. One of the main differences with demand fulfillment & ATP is that RM software focuses on revenues rather than costs. Furthermore, RM systems usually forecast demand in much more detail than demand fulfillment modules, e.g., for each flight, on each day, and for each customer class. These forecasts require a large amount of historical sales data in order to be reliable. Modern revenue management systems can handle many additional industry-specific issues, such as overbooking and connecting flights in the airline context (Talluri and van Ryzin, 2004, Sect. 10.1.3, 11.2).

Chapter 4

Demand Management Models in MTS Manufacturing

In this chapter, we align the identified general types of demand management described in Chapter 3 with the characteristics of manufacturing environments. By this, we can further narrow the domain of demand management models by excluding those ones that appear hardly suitable for MTS production systems. After identification of the most suitable models, we complement the general review from the previous chapter by a more detailed review of specialized papers taking into account the characteristics of manufacturing environments.

4.1 Matching of Model and Software Types to the Requirements of MTS Manufacturing

In this section, we identify alignments and misalignments between models and software within the domain of MTS manufacturing. Specifically, the goal of this section is to identify the most appropriate models and software types for DM decisions in MTS manufacturing. We also seek to highlight remaining research needs and provide the motivation for the models presented in Chapter 5.

We build our discussion around the structure of Figures 3.2 and 3.3. Specifically, we compare the supply flexibility in MTS manufacturing with the way that replenishment decisions are supported by different model and software types. Similarly, the demand flexibility is tied to the supported demand management. In this way, we identify the most appropriate cell(s) in Figures 3.2 and 3.3. This allows us to recognize empty spots and future research needs.

In manufacturing, production processes are the most important—and usually most costly—process steps. The customer order decoupling point as the interface between forecast-driven demand planning and customer-oriented demand fulfillment describes whether a certain production process is operated under demand (un)certainty, what type of stocks (raw material, components, final products) have to be held, where the main bottlenecks (stocks, production capacity) can be expected, and how long customer service times will be.

In MTS environments, all production processes are executed in a forecast-based way. Due to upstream capacity limitations, production planning decides on short-term replenishment of CODP inventories in a push-based, "vendor-driven" manner. Thus, models including replenishment decisions (third column of Fig. 3.2) can only support the mid-term, forecast-based demand planning, but not the short-term demand fulfillment. In order to make use of the (uncertain) information on future CODP inventory replenishments, as implied by the production plans, demand fulfillment models of the second column appear the most appropriate.

Because of the MTS market conditions and contracting practice, pricing decisions typically have to be taken on a mid-term basis. For example, the Demand Planning module of an APS forecasts several price-demand scenarios, including different alternatives for price discounts or promotions. These scenarios are passed on to a master planning module, which checks each of them with respect to supply chain constraints, selects the most profitable one, and generates directives for the (forecast-based) short-term production planning. Thus, short-term pricing flexibility is rather limited, which rules out the models on the second row of Fig. 3.2. Price-based approaches appear mainly applicable on the mid-term planning level, e.g. to determine demand forecasts in conjunction with optimal prices.

The remaining models are order promising and aATP models as the most applicable ones for DM in MTS manufacturing. Both of them consider the current level of CODP inventory. Order promising in an MTS environment searches through the ATP quantities in an FCFS manner to be able to fulfill a customer order. Newer approaches process several customer orders in a batch and allocate ATP to the most profitable customer orders. aATP models overcome the disadvantage of batch order promising, namely not providing a real-time order promise and forcing the customer to wait. However, they are dependent on forecast-based information on CODP inventories that is provided by the master and production plans, and on the possibility of customer segmentation. The ATP search rules that are used to consume the allocated ATP quantities of the different customer classes follow similar ideas as traditional RM methods. However, since products in MTS manufacturing are durable and can be stored, they also have to be able to "search over time", i.e. to take future inventory replenishments into account.

The results of this section can be summarized as follows: Replenishment decisions are not relevant for short-term demand fulfillment in MTS manufacturing, which rules out the third column in Fig. 3.2. The second row is also not appropriate for short-term applications due to the low pricing flexibility. Traditional RM methods do not consider storability of inventory. The

	Replenishment consideration		
	None	**Data**	**Decision variable**
Quantity-based	Traditional RM *+ storability* *+ several replenishments*	aATP *+ stochastics*	Inventory Rationing *+ deterministic supplies* *+ no ordering*

Figure 4.1: Quantity-Based Demand Management Models

matching of the generalized model and software types of Chap. 3 to the specific characteristics of MTS manufacturing leads to the following research questions:

How can demand management models be adapted to the specific needs of make-to-stock manufacturing? Unlike in service environments, order promising in manufacturing industries is a multi-period problem, i.e. production earlier or deliveries later than the customers' requested date are possible. Therefore, traditional RM techniques typically cannot be applied as is in MTS manufacturing industries. They have to be adapted to deal with the holding and (future) replenishment of CODP inventory and costs. The allocation and ATP consumption rules currently used in APS serve this purpose, but are very basic. Furthermore, stochastic influences from the demand side are usually ignored. Inventory rationing models cannot be applied as is to MTS manufacturing due to their short-term replenishment decisions. Excluding replenishment decisions from IR models and using the "remaining" rationing policies for demand fulfillment seems to be a way of adapting such models. Fig. 4.1 summarizes the match of models and software to the requirements of MTS manufacturing. Subsequently, such new models are shown in Chap. 5.

Since it is not clear how different models perform under realistic conditions, a comprehensive performance analysis considering the specific characteristics of MTS manufacturing will be made in Chap. 7. The analysis should help to assess the different models and rules taken from commercial software solutions and should determine the main influence factors on the performance.

4.2 Quantity-Based Demand Management in Manufacturing

We will discuss the literature of the three identified types in more detail, as basically review papers have been mentioned before. Additionally, we take into account the characteristics of MTS manufacturing when reviewing the literature.

Table 4.1: Overview of Publications on TRM in Manufacturing (Method: C=Conceptual, M=Simulation/analytical models, R=Review, S=Case study)

Publication	CODP	Classes	Method
Harris and Pinder (1995)	ATO	2	C,M
Kalyan (2002)	MTO/ATO/MTS	–	C
Kuhn and Defregger (2004)	MTO	2	S
Rehkopf and Spengler (2004)	MTO	several	C,M
Barut and Sridharan (2005)	MTO	several	M
Kimms and Klein (2005)	MTO	–	C
Jalora (2006)	MTO	several	M
Kolisch and Zatta (2006)	MTO	–	C
Rehkopf (2006)	MTO	–	C,M,R
Kumar and Frederick (2007)	MTO/MTS	3	S
Spengler et al. (2007)	MTO	several	M
Chiang et al. (2007)	–	–	R
Specht and Gruß (2007)	ATO	–	C,S

4.2.1 Traditional Revenue Management

Overviews of *TRM* and its applications in different industries (including manufacturing) are provided by Kimms and Klein (2005) and Chiang et al. (2007). These overviews reveal that the literature on quantity-based RM in manufacturing is basically limited to MTO and ATO production environments. This can be explained by the correspondence of *production capacities* and *perishable assets* which are the building blocks of RM in the service industries (Weatherford and Bodily, 1992). Usually, TRM papers for manufacturing determine optimal protection levels for production capacities (located downstream of the CODP).

Table 4.1 shows important papers on TRM in manufacturing classified according to the CODP, the number of customer classes considered and the methodology applied in the paper. We distinguish between four methodologies: *conceptual* (C), *simulation/analytical models* (M), *review* (R), and *case studies* (S). Conceptual papers are understood as those describing and developing new concepts and ideas without defining a specific model. This is done in the next methodology of defining simulation- or analytical models. Review papers focus on providing a comprehensive state-of-the-art of the literature within a special field of research. They are often combined with conceptual work, e.g., the development of a classification framework. Finally, case studies focus on a detailed description of real-world applications.

A seminal paper for the adoption of RM concepts in manufacturing is the one from Harris and Pinder (1995). The authors describe the analogies between ATO production and the service industries and proposes a TRM model for a repair facility and a sports apparel manufacturer. Unlike many papers in TRM, the author describes not only how to determine protection levels for a two-class problem, but also how to determine the optimal selling prices.

Similar to the previous paper, Kalyan (2002) establishes a relationship between airline revenue management and its counterparts in manufacturing. The author introduces the notion of MAV (minimal acceptable value) and shows how MAV can be used in many different applications. MAV is understood as the value of a resource and is known in revenue management as the bid-price, a threshold for accepting those orders that generate higher revenues than the bid-price. The basic idea of the paper is that all assets or resources are associated with a certain value (MAV). If this value is known, it can be compared to any incoming order. If the price of the order is higher than the MAV, the order is accepted, and rejected otherwise. The paper gives many examples and shows how MAV can be calculated in manufacturing applications.

Kuhn and Defregger (2004) discuss a case of a paper production company with a fixed capacity on the short-term. Production is triggered by incoming orders (MTO) and customers are divided into two classes differentiated in resulting revenues (€ 50,000 vs. € 10,000) and required lead times (2 days vs. 3 days). If a customer order is accepted, the paper machine is busy for two days. The problem is to decide which of the low-margin customers to reject in anticipation of later arriving high-margin customers. The authors propose a Markov decision process solved by means of a linear program. A numerical study shows a profit increase of 5.4% compared to a simple FCFS policy.

The work of Rehkopf and Spengler (2004) is a further paper identifying the characteristics between the service industries and MTO manufacturing according to the application of revenue management. The authors focus on the iron and steel industry and show how a network revenue management problem (Talluri and van Ryzin, 2004) can be solved with a linear program in order to allocate capacity. This conceptual work is deepened in the later released paper of Spengler et al. (2007) which is discussed further below.

The work of Barut and Sridharan (2005) is selected as a representative of an entire line of research in scheduling and accepting orders in an MTO manufacturing setting. Rather than to focus just on the acceptance decisions, the authors—in contrast to the previously mentioned papers—take into account the scheduling and exact due date determination of incoming orders. They propose a heuristic procedure (called DCAP) that is able to process orders in distinct lots and handles more than two customer classes. The results indicate that DCAP performs better than an FCFS policy. Jalora (2006) presents a similar model as shown in Barut and Sridharan (2005) but extends their work by showing a dynamic order acceptance and scheduling policy evolving over time when the exact demand realizations are known.

Kolisch and Zatta (2006) present a short introduction into revenue management for the process industry. Their work includes an empirical study over 124 companies of the process industry. The large majority of companies confirmed that revenue management is a suitable method to cope with overcapacities and increasing competition. 80% of the surveyed companies currently apply methods of revenue management, the majority of them (74%) for capacity management and 15% price management.

Kumar and Frederick (2007) show the case of Andersen, an American window manufacturer. The case describes a simplified decision problem Andersen is facing. The company sells its products over three distinct distribution channels. In two of the three channels, Andersen produces windows upon order placement and generates only low or medium margins due to long lead times. In the third channel, the customer buys the window directly in a warehouse and pays a surplus due to the short lead times. Andersen is producing on-stock in this third channel. The aim is to find an optimal amount of inventory stored in the warehouse. A closed-form solution is presented in this study resembling the famous newsvendor problem.

Spengler et al. (2007) propose a model for the iron and steel industry in an MTO setting. The authors define a stochastic dynamic program based on a vector of CTP quantities. The optimal policy is to accept an order if its current contribution margin exceeds the expected marginal profits. As the problem size is too large to be solved directly with dynamic programming, the authors approximate the expected marginal profits by a multi-dimensional knapsack formulation. In numerical tests the proposed method results in increased contribution margins of 5.3% compared to a simple FCFS rule. This work as well as the previous mentioned work of Rehkopf and Spengler (2004) is included in the dissertation of Rehkopf (2006).

Specht and Gruß (2007) describe the successful application of a revenue management system in the Ford Motor Company. The described system consists of three distinct tools: (1) a package optimizer to create bundles of promising car accessories, (2) a price optimizer to generate incentive schemes, and (3) a decision support tool for car dealers that provides information about what cars to order. Additionally to this case study, Specht and Gruß (2007) discuss the requirements of future revenue management systems in the automotive industry. The authors mention that such a system should generate buying alternatives based on the current capacity utilization in the supply chain and acceptable lead times.

Table 4.2: Overview of Publications on aATP in Manufacturing (Method: C=Conceptual, M=Simulation/analytical models, R=Review, S=Case study)

Publication	CODP	Classes	Method
Chen et al. (2001)	MTS	–	M
Fischer (2001)	MTS	several	C,M,R
Chen et al. (2002)	MTS	–	M
Gordon et al. (2002)	MTO	–	R
Ball et al. (2004)	–	–	C,R
Fleischmann et al. (2004)	–	–	C,R
Keskinocak and Tayur (2004)	MTO	–	R
Pibernik (2005)	–	–	C,R
Lee (2006)	MTO/ATO	4 to 8	M,S
Pibernik (2006)	MTS	several	C,M
Pibernik and Yadav (2009)	MTS	2	M
Kilger and Meyr (2008)	–	–	C,R
Meyr (2009)	MTS	several	C,M

4.2.2 Allocated Available-to-Promise

Models of the type aATP allocate capacity/inventory to customers according to their profitability. These models are usually found in manufacturing environments and are often directly applicable in APS to be used in real-world applications. In this section, we complement the review of aATP models by discussing important examples of this type of models.

The most relevant paper in this thesis is the one by Meyr (2009). The model presented here follows a two-step approach: In a first step, quotas are assigned to customer classes (Allocation Planning) which are consumed later on in real-time by the incoming orders (ATP consumption). Due to the importance of this paper, we give a detailed description of the presented model and research approach in the subsequent Section 4.3.

In contrast to the two-step approach of Meyr (2009), batch order promising models use batch intervals to be able to select the most profitable orders. Examples of batch models can be found in the work by Chen et al. (2001), Chen et al. (2002), and Fischer (2001). As shown in these articles, the general drawback of batch models—the long response time to customer requests—is usually handled by first answering the request with an approximative due date and then refining this date in a subsequent step.

Lee (2006) describes a simulation tool developed for IBM's hardware business in order to evaluate the performance of the entire demand management activities—from calculating ATP quantities over scheduling of orders up to due date promising. The author claims that this is one of only a few works considering the entire process, including ATP generation. The considered dimensions of ATP are the type of product, demand classes, supply classes and time buckets. ATP quantities are calculated according to information about component availability, current inventory, work-in-process, the master plan, supplier commitments and production capacity. When a customer order arrives, the model searches through the ATP dimensions according to predefined search rules. The aim of the study is to show the change in key performance indicators when shifting from an MTO to a configure-to-order (CTO) business. The study reveals that customer service increases dramatically in the CTO setting.

Pibernik (2006) discusses order fulfillment strategies in case of stock out situations. This work is one of the few papers taking deterministic future replenishments into account. The author proposes a model to allocate a set of orders to ATP quantities when the costs of short- and long-term consequences of delaying or rejecting an order can be quantified. Similar to the work of Meyr (2009), the author describes a way to pre-allocate ATP quantities to customer classes in order to increase profitability. The author also mentions the *rank-based* allocation strategy as earlier mentioned in Section 2.3.2. It starts allocating all available quantities to the highest customer class. Then, it iterates in descending order through the lower classes allocating the remaining quantities.

Together with the previous described work, the paper of Pibernik and Yadav (2009) is the second paper found considering customer classes and deterministic future replenishments . The authors propose a model that selects among two customer classes under a service-level constraint. The described model in this paper is closely linked to our setting, but reveals some distinctive features. The most prominent distinction is the service-level objective as we maximize the expected profit. Furthermore, the model assumes stochastic due dates, two customer classes and lost sales where we allow more than two classes and both, lost sales and backlogging.

4.2.3 Inventory Rationing

There are two broad research streams within the type of IR models. Ha (1997a) and De Véricourt et al. (2002) propose models with multiple demand classes and stochastic replenishment times, thus assuming limited production (=replenishment) capacities. In contrast, Melchiors et al. (2000) and Arslan et al. (2007) model deterministic replenishment lead times and unbounded replenishment quantities. All of these models take decisions on ordering and rationing

Table 4.3: Overview of Publications on IR in Manufacturing (Method: C=Conceptual, M=Simulation/analytical models, R=Review, S=Case study)

Publication	CODP	Classes	Method
Ha (1997b)	MTS	2	M
Ha (1997a)	MTS	several	M
Kleijn and Dekker (1998)	–	–	R
Melchiors et al. (2000)	MTS	2	M
De Véricourt et al. (2002)	MTS	several	M
Arslan et al. (2007)	MTS	several	M
Gupta and Wang (2007)	MTO/MTS	2	M
Möllering and Thonemann (2007)	MTS	2	M
Defregger and Kuhn (2007)	MT0	several	M
Teunter and Klein Haneveld (2008)	MTS	2	M,R

levels, which are typically expressed in policies like (s, S, R) where s is the reorder point, S the order-up-to level, and R the protection level between customer classes. When inventory falls below s, it is filled up to S. In a two-class setting, demand from the low margin class is fulfilled as long as the inventory is above the protection level R.

Although some of the following work is also linked to revenue management, we classify all models deciding about replenishments as IR models. Defregger and Kuhn (2007) propose a model in an MTO setting using a Markov decision process. The authors consider a decision maker who has to decide whether to accept an order—taking into account the order specific profit and the orders maximum lead time—and whether to raise the inventory level by additional production. In contrast to the conventional approaches in MTO settings, the authors include a finished goods inventory in their model in order to be able to fulfill high-margin orders with a short lead-time. However, it is still an MTO setting since production is triggered by incoming customer orders.

Gupta and Wang (2007) study a setting with two customer classes, distinguished in transactional and more valuable contractual orders. The manufacturer can choose which transactional orders to fulfill but has to meet the demand of contractual orders at a short notice. The authors study two scenarios, one in which the contractual orders are produced-to-stock and one with make-to-order production. In the MTS scenario, the manufacturers decision is twofold: (1) how many units to accept from the transactional orders (contractual have to be fulfilled) and (2) how much to produce to raise finished goods inventory.

Möllering and Thonemann (2007) focus on analyzing optimal backorder clearing in critical level policies. In contrast to models assuming lost sales, backorder models have to decide about which backorders to fulfill under different inventory levels. In the more realistic setting of order sizes greater than one, the authors prove an optimal way of backorder clearing.

The work of Teunter and Klein Haneveld (2008) includes an up-to-date literature review and classification of inventory rationing models. Additionally, the authors propose a dynamic rationing model with two customer classes taking into account the remaining time until the next customer order arrives. The authors mention the easy implementation of their approach as rationing levels are provided in charts and lookup-tables.

Table 4.3 gives an overview about models on IR. Although the mentioned papers in the table are not exhaustive, it represents an overview about current research in this field. The papers in the table suggest that there is a further distinction in research between papers considering two customer classes and papers considering more than two classes. Ha (1997b) explains this when he states "as the number of customer classes increases, the optimal policy will be difficult to compute because of the curse of dimensionality and will be even more difficult to implement". For practical applications, many of these models are tailored to a specific problem and usually not applicable in general settings considered by APS.

4.3 A Selected Deterministic Allocation and Order Promising Model

In this section we discuss the work of Meyr (2009) in which an LP model for demand fulfillment is presented which is the building block for the later developed stochastic models of Chapter 5. The author distinguishes between two different types of models: models with customer segmentation and models without customer segmentation. The models support the demand fulfillment functionality of APS as described in Sect. 2.2. They receive the ATP information from a production planning module and promise due dates to incoming customer orders as shown in Fig. 4.2. In the following, we provide a mathematical formulation of these models. In addition, we propose a classification of search rules for ATP consumption which consume allocated ATP quantities. Due to an aggregated or disaggregated consumption of aATP quantities, we analyze how far these rules are applicable in stochastic environments.

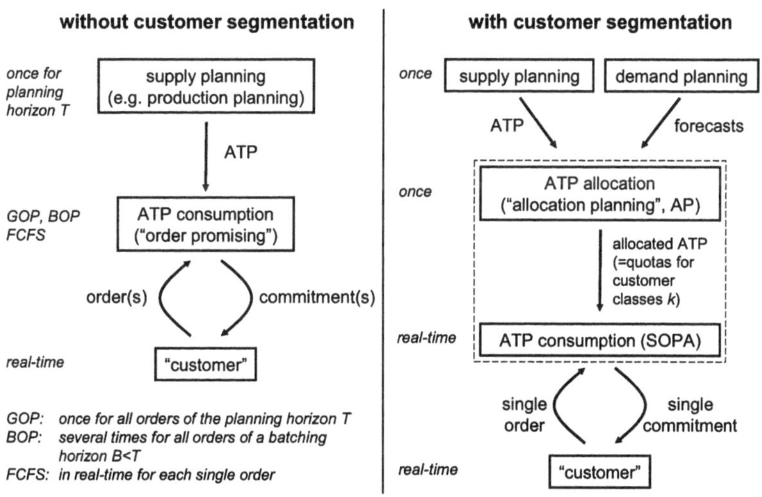

Figure 4.2: Modeling Environment (Meyr, 2009)

4.3.1 Models Without Customer Segmentation

The following basic order promising model without customer segmentation assigns customer orders to ATP quantities according to profitability. In order to model the successive arrival of customer orders the proposed LP formulation has several iteration steps. Meyr (2009) defines a set I^s of currently known orders in iteration s and distinguishes accordingly between three different cases: (1) if the model is executed after each order, i.e., I^s contains only the new order, the model resembles an FCFS policy. One can imagine that this model does not lead to an optimal profit as customers with a low level of profitability might buy units better kept for later arriving high margin customers. (2) If the model is executed after a certain *reasonable* amount of time, i.e., I^s contains all orders arrived in that certain time period, the approach is called *batch order processing* (BOP) referring to a batching horizon B in which the orders are collected to be processed in the next run. (3) If the batching horizon equals the total planning horizon, the model is not executed until all orders are known. This approach results in an optimal solution and is therefore called *global order processing* (GOP). The following equations show the *basic order promising model*:

$$\max \sum_{i \in I^s} \sum_{t=1}^{T+1} p_{it} o_{it}^s \tag{4.1}$$

subject to

$$\sum_{t=1}^{T+1} o_{it}^s = q_i \ \forall i \in I^s \tag{4.2}$$

$$\sum_{i \in I^s} o_{it}^s \leq ATP_t^s \ \forall t = 1, \dots, T. \tag{4.3}$$

The objective function 4.1 maximizes the profit over the planning horizon when satisfying the orders of set I^s. The profit p_{it} includes the revenues p_i generated by the customer i minus optional backlogging costs b_i or holding costs h, i.e., $p_{it} = p_i - h(d_i - t)$ if the required delivery date d_i of the order is after the fulfillment date t and $p_{it} = p_i - b_i(t - d_i)$ in case of a late delivery (and $p_{it} = p_i$ otherwise).

The model includes two constraints. 4.2 guarantees that the total quantity q_i of each order is fulfilled (either from *real* supply or from the infinite supply of period $T+1$). 4.3 guarantees that, in each period, not more than the total supply ATP_t is assigned to all orders.

In the cases of BOP or FCFS where several iterations are executed, the ATP quantity has to be updated after each iteration in order to cope for already assigned demand quantities. This step corresponds to the previously described *Netting* activity (see Sect. 2.2). Formally, the ATP quantities are updated after iteration s with the following formula: $ATP_t^{s+1} = ATP_t^s - \sum_{i \in I^s} o_{it}^s \ \forall t = 1, \dots, T$. Table 4.4 summarizes the used symbols and notation.

Table 4.4: Notation of the Basic Order Promising Model

Indices:	
$s = 1, \ldots, S$	Iterations
$t = 1, \ldots, T+1$	Periods of the planning horizon (T+1: dummy period)
$i = 1, \ldots, I$	Customer orders
I^s	Set of orders that are promised in iteration s
Decision variables:	
$o_{it}^s \geq 0$	Part of order i which is served by ATP of period t and promised during iteration s
Data:	
ATP_t^s	Not yet assigned supply that becomes available in period t and can still be promised to customers during iteration s
q_i	Requested order quantity of order i
p_{it}	Per unit profit of order i if satisfied by ATP of period t
p_i	Per unit revenue of order i
d_i	Requested delivery date of order i
b_i	Per unit and period backlogging costs of order i
h	Per unit and time holding costs

For the sake of comparability with the ongoing development of stochastic models, we slightly reformulate the basic order promising model. In the current formulation, holding and backlogging costs are part of the profit term p_{it}. This leads to the situation that the costs are only charged when a customer order is fulfilled. In case of backlogging, this seems intuitive, but not for holding costs. Therefore, we introduce a fictitious order ϕ with a delivery date $d_\phi = T$ where all remaining quantities of ATP are assigned to. The profit term $p_{\phi t}$ only includes the holding cost term, i.e., $p_{\phi t} = -h(T-t)$. The *adapted order promising model* can be stated as

$$\max \sum_{i \in I^s \cup \phi} \sum_{t=1}^{T+1} p_{it} o_{it}^s \tag{4.4}$$

subject to

$$\sum_{t=1}^{T+1} o_{it}^s = q_i \; \forall i \in I^s \tag{4.5}$$

$$\sum_{i \in I^s \cup \phi} o_{it}^s = ATP_t^s \; \forall t = 1, \ldots, T. \tag{4.6}$$

Table 4.5: Notation of the Network Flow Model

Indices:	
I_t^s	Set of orders i with a desired delivery date in period t
Decision variables:	
$x_t^s \geq 0$	Downstream flow of inventory in period t and iteration s
$y_t^s \geq 0$	Upstream flow of inventory in period t and iteration s
$z_i^s \geq 0$	Lost sales quantity of order i and iteration s
Data:	
b	Per unit and period backlogging costs (independent of order i)

Note that the original and the adapted formulation result in equal profits in case of high scarcity (for which the model was intended). Even if large LP models can be solved with modern LP solvers, calculation time increases rapidly when solving the GOP model. Especially in the rolling horizon simulations of Chapter 7, the problem size gets very large. We propose a network flow formulation of the above adapted order promising model that can be solved for larger instances within a reasonable time. However, this model comes with the disadvantage that the backlogging costs are not order dependent and, therefore, have to be changed to b. Additionally, this model is not able to show from which ATP quantity a certain order is fulfilled.

For the mathematical model formulation, we define a subset $I_t^s \subseteq I^s$ with $I_t^s := \{i \in I^s | d_i = t\}$ as the set all orders $i \in I^s$ with a desired delivery date in period t. The *network flow order promising model* is henceforth given as

$$\max \sum_{i \in I^s} p_i(q_i - z_i^s) - \sum_{t=1}^{T+1} (hx_t^s + by_t^s) \tag{4.7}$$

subject to

$$x_{t+1}^s - y_{t+1}^s - x_t^s + y_t^s = ATP_t^s - \sum_{i \in I_t^s} (q_i - z_i^s) \ \forall t = 1, \ldots, T \tag{4.8}$$

$$z_i^s \leq q_i \ \forall i = 1, \ldots, I^s \tag{4.9}$$

$$x_1^s = 0, y_1^s = 0, y_{T+1}^s = 0. \tag{4.10}$$

The symbols and notation of the network flow problem are shown in Table 4.5.

The objective function 4.7 maximizes the profit resulting from a flow of ATP quantities between the periods towards incoming orders. If the ATP quantities flow downwards (i.e., to later periods) holding costs are charged. If the flow goes to the opposite direction, backlogging costs are charged. The inventory balance constraint 4.8 controls the flow between the periods. Incoming quantities are consisting of the current period's ATP quantities (ATP_t^s), the downstream flow from the previous period (x_t^s) and the upstream flow from the next period (y_{t+1}^s). Outgoing quantities are consisting of the downstream flow to the next period (x_{t+1}^s), the upstream flow to the previous period (y_t^s) and the flow to the orders arriving in this period (minus lost sales) ($\sum_{i \in I_t^s}(q_i - z_i^s)$). Fig. 4.3 illustrates the flow of quantities. The further constraints in 4.10 set the initial quantities of the first and last period. x_1^s can also be used to set the initial inventory.

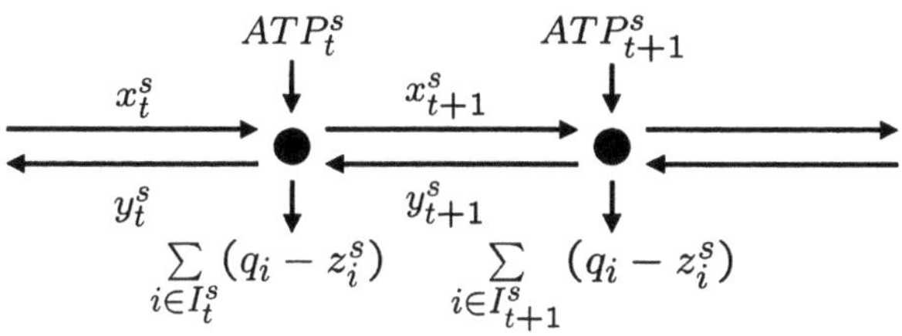

Figure 4.3: Illustration of the Inventory Balance Constraint

4.3.2 Models With Customer Segmentation

The models with customer segmentation try to overcome the disadvantages of the previous models. In case of FCFS, it is not guaranteed that a reasonable solution is reached. BOP models overcome this drawback but result in longer waiting times for the customer (as due dates are not determined until the end of the batch interval is reached). The general structure of models with customer segmentation is shown on the right side in Fig. 4.2. These models usually follow a two-step approach: in a first step (*allocation planning*), quotas are assigned to a given number of customer classes based on ATP quantities and demand forecasts. In a second step (*ATP consumption*), the quotas are consumed in real-time by incoming customer orders.

In the following, we present an approach by Meyr (2009) based on an LP model. Instead of a rule-based approach to determine the quotas (as described in Section 2.3.2), the author proposes a model allocating ATP quantities according to the profitability of customer classes. The determined quotas in the AP step are subsequently called *aATP*. Meyr (2009) uses the acronym *SOPA* for his approach, referring to ***s***ingle ***o***rder ***p***rocessing after ***a***llocation planning.

Table 4.6: Notation of the Allocation Planning Model

Decision variables:	
$z_{kt\tau} \geq 0$	Part of demand of priority class k in period τ which is satisfied by ATP of period t
$f_t \geq 0$	Still unallocated part of ATP of period t
Data:	
$d_{k\tau}^{min}$	Lower bound on sales to priority class k in period t
$d_{k\tau}^{max}$	Upper bound on sales to priority class k in period t
$p_{kt\tau}$	Per unit profit if ATP of period t satisfies demand of priority class k in period τ

With the symbols and notation of Table 4.6 we can formulate the *allocation planning model* as

$$\max \sum_{k=1}^{K} \sum_{t=1}^{T+1} \sum_{\tau=1}^{T} p_{kt\tau} z_{kt\tau} \tag{4.11}$$

subject to

$$d_{k\tau}^{min} \leq \sum_{t=1}^{T+1} z_{kt\tau} \leq d_{k\tau}^{max} \;\forall k, \tau = 1, \ldots, T \tag{4.12}$$

$$\sum_{k=1}^{K} \sum_{\tau=1}^{T} z_{kt\tau} + f_t = ATP_t^1 \;\forall t = 1, \ldots, T. \tag{4.13}$$

The profit resulting from allocating ATP quantities to customer classes is maximized in the objective function 4.11. Differently to p_{it} in the basic order promising model, the profit term $p_{kt\tau}$ represents the profit of a customer class and not an individual order. Meyr (2009) suggests to calculate $p_{kt\tau}$ as the average profit of all orders assigned to customer class k. Constraint 4.12 assures that not more than the maximum expected demand is allocated to a customer class and period (or not less than the minimum, respectively). In this constraint, the demand forecasts generated by the demand planning activity are considered in the model. Constraint 4.13 restricts the allocated quantities to the available ATP.

In the following, we show how the quotas or aATP quantities, respectively, can be extracted from the optimal solution of the AP model, denoted by "*". Meyr (2009) proposes two different granularities of aATP quantities. Firstly, a fine granularity in which the aATP quantities are structured according to the customer class k, the availability time of ATP t and the assignment of ATP to a time slot τ. The aATP in this granularity can directly be taken from the optimal values of the decision variables $z_{kt\tau}$ as shown in 4.14.

$$aATP^1_{kt\tau} := z^*_{kt\tau} \ \forall k, t, \tau. \tag{4.14}$$

The second granularity represents an aggregated version of the aATP quantities in which the time slots τ are aggregated to one time period. Equation 4.15 shows how the aggregated aATP quantities are extracted from the optimal values of the decision variables $z_{kt\tau}$. This version especially makes sense when forecast accuracy is low and the allocation of ATP to certain time slots results in poor profits. The proposed aggregation provides a way to compensate forecast errors. However, this aggregation allows customers to consume ATP quantities far away from their desired delivery date.

$$aATP^1_{kt} := \sum_{\tau=1}^{T} z^*_{kt\tau} \ \forall k, t. \tag{4.15}$$

Additionally to the aATP quantities, the AP model might also result in unallocated ATP, e.g., when the maximum expected demand is low in comparison to available ATP. These quantities are henceforth called uATP as shown in 4.16.

$$uATP^1_t := f^*_t \ \forall t. \tag{4.16}$$

The second step of the SOPA approach processes the incoming customer orders in real-time according to the aATP quantities. Let Ξ_i be the set of accessible priority classes from order i. Additionally, let $\hat{\imath}(s)$ denote the current (and only) order processed in the iteration step s. Accordingly, we define the *order processing model* as

$$\max \sum_{k \in \Xi_{\hat{\imath}(s)}} \sum_{t=1}^{T+1} p_{\hat{\imath}(s),t} \overline{o}^s_{kt} + \sum_{t=1}^{T} p_{\hat{\imath}(s),t} x^s_t \tag{4.17}$$

Table 4.7: Notation of the SOPA Model

Indices:	
Ξ_i	Set of priority classes which can be consumed by order i
Decision variables:	
$\overline{o}^s_{kt} \geq 0$	Part of allocated ATP of period t for priority class k which is in iteration s assigned to order $\hat{\imath}(s)$ showing a desired delivery date $d_{\hat{\imath}(s)}$
$x^s_t \geq 0$	Part of unallocated ATP of period t which is in iteration s assigned to order $\hat{\imath}(s)$ showing a desired delivery date $d_{\hat{\imath}(s)}$
Data:	
$aATP^s_{kt\tau}$	ATP that becomes available in period t and has been allocated to orders in priority class k with a requested delivery date in period τ
$uATP^s_t$	ATP that becomes available in period t but has not yet been allocated to any priority class or planned delivery date
$\hat{\imath}(s)$	The (single) order considered in iteration s

subject to

$$\sum_{k \in \Xi_{\hat{\imath}(s)}} \sum_{t=1}^{T+1} \overline{o}^s_{kt} + \sum_{t=1}^{T} x^s_t = q_{\hat{\imath}(s)} \tag{4.18}$$

$$\overline{o}^s_{kt} \leq aATP^s_{ktd_{\hat{\imath}(s)}} \quad \forall k \in \Xi_{\hat{\imath}(s)}, t = 1, \ldots, T \tag{4.19}$$

$$x^s_t \leq uATP^s_t \ \forall t = 1, \ldots, T. \tag{4.20}$$

Table 4.7 summarizes the symbols and notation of the above model. 4.17 maximizes the profit of the quantities assigned to order $\hat{\imath}(s)$. 4.18 guarantees that the assigned quantities to order $\hat{\imath}(s)$ are equal to the demand (if not enough supply is available, the order is fulfilled from the fictitious supply of period $T+1$). 4.19 and 4.20 restrict the consumed quantities of order $\hat{\imath}(s)$ to the available allocated and unallocated quantities. The SOPA model takes as input a given number of customer classes and corresponding assignments of orders to classes. The assignment of orders to classes has to be done before the actual order arrives, otherwise the SOPA approach will not work. As this seems to be confusing on the first sight, Meyr (2009) argues that not a single order has to be assigned to a class, but the associated customer handing in this order. Long-term relationships between vendors and their customers usually make it possible for such an assignment to be done before the actual order processing starts. All orders i of a customer assigned to class k are then also part of this class. The set Ξ_i of accessible classes of order i includes at least the class of the customer posting the order i, but might be extended when a customer is allowed to consume quantities of lower classes. Meyr (2009) analyzes which approaches perform best.

As the above order processing model solves an LP for each single order that arrives, it seems reasonable for practical implementations to mimic the SOPA search process through the aATP quantities by using simple rules. A description of such rules can be found in the following Section 4.3.3.

A remaining task is still to determine an appropriate number of customer classes k. As the number of classes gets larger, a finer determination of quotas is possible. However, the demand forecast $d_{k\tau}^{max}$ becomes less accurate with increasing k. As this is a medium-term planning task and is usually not part of the short-term demand fulfillment, we will not focus on this trade-off but nevertheless provide some insights to this problem in the numerical studies of Chapter 7.

The benefits of SOPA result from the immediate response to customer requests and the ability to increase profitability by selecting among customer classes. The major drawback of this model is the negligence of demand variability as it assumes demand as deterministic.

4.3.3 Search Rules for ATP Consumption

This section builds on the model described in Sect. 4.3.2, but instead of using an LP for the ATP consumption step, simple rules are proposed. The rules take as input the $aATP$ quantities generated in the Allocation Planning step. The presented rules emulate the order processing step for the disaggregated $aATP$ quantities (cf. Equation 4.14) and for the aggregated quantities (cf. Equation 4.15). Additionally, we show a modified rule adapted to the specifics of stochastic environments.

Disaggregated Single Order Processing

The search rule presented in this section takes as input the disaggregated quantities $aATP_{kt\tau}^{1}$. When not otherwise stated, we use the notation of Section 4.3, hence $\hat{i}(s)$ denotes the currently processed order. The order is allowed to consume $aATP$ quantities from its own and lower priority classes reserved for the requested delivery date $d_{\hat{i}(s)}$. The search rule and the order of execution is depicted in Fig. 4.4. The rule starts searching in the orders own priority class

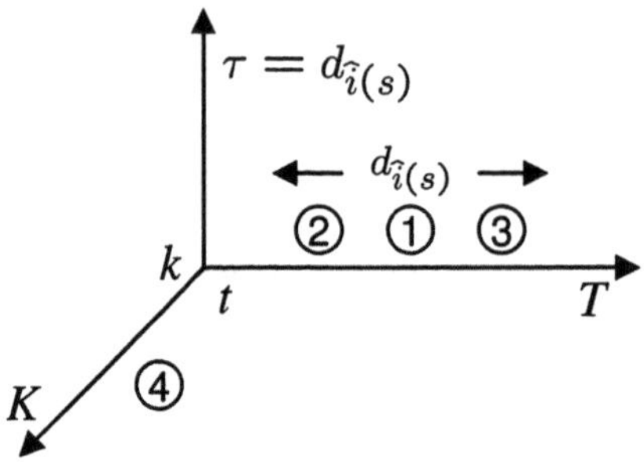

Figure 4.4: Rule-Based Order Processing (Disaggregated)

in quantities reserved for the requested delivery date ($\tau = d_{\hat{i}(s)}$) and moves through the availability times starting at the delivery date ($t = d_{\hat{i}(s)}$) (cf. ①), then before ($t < d_{\hat{i}(s)}$) (cf. ②) and then after the delivery date ($t > d_{\hat{i}(s)}$) (cf. ③). Then it searches through all availability times in lower classes (cf. ④) at the delivery date. If not all requested quantities can be fulfilled, it is searched through the unallocated quantities available at the delivery date of the order, then through quantities available prior to the delivery date and then through the quantities available after the delivery date.

Aggregated Single Order Processing

In contrast to the disaggregated $aATP$, the quantities reserved for a specific period τ are aggregated and can be consumed by all incoming orders. The corresponding aggregated search rule hence merely searches in the dimensions t (availability time of ATP) and k (customer class). Again, consumption of quantities from lower classes is allowed. The search procedure is depicted in Fig. 4.5. In order to prevent high backlogging costs, the search rule starts searching through those quantities available at the requested delivery date of the order ($t = d_{\hat{i}(s)}$) (cf. ①). If there are no quantities available in the orders own priority class, then the search moves to lower classes (cf. ②). If the order is still not completely fulfilled, the search goes to ATP quantities (of the orders own priority class) available before the delivery date ($t < d_{\hat{i}(s)}$) (cf. ③). The search is repeated for $aATP$ quantities reserved for lower classes and available before the delivery date. If there are still quantities requested, it is searched through the $aATP$ quantities available after the delivery date ($t > d_{\hat{i}(s)}$) (cf. ④), first in the orders own priority class and then in lower

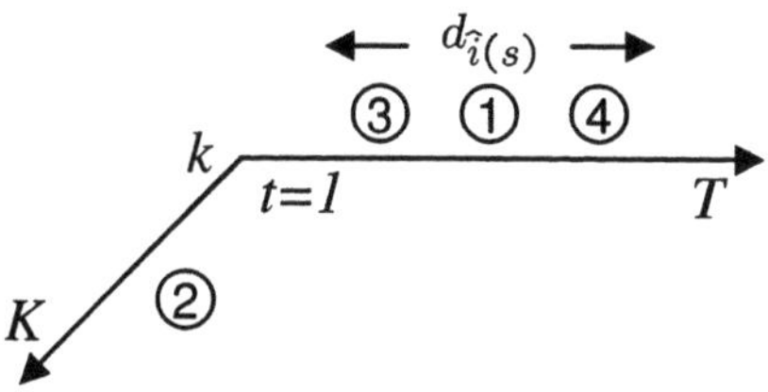

Figure 4.5: Rule-Based Order Processing (Aggregated)

classes. If not all requested quantities can be fulfilled, it is searched through the unallocated quantities as described in the previous section.

A Classification of Search Rules

We have seen two different search rules that mimic the behavior of the order processing model of Sect. 4.3.2. In order to classify different search rules and their performance in stochastic environments, we propose a classification of search rules according to the following set of attributes. All search rules are based on the disaggregated $aATP$ quantities of Equation 4.14.

First, we distinguish search rules according to the attribute *nested aATP*. If the search is nested, consumption of quantities from lower classes is allowed.

The second and third attributes concern the aggregation according to the requested delivery date of the order. As in the case of the search rule described 4.3.3, an order is only allowed to consume quantities reserved for the order's own delivery date. However, as backlogging of orders is usually much more expensive than an early availability of goods (and associated holding costs), we distinguish the aggregation according to quantities reserved for periods after the delivery date of the current order and quantities reserved for periods before the delivery date. These attributes are called *aggregate future aATP* or *aggregate past aATP*, respectively. For instance, in case *aggregate future aATP* is not, but *aggregate past aATP* is allowed, an order is allowed to consume all quantities reserved for periods at and prior to its delivery date. In this way, the expensive backlogging of orders is limited to a minimum. If both attributes are set to true, then the order is allowed to consume both quantities, prior to and after the requested delivery date.

Since the allocation planning step might also result in unallocated ATP quantities ($uATP$), search rules have to define how these quantities are consumed. Since $uATP$ is allocated to neither delivery dates nor customer classes, the only way to differentiate it is the availability time. The attribute *future uATP available* states whether $uATP$ available after the delivery date of the order can be consumed or not.

Table 4.8: Classification of Search Rules

Attribute	SOPA_D	SOPA_A
nested $aATP$	✓	✓
aggregate future $aATP$	–	✓
aggregate past $aATP$	–	✓
future $uATP$ available	✓	✓

According to these attributes, we classify two different search rules. First, we denote the search rule of Sect. 4.3.3 as SOPA_D, referring to a disaggregated single order processing after allocation planning. As access to lower classes is allowed, *nested aATP* is set to true. Accordingly, *aggregate future/past aATP* both are set to false, as only the quantities reserved for the delivery date can be consumed. Also, *future uATP available* is set to true as consumption of all unallocated quantities is allowed.

Second, we denote an aggregated version of SOPA as SOPA_A. This rule resembles the search rule described in Sect. 4.3.3, but is slightly different. In contrast to Sect. 4.3.3, SOPA_A takes as input the disaggregated $aATP$ quantities (cf. 4.14), but is allowed to consume all quantities reserved for periods prior and after the requested delivery date. The search proceeds as follows: First, SOPA_A searches through the disaggregated quantities like the rule SOPA_D. Then it moves to quantities reserved for periods prior to the delivery date ($\tau < d_{\hat{i}(s)}$). Afterwards, it searches through quantities reserved for periods after the delivery date. An overview of the discussed search rules is given in Table 4.8.

4.4 Summary

The discussion of selected papers revealed that only very little research exists for the specific setting described in this work. When it comes to stochastic approaches, nothing was found so far. The literature on TRM features many papers with a manufacturing focus, but nearly all models are developed for an MTO setting. There was only one paper considering stochastic demand and a similar setting as ours (Pibernik and Yadav, 2009), but it differs in terms of focusing on a service level objective. The manifold literature on inventory rationing shows that there is much research in this field, but usually the approaches are adapted to very specific settings and not generally applicable. This is—on the other hand—the advantage of aATP models, as they are developed to be used in APS. However, these models are usually kept simple in order to preserve general applicability. Thus, these models still offer many possibilities for further improvements.

Chapter 5

New Demand Management Approaches

In this chapter, we address the identified shortcomings of the TRM, aATP and IR models and show new approaches designed specifically for the characteristics of MTS manufacturing. First, we show an approach based on revenue management ideas and show the optimal demand fulfillment policy. However, for large problem sizes this approach soon reaches its limits since it requires extensive calculation time. In addition, we propose an approximative model based on an adapted version of the SOPA approach which uses ideas from the network revenue management literature, called randomized linear programming (RLP). Due to the high applicability of LP models, randomized linear programming combines a conventional LP with stochastic demand information.

5.1 A Revenue Management Approach

5.1.1 Model formulation

Recall our setting of a make-to-stock manufacturing system facing demand from multiple customer classes. Customer classes differ in the price per unit that they pay. Scheduled inventory replenishments are known. Given this information, the manufacturer decides for each order whether to satisfy it from stock, backorder it at a penalty cost, or reject it. The objective is to maximize profit over a finite planning horizon, taking into account sales revenues, inventory holding costs, and backorder penalties.

In order to achieve this goal the manufacturer has to make a trade-off for each order whether to satisfy it or whether to save the supply for potentially more profitable future orders. We make the following assumptions to model this situation.

Assumption 5.1. *Orders from a given customer class follow a compound Poisson process. The order processes of different classes are mutually independent and they are independent of the available supply.*

Let λ denote the expected number of orders of the Poisson process in a given period, then the probability that exactly k orders arrive can be calculated with

$$f(k, \lambda) = \frac{\lambda^k e^{-\lambda}}{k!}. \tag{5.1}$$

The Poisson assumption is common in many RM models, specifically in so-called dynamic demand models (see Talluri and van Ryzin (2004)). As Lautenbacher and Stidham (1999), we allow non-unit order sizes, which appears appropriate in a manufacturing environment. In our analysis, we discretize the planning horizon in such a way that the probability of receiving multiple orders within a single period is negligible. Let T denote the length of the planning horizon and t the period index. Moreover, let $c = 1, \ldots C$ identify the different customer classes.

Assumption 5.2. *Inventory replenishments are exogenous and known.*

This assumption reflects the APS planning hierarchy. Inventory replenishments are determined in mid-term and short-term production planning and then serve as input for order promising decisions. Let x_i be the available supply arriving at the beginning of period i, $i = 1, \ldots, T$ and let $\bar{x} = (x_1, \ldots, x_T)$ be the vector of all of these replenishments. Note that at time t, x_i corresponds with inventory on-hand if $i \leq t$ and with a future scheduled replenishment otherwise. In APS terminology, $\bar{x}$ denotes the ATP quantities.

Assumption 5.3. *Order due dates are equal to order arrival times, but orders can be backlogged at a price discount.*

This assumption reflects the MTS context. Customers expect immediate delivery, in principle. Late deliveries are only acceptable at a price discount. Let r_c denote the unit revenue from satisfying an order of class c from stock. Delaying an order gives rise to unit backorder costs b per period. Analogously, holding costs h are incurred for all units of inventory on hand at the end of a period. Note that unit backorder and holding costs are independent of time and customer class.

Assumption 5.4. *Partial order fulfillment is allowed.*

This assumption includes splitting an order for partial delivery in different periods. This is a technical assumption, which we need for tractability. We discuss its impact and potential relaxations later on. Let d denote the order quantity, u_i the amount of supply arriving in period i used to satisfy a given customer order, and let $\bar{u} = (u_1, \ldots, u_T)$. Note that for an order arriving in period t, u_i corresponds with delivery from stock if $i \leq t$ and with backlogging otherwise.

Table 5.1 summarizes the above notation. We can now formulate our problem as a stochastic dynamic program with state variable $\bar{x}$ and decision variable $\bar{u}$. In principle, one can drop all entries from these vectors, for which $x_i = 0$. I.e., the dimension of the state space corresponds with the number of scheduled replenishments. However, for ease of notation we use $\bar{x}$ and $\bar{u}$ as defined above.

The profit $\hat{P}_t(\bar{x}, d, c, \bar{u})$ earned in period t depends on the available supply, order size, customer class, and fulfillment decision as follows

$$\hat{P}_t(\bar{x}, d, c, \bar{u}) = r_c \sum_{i=1}^{T} u_i - b \sum_{i=1}^{T} u_i(i-t)(1-\delta_{it}) - h \sum_{i=1}^{T} (x_i - u_i)\delta_{it}, \quad (5.2)$$

where δ_{it} is defined as 1 if $i \leq t$ and 0 otherwise, and $\bar{u}$ has to satisfy $u_i \leq x_i$ for all i and $\sum_i u_i \leq d$.

The first term in Equation 5.2 calculates the revenues received from satisfying the current order of class c. The second term computes backlogging costs that occur when using supply that arrives later than the customer order, i.e. when $\delta_{it} = 0$. These costs are computed for the total length of the delay $(i-t)$. The third term represents holding costs that are charged for the on-hand inventory at the end of period t. Note that unlike the backlogging costs, which are charged for the total customer waiting time, holding costs only cover the current period t. To simplify subsequent calculations, we define $P_t(i, c)$ as the incremental profit per unit of supply i used to satisfy one unit of an order of class c in period t. Collecting the terms in Equation 5.2 that depend on u_i yields

$$P_t(i, c) = r_c - b(i-t)(1-\delta_{it}) + h\delta_{it} \quad (5.3)$$

and

$$\hat{P}_t(\bar{x}, d, c, \bar{u}) = \sum_{i=1}^{T} P_t(i, c)u_i - h \sum_{i=1}^{T} x_i\delta_{it}. \quad (5.4)$$

In addition to the current period's profit, we also have to take into account the impact of a fulfillment decision $\bar{u}$ on future profits. The state transition is given by $\bar{x} \rightarrow \bar{x} - \bar{u} = (x_1 - u_1, \ldots, x_T - u_T)$. Letting $V_t(\bar{x})$ denote the maximum

Table 5.1: Notation of the Revenue Management Approach

Indices:	
$t = 1, \dots, T$	Periods of the planning horizon
$i = 1, \dots, T$	Period of inventory replenishment
State variables:	
$\bar{x} = (x_1, \dots, x_T)$	Vector of available supply quantities
Decision variables:	
$\bar{u} = (u_1, \dots, u_T)$	Vector of supply quantities used to fulfill a given order
Random variables:	
c	Customer class
d	Order quantity
$F(c, d)$	Joint CDF of customer class c and order quantity d
Data:	
r_c	Unit revenue from customer class c
b	Unit backorder costs per period
h	Unit holding cost per period

expected profit-to-go from period t to the end of the planning horizon T for a given supply vector $\bar{x}$ we then obtain the following Bellman recursion

$$V_t(\bar{x}) = E_{d,c}\left[\max_{\substack{\bar{u} \\ 0 \le u_i \le x_i, \sum_{i=1}^{T} u_i \le d}} \left\{\sum_{i=1}^{T}(u_i P_t(i,c) - h x_i \delta_{it}) + V_{t+1}(\bar{x} - \bar{u})\right\}\right] \quad (5.5)$$

with the boundary condition $V_{T+1}(\bar{x}) = 0$.

5.1.2 Structural properties and optimal policy

We now analyze structural properties of the value function of the dynamic program defined in the previous section. This will then allow us to characterize the optimal fulfillment policy. All proofs of this section are given in the appendix. We start by defining marginal profits:

Definition 5.1. $\Delta_i V_t(\bar{x}) := V_t(\bar{x}) - V_t(\bar{x} - \bar{e}_i)$ *for* $x_i \ge 1$,

where $\bar{e}_i$ denotes the i-th unit vector. Definition 5.1 concerns the expected marginal value of a unit of supply arriving in period i or, equivalently, the opportunity costs of selling this unit. Using this definition, we can rewrite the Bellman recursion of Equation 5.5 as follows.

$$\begin{aligned}
V_t(\bar{x}) &= E_{d,c}\left[\max_{\substack{\bar{u}\\ 0\le u_i\le x_i,\sum_{i=1}^T u_i\le d}}\left\{\sum_{i=1}^{T}(u_iP_t(i,c)-hx_i\delta_{it})+V_{t+1}(\bar{x}-\bar{u})\right\}\right]\\
&= E_{d,c}\left[\max_{\substack{\bar{u}\\ 0\le u_i\le x_i,\sum_{i=1}^T u_i\le d}}\left\{\sum_{i=1}^{T}(u_iP_t(i,c)-hx_i\delta_{it})\right.\right.\\
&\quad\left.\left.+V_{t+1}(\bar{x})-\sum_{i=1}^{T}\sum_{z=1}^{u_i}\Delta_iV_{t+1}\left(\bar{x}-\bar{e}_i(z-1)-\sum_{j=1}^{i-1}(\bar{e}_ju_j)\right)\right\}\right]\\
&= V_{t+1}(\bar{x})-h\sum_{i=1}^{t}x_i+E_{d,c}\left[\max_{\substack{\bar{u}\\ 0\le u_i\le x_i,\sum_{i=1}^T u_i\le d}}\left\{\sum_{i=1}^{T}\left(\sum_{z=1}^{u_i}(P_t(i,c)\right.\right.\right.\\
&\quad\left.\left.\left.-\Delta_iV_{t+1}(\bar{x}-\bar{e}_i(z-1)-\sum_{j=1}^{i-1}(\bar{e}_ju_j))\right)\right\}\right].
\end{aligned} \tag{5.6}$$

Note that this formulation decomposes $\bar{u}$ into single-unit steps. In this way, the maximization in Equation 5.6 reflects the trade-off between the profit of selling a unit of supply now and the corresponding opportunity cost. Also note that a similar decomposition is well-known for the classical single-leg airline yield management problem (see Talluri and van Ryzin (2004), page 59). What is different in Equation 5.6 is the summation over i, which introduces an additional dimension into the problem.

We now identify properties of the value function that help us evaluate the above maximization expression. The first step is to compare the marginal values of supplies arriving in different periods.

Proposition 5.1. *For all $m < n$ and for all $\bar{x}$ with $x_m, x_n \geq 1$ the value function satisfies:*
a) $\Delta_m V_t(\bar{x}) - \Delta_n V_t(\bar{x}) \leq b(\max(n,t) - \max(m,t)) = b(n - m + \delta_{nt}(t-n) + \delta_{mt}(m-t))$
b) $V_t(\bar{x} + \bar{e}_m) - V_t(\bar{x} + \bar{e}_n) \leq b(n - m + \delta_{nt}(t-n) + \delta_{mt}(m-t))$.

Proposition 5.1 states that the difference between the marginal value of one unit of a supply arriving in period m and one unit arriving in period n is bounded by the difference in backordering costs of using each of these supplies in period t. This relationship implies the following important monotonicity property, regarding the alternative fulfillment options.

Proposition 5.2. *For all $m < n$ and for all $\bar{x}$ with $x_m, x_n \geq 1$ it holds that* $P_t(m,c) - \Delta_m V_{t+1}(\bar{x}) \geq P_t(n,c) - \Delta_n V_{t+1}(\bar{x}), \forall c$.

The terms on the left-hand-side of the inequality can be interpreted as the net benefit of the current revenues from selling a unit of supply arriving in period m minus the opportunity cost of not having that unit available in the future. Proposition 5.2 states that this net benefit is decreasing in the arrival time of the supply. Therefore, an order should always be either fulfilled using the earliest available supply or not at all (if the left-hand-side becomes negative). The next important property concerns the concavity of the value function along certain axes.

Proposition 5.3. *Let $\bar{x}$ be such that $\sum_i x_i \geq 2$. Furthermore, let $m = \min\{i|x_i > 0\}$ and let $n = m$ if $x_m > 1$ and $n = \min\{i|i > m, x_i > 0\}$ otherwise. Then*
$P_t(m,c) - \Delta_m V_{t+1}(\bar{x}) \geq P_t(n,c) - \Delta_n V_{t+1}(\bar{x} - \bar{e}_m), \forall c$.

Proposition 5.3 implies in particular that the value function V_t is concave in the quantity of the earliest available supply. This is intuitive since one would expect available supply to have decreasing marginal benefits.

The above properties allow us to characterize the optimal fulfillment policy. The optimal policy turns out to be a generalization of the well-known booking-limit policies in traditional revenue management (Talluri and van Ryzin (2004)). We summarize this result in the following theorem.

Theorem 5.1. *Define the following set of critical levels:*
For $i = 1, \ldots, T$ let $\bar{y}_i = \bar{x} - \sum_{k=1}^{i} \bar{e}_k x_k$,
and let $L_t(c,i,\bar{y}_i) = \max\{k|P_t(i,c) < \Delta_i V_{t+1}(\bar{y}_i + k\bar{e}_i)\}$.
Then the following fulfillment decision is optimal in period t, given an order quantity d from customer class c:
Start with $i = 1$;
set $u_i = \max\left(\min\left(x_i - L_t(c,i,\bar{y}_i), d - \sum_{k=1}^{i-1} u_k\right), 0\right)$;
if $u_i < x_i$ set $u_k = 0$ for all $k > i$ and stop, otherwise repeat for i+1.

Intuitively, this policy successively consumes units of supply, in the order of their arrival, until the immediate marginal profit drops below the opportunity costs. This very much resembles a traditional booking-limits policy. The values $L_t(c,i,.)$ set nested protection levels that bar some amount of supply i from consumption by classes c and higher. Note that we have separate protection levels for each class and supply arrival. Also note that the protection levels of supply i depend on the available quantities of subsequent arrivals $\bar{y}_i$. However, $L_t(c,i,.)$ is independent of x_i (and of all earlier arrivals x_j for $j < i$) and therefore indeed acts as a protection level. The amount of supply i exceeding

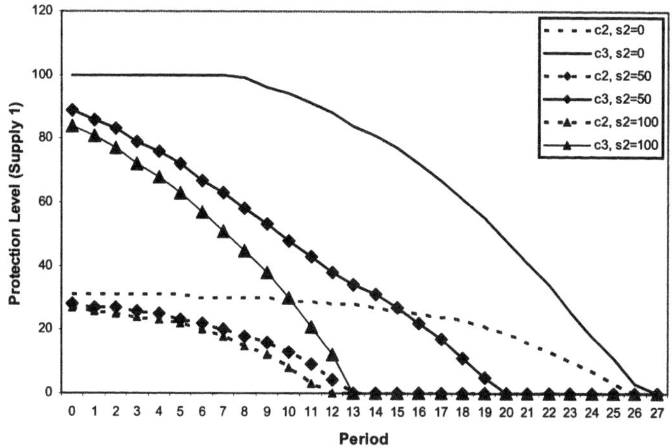

Figure 5.1: Non-Increasing Protection Levels

$L_t(c, i, .)$ is available for consumption by customer class c at time t. It is worth pointing out that even the most valuable customer class, i.e. $c = 1$, may face non-trivial booking limits for future supplies, i.e. for $i > t$: While this class can always consume supply on hand it is not necessarily optimal to backlog demand from this class, due to the incurred backorder penalties. We illustrate the various protection levels $L_t(c, i, .)$ graphically in an example in the next section.

The following proposition shows that, as in the classical case, protection levels decrease in time. This is intuitive since a shorter remaining planning horizon implies less selling opportunities and therefore available supply is of less value. It is worth mentioning, however, that this result is only true for stationary demand. Unlike in traditional revenue management models, the holding cost term in our model may destroy the monotonicity of the protection levels if the demand distribution changes across periods.

Proposition 5.4. *The protection levels $L_t(c, i, \bar{y}_i)$ defined in Theorem 5.1 are non-increasing in t.*

5.1.3 A Numerical Example

Fig. 5.1 illustrates the protection levels of supply one for different customer classes and different levels of the second supply. For example, the line "$c2, s2 = 0$" shows the protection levels for class two and no remaining quantities of the second supply. In the first period, 31 units of supply one are protected from consumption of class two (and, accordingly, class three). As the value of supply

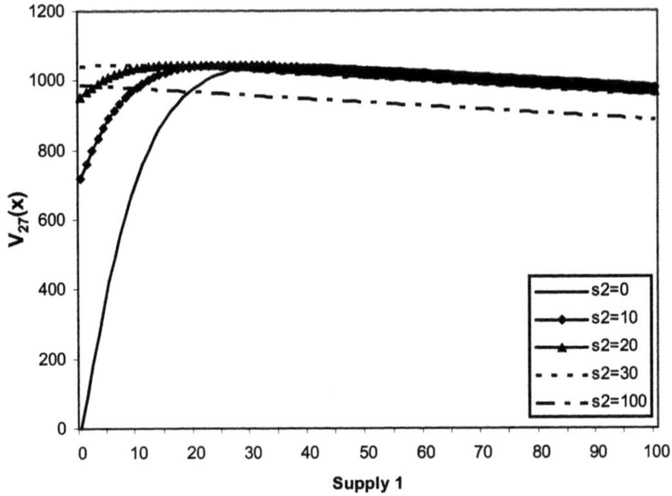

Figure 5.2: Concave Value Function

decreases as times goes on, the protection levels decrease. At the end of the planning horizon (period 27), no supplies have to be protected anymore. As seen in Proposition 5.4, protection levels are non-increasing in time.

Proposition 5.3 states that the value function is concave. This behavior is illustrated in Fig. 5.2 which shows the values of $V_t(x)$ in period 27 for different remaining quantities of the second supply. In case of $s2 = 0$ and small amounts of the first supply, each additional unit of supply one contributes much to the expected profit which explains the huge slope of the line from $s1 = 0$ to 20. After the maximum is reached the slope of the line becomes negative as holding costs are expected that reduce the expected profit. In the extreme case of $s2 = 100$ each additional unit of supply never contributes in a positive way to the profit and the line steadily decreases.

5.2 Approximations Based on Linear Programming

The idea behind the models presented in this section originates from the work on network revenue management, as described in Talluri and van Ryzin (2004). In network revenue management, resources are bundled together to form the products that customers buy. As an example, airlines offer so-called *origin-destination-fares* (ODF), wich often consist of several single flight legs. The complexity of network RM results from the fact that single flight legs might be part of more than one ODF. If two customers want to buy the same flight leg, for example the first customer from Vienna to Chicago over Amsterdam and the second customer from Vienna to Amsterdam, it has to be decided which customer brings more profit.

Many factors contributed to the development of these approaches. First, optimal solutions of realistically-sized networks can not easily be computed as the curse of dimensionality prevents fast computations. Second, as airlines usually have an enormous amount of demand information available, approximating the optimal solution via deterministic approaches would simply mean a waste of resources. Third, methods of linear programming are known to be efficient and are easily to be implemented. As an introduction to the randomized linear programming approach of Section 5.2.2, we first introduce a deterministic linear programming model (DLP) which also serves as an approximation method to the optimal solution but does not take into account demand variability.

5.2.1 Deterministic Linear Programming

The following deterministic linear programming model resembles the allocation planning model described in Sect. 4.3.2, only differing in the demand constraint (5.8). Instead of restricting the allocated quantities to the demand forecast, the *deterministic linear program* uses the expected demand $E[d_{k\tau}]$ and is formulated as shown in the following.

$$\max \sum_{k=1}^{K} \sum_{t=1}^{T+1} \sum_{\tau=1}^{T} p_{kt\tau} z_{kt\tau} \tag{5.7}$$

subject to

$$d_{k\tau}^{min} \le \sum_{t=1}^{T+1} z_{kt\tau} \le E[d_{k\tau}] \ \forall k, \tau = 1, \ldots, T \tag{5.8}$$

$$\sum_{k=1}^{K} \sum_{\tau=1}^{T} z_{kt\tau} + f_t = ATP_t^1 \ \forall t = 1, \ldots, T. \tag{5.9}$$

Despite the fact that the DLP is very efficient to solve and is easily applicable in practical settings, it is not the final answer for stochastic problems as it has an important disadvantage: the DLP neglects demand variations and simply considers the expected demand. All information included in demand distributions are not taken into account.

To illustrate the weaknesses of the DLP approach, consider a case with extreme supply shortage, two customer classes and a large difference between the profits of class one and class two. The DLP will certainly allocate the highest possible number of units to class one—as this is the most profitable class—which equals the expected demand of this class. The rest will be allocated to the less profitable class two. In the case that the demand of class one exceeds the expected demand, the DLP results in poor profits since not all class one customers are satisfied. The profit loss in not satisfying class one customers is substantial as class two generates only very low profits compared to class one.

This example resembles the situation in the famous newsvendor problem. Here, one has to decide how many newspapers to order on the day before the actual demand is realized. It is assumed that the distribution of the demand is known when the decision about the quantity is made. An intuitive solution to this problem is to order exactly the expected demand as the probability of resulting in too high or too low inventory is minimized. However, this intuitive solution does not always yield the highest profit, only in case the costs of having too much or too less are equal. In a situation in which it is very important to satisfy all customers because costs for loss of goodwill are high, the optimum order quantity will be higher than the expected demand. In the following numerical example, we show that this argumentation is also valid for a simple allocation planning and order promising problem.

Example 5.1. Consider a two-customer class problem with an expected demand per period of class one and two of $E[D] = 5$. Available supply is 10 units per period. For the sake of simplicity, all units that are not consumed are lost at the end of a period. We consider three scenarios of different profitabilities: (1) class one yields a profit of $p_1 = 5$, class two of $p_2 = 1$, (2) $p_1 = 2$ and $p_2 = 1$ and (3) $p_1 = 1$ and $p_2 = 1$. Furthermore, we illustrate the effects of different allocation strategies, from the one extreme making all units available to the first class to the other extreme case of allocating everything to the second class. We do not consider nesting, i.e. class one is not allowed to consume from class two. To calculate profitability of each scenario and allocation strategy, we simulated a Poisson distributed demand stream over 10,000 periods.

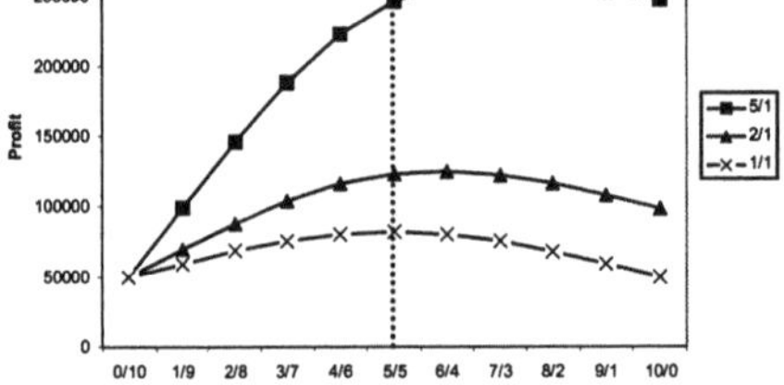

Figure 5.3: DLP and the Optimal Solution

Fig. 5.3 illustrates the effects of the different allocation strategies. In case of equal profitabilities, the best allocation strategy is the one from the DLP approach, which means allocating the expected demand quantities. However, if class one is more profitable as class two, it is beneficial to make more units available to class one. In these cases, the DLP strategy does not perform well as the optimum moves away from the expected demand quantities. These results are in compliance with the previously discussed newsvendor problem.

5.2.2 Randomized Linear Programming

We have seen that the optimal solution may not be reached by simply inserting the expected demand in the AP step. The RLP approach combines the easy to use LP formulation of the DLP, and the available stochastic demand information. The idea is to repetitively solve the DLP, not with the expected, but with a random demand drawn from the known stochastic demand distribution. Let $D^i_{k\tau}$ denote a random variable following a known stochastic distribution of the demand quantity. Then we can formulate the *randomized linear programming problem* as

$$H_t(D^i_{k\tau}) = \max \sum_{k=1}^{K} \sum_{t=1}^{T+1} \sum_{\tau=1}^{T} p_{kt\tau} z^i_{kt\tau} \tag{5.10}$$

subject to

$$d^{min}_{k\tau} \leq \sum_{t=1}^{T+1} z^i_{kt\tau} \leq D^i_{k\tau} \ \forall k, \tau = 1, \ldots, T \tag{5.11}$$

$$\sum_{k=1}^{K} \sum_{\tau=1}^{T} z^i_{kt\tau} + f_t = ATP^1_t \ \forall t = 1, \ldots, T. \tag{5.12}$$

Note that the resulting optimal solution $H^*_t(D^i_{k\tau})$ is a random variable. The optimal solution of the stochastic problem can be approximated by calculating the expected value $E[H^*_t(D^i_{k\tau})]$. We estimate the allocated quantities $z_{kt\tau}$ by using the weighted average of the resulting quantities over N simulation runs, as shown in 5.13.

$$z_{kt\tau} = \frac{\sum_{i=1}^{N} H^*_t(D^i_{k\tau}) \times z^i_{kt\tau}}{\sum_{i=1}^{N} H^*_t(D^i_{k\tau})} \tag{5.13}$$

In the subsequent numerical analysis of the RLP approach, we choose $N = 30$ which showed robust results in some preliminary tests. This is in line with the chosen parameters of Talluri and van Ryzin (1999, p. 213), although he mentions that this behavior might also be problem dependent.

Numerical studies of RLP applications in the airline industry does not show promising results. It is often the case that the DLP approach dominates the RLP solution. De Boer et al. (2002) analyzed this result in more detail and found an answer to this problem. The authors state that "... the observed domination of the deterministic model over probabilistic techniques is a fortunate by-product of ignoring the uncertainty related to demand. This phenomenon is based on nesting".

As the RLP approach is an alternative version for the allocation planning step, we still have to decide about how to consume the resulting aATP quantities. In Section 4.3.3 we discussed different consumption rules and mentioned that SOPA_D might be fragile to stochastic demand streams. In contrast, SOPA_A aggregates the aATP quantities in order to compensate forecast errors. Thus, we choose SOPA_D as the consumption rule after running the RLP because RLP already considers stochastic demand.

Chapter 6

Simulation Environment

In order to prepare the numerical studies of Chapter 7, we start by introducing the developed simulation environment. We divide this chapter into two parts. First, we discuss the technical settings and issues regarding the implementation, and second, we introduce the parameter set required to run simulations.

6.1 Technical Settings and Implementation Issues

6.1.1 Test Environment

All models and algorithms are part of a single simulation environment implemented in C++ and compiled under Microsoft Visual Studio 2005. The LP models (AP and GOP) are solved using the open source GNU Linear Programming Kit (GLPK) version 4.28. The GLPK library is accessed over a C++ interface in order to run a large number of simulations consecutively. All simulations are executed on a standard PC with a 2.4GHz Intel Core 2 CPU and 512MB memory.

Uniform random numbers are generated using the "Mersenne Twister" algorithm provided by the open source GNU Scientific Library (GSL) version 1.9. In extensive simulations, it was realized that the standard C++ random number generator does not yield satisfying results, so we turned to the Mersenne Twister algorithm described by Matsumoto and Nishimura (1998). To generate random numbers, we use the *inverse transformation method*: when X is a random variable with a cumulative distribution function F, and U is a Uniform distributed random number between 0 and 1, then X can be computed with $X = F^{-1}(U)$.

6.1.2 Implementation Issues

As the implementation usually bears some complications, we illustrate the RM approach of Section 5.1 in pseudo code. In particular, we show how to compute the value function of Equation 5.5 which is required to compute the critical levels $L_t(c, i, \bar{y}_i)$. The value function $V_t(\bar{x})$ has to be computed for all realizations of $\bar{x}$ in all periods t. As $V_t(\bar{x})$ can only be computed when $V_{t+1}(\bar{x})$ is known, the algorithm iterates from the last period T to the first period.

This step is illustrated in Algorithm 1. The algorithm *recursion* as shown in Line 2 contains the iterations through $\bar{x}$ and is explained below.

Algorithm 1: Stochastic Dynamic Program

---

input : The $ATP(t)$ quantities
input : The number of periods T
input : A zero-initialized capacity vector $\bar{x}$
input : A zero-initialized vector $v_t(\bar{x})$ for the value function
output: The vector $v_t(\bar{x})$ filled with the expected profit-to-go for each realization of $\bar{x}$

1 **for** $t \leftarrow T$ **to** 1 **do**
2   `recursion`$(0, t, \bar{x}, v_t(\bar{x}))$;
3 **end**

Algorithm 2 shows a recursive iteration through all realizations of $\bar{x}$. A recursive algorithm is necessary because the number of periods T—and accordingly, possible supply arrivals—might change from one run of the algorithm to another one, and for each period a loop through the supply quantities arriving in this and all other periods is required.

For each specific realization of $\bar{x}$, the expected value $E_{d,c}$ has to be computed. This is done by iterating through all possible demand realizations d and c. As the theoretical limit of d goes to infinity, we have to find an upper limit for d, denoted by D. If the limit D is chosen too high, the computation time is above practical limits. If the limit is chosen too low, the results are not satisfying. In all simulations in this work we chose a limit D such that 99.9% of all possible values d are in the range between 0 and D. D can be computed easily with the *inverse transformation method*: $D = F^{-1}(0.999)$.

In the following, we go through the steps of the algorithm and explain the data variables. In Line 1, the algorithm iterates through the supply quantities arriving in the period *atp_arrival_time*. In Line 2, the current supply quantity of ATP arriving in *atp_arrival_time* is stored in the vector $\bar{x}$. In the next step, the stopping criteria is checked: when the last period is reached, there are no further supplies to be considered. Prior to the last period, a new recursion is started (Line 4) with the next arriving supply. At the time the stopping criteria is met and the "else" sector is reached (Line 5), the vector $\bar{x}$ contains the supply information of all arriving supplies. In the next steps, the expected value is calculated by iterating through all possible demand quantities (Line 6) and customer classes (Line 7).

In Line 8, the policy of Theorem 5.1 is evaluated in the Function *acceptance Rule*. An order is accepted stepwise as long as the profit is larger than the opportunity costs. Note that in this step, any other policy can also be used,

Algorithm 2: recursion(atp_arrival_time, period, $\bar{x}$, $v_t(\bar{x})$)

input : The *atp_arrival_time* of the current considered ATP quantity
input : The current considered period t
input : The vector of the current considered capacities $\bar{x}$
input : A zero-initialized vector $v_t(\bar{x})$ for the value function
output: The vector $v_t(\bar{x})$ filled with the expected profit-to-go for each realization of $\bar{x}$ in the current period t

```
1  for cap ← 0 to ATP_{atp_arrival_time} do
2      x_{atp_arrival_time} = cap;
3      if atp_arrival_time < T then
4          recursion(atp_arrival_time + 1, t, x̄, v_t(x̄));
5      else
6          for d ← 0 to D do
7              for c ← 1 to C do
8                  profit ←acceptanceRule(x̄, d, c);
9                  expprofit ← expprofit+Prob(d, c) ×profit;
10             end
11         end
12         v_t(x̄) ← expprofit;
13     end
14 end
```

e.g. FCFS or the SOPA approach. Therefore, we do not describe this step in more detail. The function *acceptanceRule* returns the profit associated with the fulfillment decisions of the current order represented by the demand quantity d and class c. For each demand realization (possible values of d and c), the probability $Prob(d, c)$ is multiplied to the profit resulting from the acceptance decision (Line 9). After the iterations through all demand realizations, the profit-to-go for the current considered realization of vector $\bar{x}$ is stored in $v_t(\bar{x})$ (Line 12).

6.2 Simulation Issues

6.2.1 Data Generation

Kimms and Müller-Bungart (2007) present a review on papers dealing with demand data generation with a focus on different assumptions on demand. The authors state that "...assuming demand data that follows a non-homogeneous

Poisson process is more or less standard nowadays". However, the Poisson assumption requires that demand and variance are equal, which might not be true in many applications. For instance, Lawless (1987) states that count data often display extra variation beyond the scope of Poisson distributions. In such cases, the negative Binomial distribution (NB) exhibits certain advantages, as NBs have a long tradition in the marketing and operations literature. It is often mentioned that NBs fit best to observed customer demand (e.g. Ehrenberg, 1959, Agrawal and Smith, 1998).

We distinguish two settings of demand data streams. First, we present a general setting representing demand fulfillment decisions of one year executed on a rolling horizon. Second, we consider a setting which is consistent with the assumptions of the RM approach of Section 5.1. For instance, in the RM setting, only one order is allowed to arrive per period. Table 6.1 displays the options considered in the two settings and shows the used symbols and underlying assumptions.

Table 6.1: Data Stream Options

Description	**Distribution**		**Symbol**
	General setting	RM setting	
Demand data stream			
#Orders per period	$Poisson(\mu)$	$Deterministic$	n_t
Order quantity	$Deterministic$	$1 + NB(\mu - 1, \sigma^2)$	d_i
Revenues per order	$U^c(a, b)$	$U^d \in (r_1, \ldots, r_K)$	r_i
Requested due date	$Deterministic$	$Deterministic$	γ_i
No-arrival probability	–	$Deterministic$	p_0
Supply data stream			
Inter-arrival time	$Deterministic$	$Deterministic$	ϕ
Supply quantity	$Deterministic$	$Deterministic$	s_t

In the general setting, the number of orders n_t arriving in period t is modeled as a Poisson process. The demand quantity per order d_i is set to a fixed value. The revenues r_i of order i are uniformly distributed in the range a to b. As we focus on make-to-stock environments, we assume in the simulation runs that an immediate order confirmation is required (i.e., $\gamma_i = 0$).

Supply data is generated in both settings without any stochastic influences. This is due to our assumption that on the short-term, supply can be considered as given. The supply quantities s arrive in specific intervals, defined by the inter-arrival time ϕ. We model the supply arrival process s_t with $s_t = s$ if $t \bmod \phi = 0$ and $s_t = 0$ otherwise.

The RM setting is different to the general setting in order to account for the different demand assumptions. First of all, the number of orders n_t is deterministic and set to 1 (cf. Assumption 5.1). However, in order to be able to capture the effects of no-arrival probabilities, we introduce p_0 denoting the probability that no customer order arrives in a period. Then, the arrival process can be modeled as such that one customer class arrives per period with an arrival probability of $(\frac{1-p_0}{\#classes})$ for each class (all classes have the same arrival probability). As the customer demand is expected to be discrete and positive, we chose an NB to model the demand quantity. Additionally, it allows us to analyze the effects of large variations in demand. The demand quantity is modeled to be strictly positive with $d_i \sim 1 + NB(\mu - 1, \sigma^2)$. Note that in contrast to the general setting, the demand quantity is always positive (i.e. > 0).

In contrast to the general setting, the revenues of all orders within the same class are equal. The assignment of orders to classes is stochastic and uniformly distributed. Due to Assumption 5.3, orders require an immediate fulfillment, but are willing to accept later deliveries with a price discount. Therefore, $\gamma_i = 0$ holds in all simulations.

To study the impact of supply shortage on the performance, we define *shortage* as a ratio of the total supply throughout the simulation horizon and the total expected demand, more formally stated as

$$sr = 1 - \frac{\sum_{t=1}^{T} s_t}{(1 - p_0) \times E[n_t] \times E[d_i] \times T}. \tag{6.1}$$

6.2.2 Simulation Options

The simulation runs of Chapter 7 can be distinguished according to the data stream options of the previous section and simulation options as shown in Table 6.2. We describe the simulation options in the following.

Table 6.2: Simulation Options

Description	**Symbol**
Number of customer classes	K
Simulation horizon	T
Planning window	W
Replanning frequency	F
Backlogging costs	b
Holding costs	h
Forecast error	e

The *number of customer classes* K is considered as a given input and can be changed from one simulation run to the next. By this, we can assess the trade-off between finer customer differentiation and increasing forecast accuracy. In this regard, the assignment of customers to classes is done based on a simple procedure which results in a well-balanced amount of customers in each class. Refer to the work of Meyr (2008) for a more detailed analysis of different clustering methods. The procedure works as follows: first, determine the average number of customers per class by dividing the number of customers by the number of classes. Second, sort all customers according to their profits. Then, assign the most valuable customer to the first class. If the first class contains the average number of customers, move to the next class. Repeat this process until all customers are assigned.

The next three options are used to define a rolling horizon. The *simulation horizon* T covers all periods of a simulation run, e.g. one year. The *planning window* W covers the periods in which the short-term demand management decisions are simulated. In practical settings, the planning window covers a few weeks to month. The *replanning frequency* F determines the amount of time that lies between two consecutive planning windows. Usually, the replanning frequency is shorter than the planning window in order to have overlapping time periods. Figure 6.1 illustrates the three options.

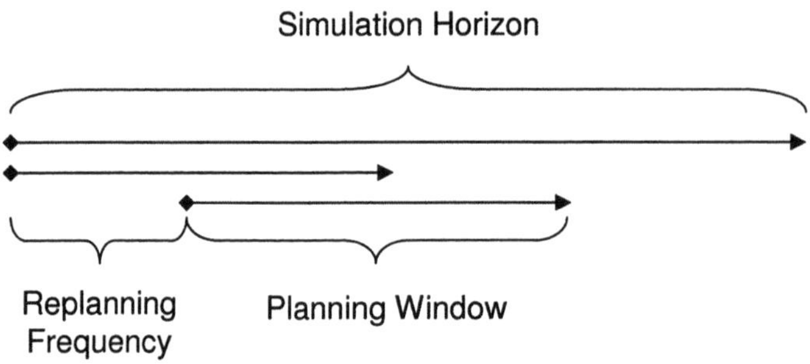

Figure 6.1: Simulation Horizon, Window and Frequency

Backlogging and *holding costs* (b and h, respectively) are not dependent on a specific order and, therefore, are part of the simulation options. We did not implement class- or order-dependent backlogging and holding cost because neither the RM approach (cf. Sect. 5.1) nor the network version of GOP (cf. Sect. 4.3.1) support it.

The last option determines how demand forecasts are generated during a simulation run. We distinguish between forecasts based on the mean demand, and forecasts that are generated according to a predefined *forecast error* e. In the first case, we assume that the mean demand is known (e.g. by exponential smoothing) and is used as a forecast for the demand in SOPA and the RM approach. In case of RM, we additionally assume that the demand variance is known as well. If the mean demand is chosen for generating demand forecasts, we denote this by M. The resulting forecast errors in this case are hence equal to the standard deviation of the demand stream. For example, if the demand is Poisson distributed with $\lambda = 10$, then the standard deviation is 3.33 which is also the mean deviation from the forecasts.

In the second case, we generate forecasts according to the predefined error and the true realization of the demand, denoted by d^*_{kt}. Let d^{max}_{kt} denote the demand forecast for class k in period t and ϵ_{kt} the forecast error, then the forecast error is distributed as

$$\epsilon_{kt} \sim Norm(0, \frac{\sigma_e}{\sqrt{K}}), \tag{6.2}$$

and the demand forecast can be calculated with $d^{max}_{kt} = \max\{0, d^*_{kt} + \epsilon_{kt}\}$. Note that negative demand is changed to 0. σ_e is chosen as a percentage of the mean demand during the planning window. Let m denote the mean demand in the planning window over all classes, then σ_e can be calculated with $\sigma_e = e \times m$.

6.2 shows that the variability of the forecast error within a specific class decreases with an increasing number of classes. However, the variability of the forecast error over all classes $\sum_{k=1}^{K} \epsilon_{kt}$ increases with an increasing number of classes. This behavior resembles common forecasting methods used in practical settings.

For illustration of this rather counterintuitive behavior, consider a mean demand of 1,000 units per period with a standard deviation of 500. If the demand is equally segmented into 1,000 individual classes, a mean of one unit per period per class can be expected. According to Formula 6.2, the standard deviation of the demand per class changes to $\frac{500}{\sqrt{1{,}000}} = 15.81$. This small example shows that the standard deviation of the demand of one class has to be smaller than the standard deviation of the total demand.

6.2.3 Output and Key Performance Indicators

Since the discussed approaches of Chapter 5 focus on profit maximization, we choose the expected profit as the key performance indicator (KPI) in order to compare the different approaches. Expected profits of the RM approach described in Section 5.1 can be directly calculated by solving the value function 5.5. An implementation of the value function is discussed in Algorithm 2. If the assumptions of the RM approach hold, expected profits of SOPA and FCFS can be calculated by means of the value function, as well, just replacing the

RM acceptance rule (Line 8 in Algorithm 2) with the SOPA or FCFS rules. Equation 6.3 shows the value function adapted to FCFS or SOPA.

$$V_t(\bar{x}) = E_{d,c}\left[\underset{0\le u_i\le x_i, \sum_{i=1}^{T} u_i \le d}{\underset{\bar{u}}{\text{FCFS / SOPA}}}\left\{\sum_{i=1}^{T}(u_i P_t(i,c) - hx_i\delta_{it}) + V_{t+1}(\bar{x}-\bar{u})\right\}\right]. \tag{6.3}$$

However, in the simulation runs of Chapter 7 we do not calculate expected profits by means of the value function, but rather run a "reasonable" large number of simulations with different random variates (drawn from the discussed distributions). Subsequently, we calculate the average profit over all simulation runs as an approximation of the real expected profit. The reasons for this are: (1) in some of the scenarios, the demand assumptions of the RM approach do not hold. (2) The GOP solution cannot be calculated by means of the value function, because the Bellman principle of optimality does not hold in this case. The principle states that the optimal decision $\bar{u}$ in period t only depends on the current state $\bar{x}$ and the expected profits in period $t+1$. However, in case of GOP, an optimal decision in period t depends on the actual demand realizations of all periods. (3) In large scenarios, computing the value function is practically not possible due to the curse of dimensionality. In these cases, the approximate expected profit is sufficient to identify trends in the numerical results.

A problem remains how to choose a reasonable number of simulation runs, denoted by Ω in the following. If Ω is chosen too large, the simulation time increases too much. If chosen too low, the approximation of the expected profits is insufficient and the results might be due to random influences. In scenarios with a large variance in the demand, Ω must be chosen high in order to prevent random outcomes. In the simulation runs of Chapter 7, we have manually chosen Ω in the way that a larger Ω would not contribute very much to the trends seen in the different figures.

In order to capture how much of the performance can be attributed to the different approaches directly and not to differences in the simulation settings, we predominantly show profit deviations to GOP in the numerical results, instead of showing absolute profits. These profit deviations, or relative profits respectively, are calculated according to the formula $\sum_{i=1}^{\Omega} \frac{GOP_i^* - S_i^*}{GOP_i^*}$, when S_i^* represents the optimal profit of a certain approach S in simulation run i and GOP_i^* the optimal profit of GOP in simulation run i.

We complement the analysis of expected profits with an analysis of service rates. We distinguish between four different service rates: (1) order quantities fulfilled *in time*, order quantities fulfilled too *early*, order quantities fulfilled too late (*backlogging*), and rejected order quantities (*lost sales*). We choose quantity-oriented service measures (Tempelmeier, 2006) adapted to our setting with simultaneous lost sales and backlogging. Furthermore, since order quantities can be split, we did not focus on orders as a whole but calculated the service measures according to single units. For instance, the amount of *backlogging* covers all units (not orders) with a delivery date in the planning window that are backlogged.

Chapter 7

Numerical Analysis

We have seen in Chapter 2 that demand fulfillment with customer segmentation is able to substantially increase profitability. However, in the literature these approaches have been analyzed only in deterministic settings neglecting stochastic demand. Further approaches have been developed in Chapter 5 to explicitly account for stochastic demand. Our aim in this chapter is to assess both types of demand management approaches under realistic conditions, i.e. to analyze the performance of the described approaches under stochastic influences. Due to technical reasons, we split the analysis in two parts: first, we analyze the different SOPA approaches in a large scenario imitating the demand management process of a company over one year. Second, we show a smaller scenario following the demand assumptions of the RM approach in Section 5.1 to show the relative performance of the approaches. The numerical results underlying the respective figures displayed in the following chapter are shown in Appendix B. Note that the exact shapes of the figures depend on the chosen input data. However, the movements of the curves under parameter changes provide interesting insights independent of the actual scenario settings.

7.1 SOPA in Stochastic Environments

We start with a detailed analysis of SOPA under stochastic demand compared with the optimal solution GOP and a simple FCFS rule. In a preliminary study, it turned out that FCFS made use of the possibility to backlog, without considering the resulting costs. Thus, for reasons of fairness, we assume that future arriving supplies are not taken into account by FCFS. Hence, orders are only fulfilled if inventory is on-hand and therefore extensive backlogging is prevented. For our analysis, we define a base case in the first step and vary the parameters in the subsequent sections. The notation and parameters follow the description of the simulation environment in Chapter 6.

Example 7.1. Consider a problem with uniform distributed revenues $r_i \sim U(90, 110)$. The customer arrival process follows a Poisson distribution with $n_t \sim P(10)$ and a fixed order quantity of $d_i = 12$ units per order. Immediate order fulfillment is assumed (i.e. $\gamma_i = 0$). The supply inter-arrival time is $\phi = 14$ periods starting in period 1, each supply with a quantity of $s = 1,000$

units. The simulation horizon is $T = 365$ periods, the planning window $W = 28$ periods and the replanning frequency is $F = 7$ periods. Per unit and period backlogging costs are $b = 10$ and holding costs $h = 1$. If not otherwise stated, we consider three customer classes ($K = 3$) and assume that the mean demand per class is known ($e = M$).

In Example 7.1, we show a demand management process executed over one year based on a rolling horizon. The parameters are chosen to mimic a realistic demand management process for a single product. In case of backlogging costs, it is not easy to find realistic assumptions. Anderson et al. (2006) show a method for determining stockout costs, which they apply in an empirical study in a retail environment. Depending on whether short- or long-term effects are included, they report stockout costs of 8.76$ and 22.69$, respectively, for a product selling for 51.06$. This corresponds to costs of 17.15% and 44.43% of the product's price. According to these findings, we decide to give roughly 10% discount ($b = 10$ and $E[r_i] = 100$) in each period a product is not immediately available (backlogging). The shortage ratio in this example is $sr = 1 - \frac{27 \times 1{,}000}{10 \times 12 \times 365} = 0.3836$ (cf. Equation 6.1), i.e., it can be expected that 38.36% of all orders are not satisfied.

7.1.1 Base Case Analysis

We start by applying FCFS, GOP, and the two versions of SOPA to the base case. The base case simulated average profit of SOPA_D equals 2,543,725, and the average profit of SOPA_A equals 1,774,840. Table 7.1 compares this value to the average profits of the two benchmark approaches GOP and FCFS. We observe that SOPA_D outperforms both FCFS and SOPA_A. However, the difference to FCFS is marginal. The profits of SOPA_A indicate that the aggregation of ATP quantities leads to poor results. We will analyze the reasons for the poor results of SOPA_A below. The second row in the table shows the relative performance of the approaches in relation to the optimal solution GOP. Note that the relative profits can not be obtained from the absolute values shown in the table, because relative profits are calculated as an average over all single simulation runs.

Table 7.1: Base Case Average Profits for Different Approaches

	GOP	FCFS	SOPA_D	SOPA_A
Absolute	2,617,006	2,515,394	2,543,725	1,774,840
Relative		3.88%	2.80%	32.18%

Figure 7.1 helps to explain the observed performance differences. The figure specifies the service levels achieved by each approach. Specifically, it shows for each policy the average fraction of orders lost and backordered of each customer class. Due to the large size of the scenario, the solution of GOP was calculated with the network flow LP (cf. 4.7 described in Section 4.3.1) which is not able to calculate class-specific service rates.

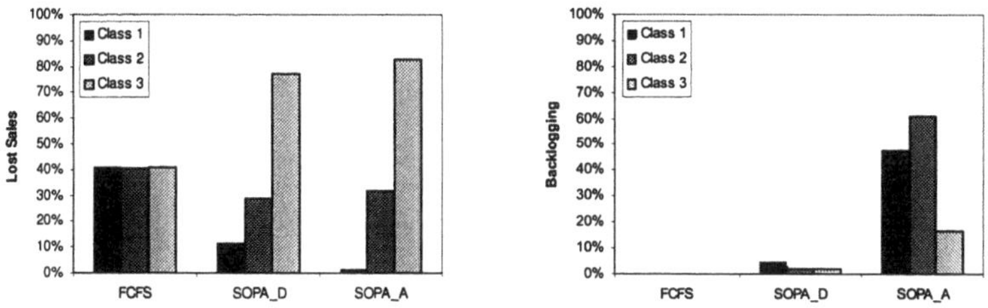

(a) Lost Sales (b) Backlogged Quantities

Figure 7.1: Base Case Service Rates I

Figure 7.1 shows that FCFS rejects customers independent of their class and results in equal amounts of lost sales (Figure 7.1 (a)). The two versions of SOPA mainly differ in terms of how they treat the most profitable class. The aggregated SOPA rejects nearly no quantities of this customer class, but this behavior does not explain the large differences in profits.

Figure 7.1 (b) displays the amount of backlogged quantities. As said before, in FCFS backlogged quantities are zero by definition because backlogging is not allowed. Similarly, SOPA_D very rarely makes use of backlogging, basically in the highest and most profitable class. In contrast, SOPA_A allows consumption of quantities reserved for all periods and therefore results in extensive backlogging. Due to the high backlogging costs, SOPA_A performs poor in terms of profitability.

In Figure 7.2, the service rates for too early and timely deliveries are displayed. As expected, SOPA_D has high rates for the on-time delivery in all customer classes. Regarding early deliveries, due to the holding costs service rates differ considerably between the highest and the lowest customer class. SOPA_A, however, produces high service rates regarding on-time deliveries in the highest class, but—due to nesting—low rates for the other two classes. Considering early deliveries, SOPA_A has low rates, especially for the two lowest classes. This effect goes in hand with the high amount of backlogging, which leaves no space for early deliveries. The results of FCFS are intuitive, since backlogging is not allowed and therefore early deliveries have the highest

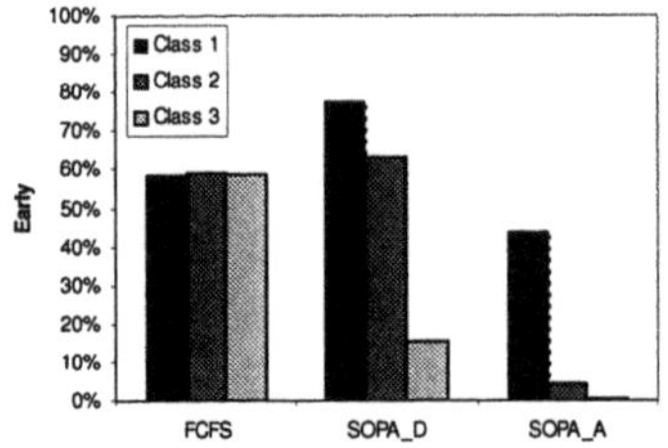

(a) Early Delivery

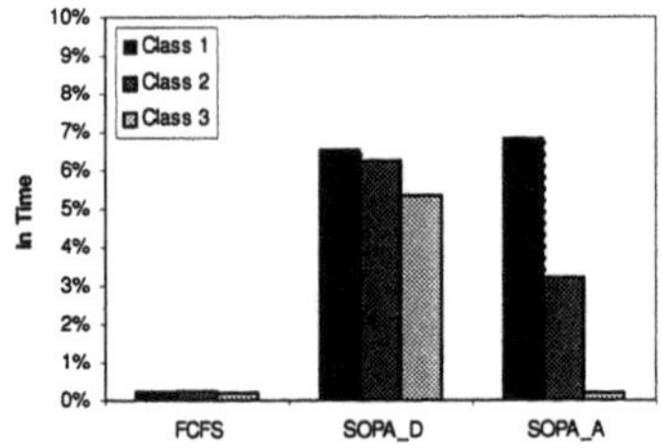

(b) On-Time Delivery

Figure 7.2: Base Case Service Rates II

probability to occur if supply quantities are available. In the following, we change parameters of the base case and analyze the resulting effects. For the sake of comparability, we include the results of the base case in the following figures. The base case is always denoted by *.

7.1.2 Impact of Customer Classes

In this section, we analyze the behavior of the profits when the number of customer classes increases. It is expected that with an increasing number of classes, the SOPA results improve due to a finer allocation, but on the other hand are negatively affected by decreasing forecast accuracy. Figure 7.3 shows the results of FCFS, GOP, SOPA_A, and SOPA_D. Note that * indicates the base case.

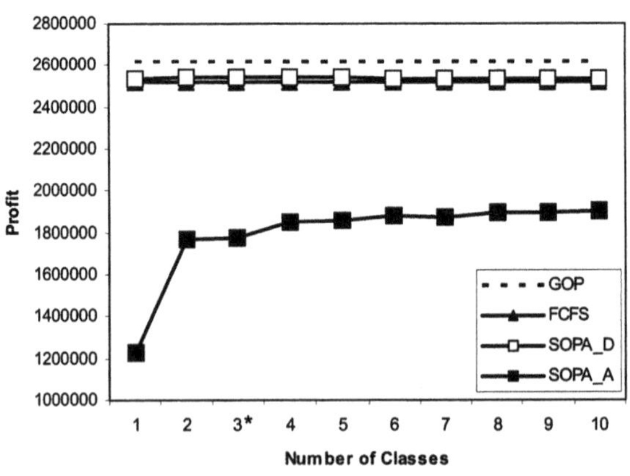

Figure 7.3: Average Profits with Varying Number of Classes

First, note that FCFS and GOP do not consider customer segmentation and, hence, are not influenced by the increasing number of classes. The figure shows that the aggregated version of SOPA is far away from the profits of FCFS, GOP and SOPA_D, which are located close together. Nevertheless, SOPA_A benefits from an increasing number of classes, especially regarding the step from one to two classes. The expected trade-off between a finer segmentation and an increasing forecast error can be seen in the case of SOPA_D where the profits first slightly increase up to two or three customer classes and then decrease again. This effect is not visible from the graph, but can better be seen in the data Table B.3 in the Appendix. Despite the small dimensions of the phenomenon, it has proven robust to parameter changes.

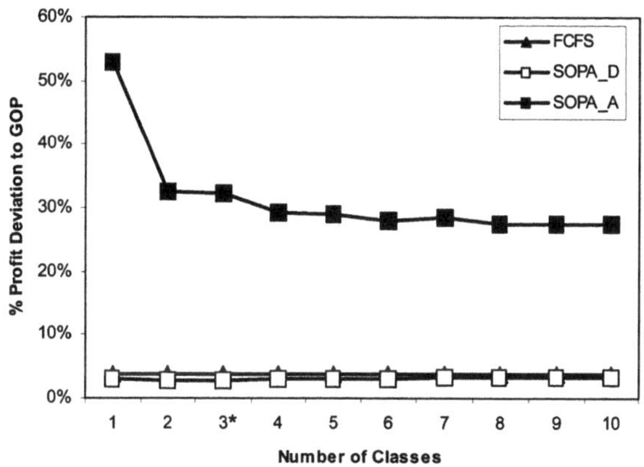

Figure 7.4: Average Relative Profits with Varying Number of Classes

Figure 7.4 displays the relative performance of the approaches compared to the optimal solution (GOP) with the same scenario as used in Figure 7.3. We see that SOPA_D and FCFS are roughly 3-4% worse than the optimal solution, whereas SOPA_A produces poor results. These are due to the high amount of backlogging which is not prevented by SOPA_A. Since FCFS seems to be highly competitive in this scenario, we will analyze further settings in the subsequent chapters.

7.1.3 Impact of Customer Heterogeneity

We have seen in the base case that FCFS is competitive to the SOPA approaches. In the following, we analyze the effect of an increased customer heterogeneity regarding profitability. We expect that higher variation in customer profitability positively influences the performance of approaches with customer segmentation. We vary the heterogeneity by changing the revenues r_i. In the base case, we had a 10% deviation from the mean, upwards and downwards ($r_i \sim U(90, 110)$). Additionally, we now consider cases with 30%, 50%, and 70% deviation.

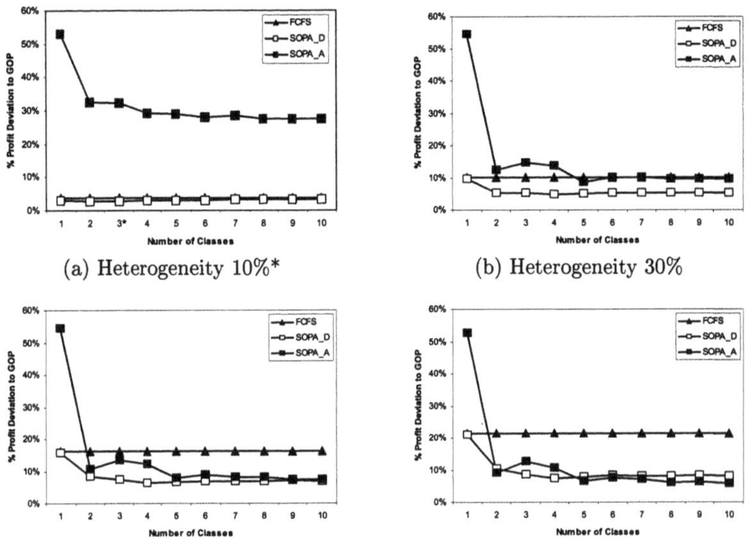

(a) Heterogeneity 10%* (b) Heterogeneity 30%

(c) Heterogeneity 50% (d) Heterogeneity 70%

Figure 7.5: Variation of Customer Heterogeneity

Figure 7.5 displays the three scenarios with varied customer heterogeneity in addition to the base case with 10% deviation (denoted by *). Again, the figure shows the deviation from the optimal solution. As expected, FCFS is not able to manage increased heterogeneity. The results get worse from (a) (with approximately 3% profit deviation to GOP) to (d) (approximately 21% profit deviation to GOP). In contrast, both SOPA approaches benefit a lot—especially around two to five customer classes. The jagged appearance of SOPA_A is due to the stochastic input data and shows that it is less robust than SOPA_D.

The trade-off between forecast accuracy and a finer segmentation can better be seen now in the curve of SOPA_D. In the case of four customer classes and high heterogeneity, SOPA_D gets closest to GOP. Interestingly, SOPA_A approaches the profits of SOPA_D in case of very high heterogeneities.

7.1.4 Impact of Forecast Errors

In this section, we analyze the influence of different forecast errors and their effect on the expected profit. In the base case, (again denoted by * in Figure 7.6), we assume that the mean demand in a customer class is known and can be used as a forecast. In addition to the base case, we analyze a setting with no forecast errors 7.6 (a), i.e., deterministic forecasts, and settings with 50% and 100% forecast errors. Note that we consciously do not want to simulate a forecast procedure, but rather choose to directly calculate forecast errors. In this respect, our analysis is independent of the chosen forecast procedure (and its resulting forecast error), which allows us to analyze a much larger spectrum of different forecast errors. The calculation of forecast errors is explained in Equation 6.2.

The setting M in the upper right corner results in forecast errors which are determined by the standard deviation of the demand data stream. In our Example 7.1, we have a Poisson distributed arrival process of customers with $\lambda = 10$ per period with a fixed quantity of 12 units each. Hence, on average 120 units are ordered per period with a standard deviation of $37.95 = \sqrt{10} \times 12$. I.e., if we use the mean demand of 120 units as forecast, we result in errors of 37.95 units on average, approximately 32%. Therefore, in Figure 7.6 we arrange the setting M in between the scenario with 0% forecast errors and 50% forecast errors.

Figure 7.6 shows the behavior of SOPA with different forecast errors. Since FCFS does not require demand forecasts, its profits are not affected by increasing forecast errors and are, hence, equal throughout all figures. The curve of SOPA_D in Part 7.6 (a) approaches the GOP solution with an increasing number of customer classes. This is intuitive since when the number of classes equals the number of orders, the AP step optimally allocates ATP quantities to each order. In case of only one class, low-margin customers might consume quantities from the single class that are better kept for later high-margin customers. Therefore, SOPA_D cannot yield optimal profits in case of few customer classes.

With increasing forecast errors, SOPA_D becomes worse and is soon outperformed by FCFS. In the cases of 50% and 100% error, SOPA_D does not benefit from a larger number of classes since the imprecision of the forecasts of each class increases, which overcompensates the finer customer segmentation.

The behavior of SOPA_A is rather different to SOPA_D. Due to the aggregation of quantities, SOPA_A even benefits from the forecast errors and the performance improves with an increasing number of classes. Nevertheless, the results of SOPA_A stay in the range between 10% and 20% deviation from the optimum and at around 10% deviation from FCFS. In the the case of very high

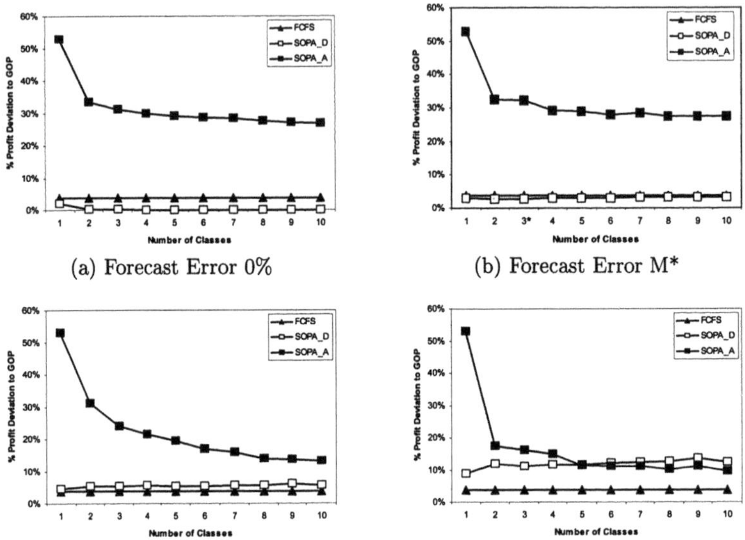

(a) Forecast Error 0%

(b) Forecast Error M*

(c) Forecast Error 50%

(d) Forecast Error 100%

Figure 7.6: Variation of Forecast Errors

forecast errors, SOPA_D is in a similar range as SOPA_A. In this respect, we conclude that in case of high errors, the allocation of ATP to customer classes in the AP step is rather a random procedure. The consumption rules based on the allocated ATP quantities reveal a random outcome a long way from an optimal solution.

7.1.5 Impact of Backlogging Costs

We have seen already in the previous sections that profits are considerably influenced by the amount of backlogged quantities. In the following, we analyze the effects of different backlogging costs. Figure 7.7 displays the behavior of FCFS, SOPA_A, and SOPA_D when backlogging costs are increased, starting from zero up to ten. Note that the last point represents the base case.

Some interesting effects are visible: First, GOP is only slightly influenced by increasing backlogging costs confirming that the optimal allocation of ATP to orders works fine. SOPA_D behaves similarly to GOP which indicates that the allocation of ATP to specific due dates works well regardless of the backlogging costs. FCFS is not influenced at all since we forbid backlogging

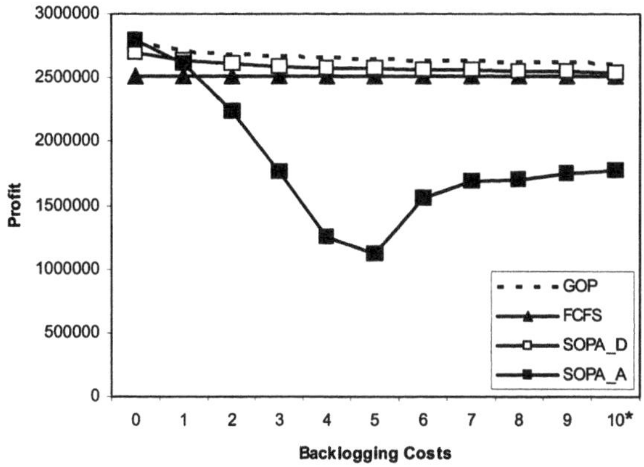

Figure 7.7: Variation of Backlogging Costs

in this case. In the case of low backlogging costs, FCFS is outperformed by GOP and SOPA_D, but both approaches approximate the curve of FCFS with further increasing backlogging costs.

SOPA_A exhibits interesting behavior. In case of no backlogging costs, the results of SOPA_A are equal to the results of GOP. This result can be explained by the fact that the aggregation compensates all forecast errors, whereas late fulfillment of orders does not influence the results due to the zero backlogging costs. Early availability of ATP actually results in holding costs, but due to the assumed scarce capacities this does not play a role in these scenarios as ATP certainly never becomes available before the actual due date. With increasing backlogging costs the profit of SOPA_A decreases drastically. However, this behavior is reversed at backlogging costs of five. We explain this behavior by the interplay of errors and backlogging costs: in the range of low backlogging costs, wrong allocations and forecast errors do not play a pivotal role as they are compensated by the aggregation of ATP quantities. With medium backlogging costs, backlogged customer orders decrease the profit. In case of high backlogging costs, the AP step allocates ATP more carefully to the different classes which results in higher profits.

7.2 Analysis of the Revenue Management Approach

In the following, we numerically analyze the revenue management approach of Section 5.1. As noted earlier, we choose a scenario following the demand and supply assumptions of Section 5.1.1. For reasons of practicability, the scenario is much smaller than in the previous analysis. This is due to the large computation time of the stochastic dynamic program. The following Example 7.2 shows the base case scenario.

Example 7.2. Consider a three-customer class problem with revenues $p_1 = 100$, $p_2 = 90$, and $p_3 = 80$. Let $h = 1$ and $b = 10$. The simulation and planning horizon is $T = 28$ periods with two receipts of supply of 100 units each, the first in the start period $t = 1$ and the second in period $t = 15$. We assume exactly one customer arrival per period ($p_0 = 0$) with the demand quantity following a negative Binomial distribution with mean $\mu = 12$ and a standard deviation of $\sigma = 8$.

In the next subsection, we evaluate our RM procedure for this base case and compare it to the FCFS, SOPA_D, and GOP benchmarks. In the subsequent sections, we investigate the impact of several key model parameters on the relative performance of RM, thereby identifying conditions that are particularly conductive to the use of revenue management in MTS demand management. Specifically, we address the impact of demand variability (Section 7.2.2), customer heterogeneity (Section 7.2.3), and supply shortage (Section 7.2.4).

7.2.1 Base Case Analysis

The base case simulated average profit of the RM policy equals 17,635.90. Table 7.2 compares this value to the average profits of the three benchmark policies. We observe that RM outperforms both FCFS and SOPA_D by about 2%. In terms of relative profits to GOP, FCFS looses more than 3% to GOP, SOPA_D roughly 3%, and RM around 1%.

Table 7.2: Base Case Average Profits for Different Approaches

	GOP	FCFS	SOPA_D	RM
Absolute	17,843.03	17,247.27	17,327.95	17,635.90
Relative		3.33%	2.91%	1.16%

Figure 7.8 helps to explain the observed performance differences by displaying the service levels graphically. Again, we measure customer service in terms of lost sales (Figure 7.8 (a)) and backlogging of orders (Figure 7.8 (b)).

A number of differences between the policies stand out. First of all, FCFS does not differentiate between customer classes, which is reflected in roughly uniform service levels across classes. All other policies clearly prioritize high-value orders. While FCFS achieves the lowest total number of lost sales, it loses relatively many high-value orders. Comparing RM and SOPA_D, we see that SOPA_D rejects even more orders of classes two and three. However, the resulting decrease in lost sales of class one—relative to RM—is insufficient to compensate the lost revenues. It appears that in the face of demand uncertainty, the prioritization of the SOPA_D rule is slightly too aggressive. Another difference between RM and SOPA_D concerns the backordering behavior. SOPA_D backorders many more orders from lower customer classes. Under demand uncertainty, it appears preferable to reserve more future supply for potential future orders, thereby avoiding backorder penalties.

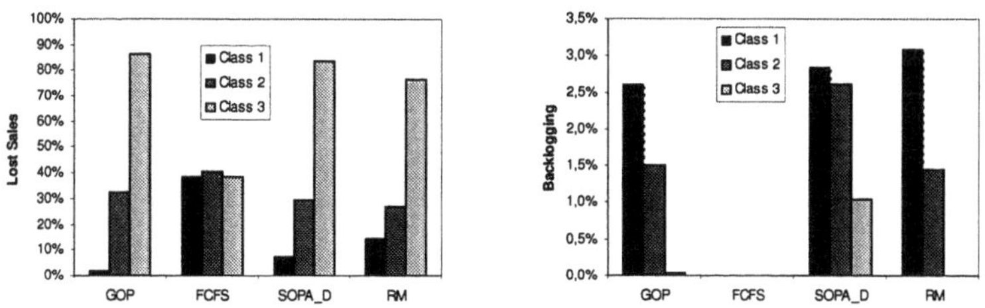

(a) Lost Sales (b) Backlogged Quantities

Figure 7.8: Customer Service Levels in the Base Case

7.2.2 Impact of Demand Variability

We now investigate how the above results depend on a number of key parameters. We start by addressing demand variability. To this end, we vary the standard deviation of the order size $\sigma$from 4 to 16. In addition, we consider the case of a constant order size of $\mu = 12$ units. This range corresponds with a CV of the order size between 0 and 1.33. The scenario $CV = 0.67$ / $\sigma = 8$ corresponds with the base case analyzed in detail in the previous section (again denoted by *). Note that in addition to the order size, we also have uncertainty in the order arrivals. Therefore, even the scenario with a constant order size is not entirely deterministic.

Figure 7.9 shows the expected profits for different CVs of GOP, RM, FCFS, and SOPA using the setting of example 7.2. We observe the following: (1) The negative effect of increasing variance is maximal if using the purely deterministic SOPA approach whereas (2) FCFS seems unaffected from the increase at least in case of low variability. (3) In the case of deterministic demand quantities ($CV = 0$), SOPA is competitive to RM. (4) Overall, the RM approach performs best, but the consideration of stochastic demand does not prevent its profit from decreasing with increasing demand variability.

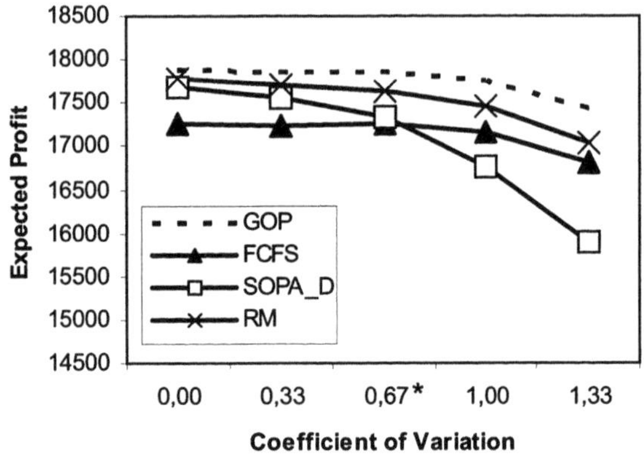

Figure 7.9: Average Profits for Different Levels of Demand Variability

To summarize, we conclude that the effectiveness of customer differentiation in demand fulfillment decreases with increasing demand variability and that forecasting errors should be taken into account in the fulfillment decision.

Note that some of the variations in the average profits can be explained by changes in the maximum attainable ex-post profit GOP. To eliminate this effect, we consider again the relative deviation of FCFS, SOPA_D, and RM with respect to GOP in the subsequent analyses.

7.2.3 Impact of Customer Heterogeneity

In Figure 7.10 we show how increasing customer heterogeneity changes the relative performance of FCFS, RM and SOPA_D under increasing demand variability. In the low heterogeneity case (7.10 (a)), RM and SOPA_D hardly outperform FCFS. In particular, SOPA_D is only competitive in cases with low variability. In the cases with medium and high customer heterogeneity (Figures 7.10 (b) and 7.10 (c)), SOPA_D and RM in general perform better than FCFS. The relative performance of RM and SOPA_D is only weakly influenced by customer heterogeneity under low demand variability (less than 0.33), but we find a strong influence under high demand variability. As expected, the difference between SOPA_D and RM rises with increasing values of heterogeneity and demand variability. Figure 7.10 (c) reveals that the deterministic SOPA_D is not able to benefit from increasing heterogeneity when the variability is high. This is in line with the previous findings. Another interesting result is that the relative performance of FCFS, though not influenced by increasing variability, is strongly affected by increasing heterogeneity. The latter is intuitive since FCFS treats all customers equally and does not care for the larger profit potential. Summarizing the results we can say that RM outperforms FCFS and SOPA_D, especially under high variability. In case of low variability, SOPA_D seems to be competitive to RM. FCFS as the simplest rule is only appropriate if heterogeneity is low. The point in which SOPA_D and FCFS approximately perform equally moves towards the upper right corner with increasing heterogeneity (from 7.10 (a) to 7.10 (c)).

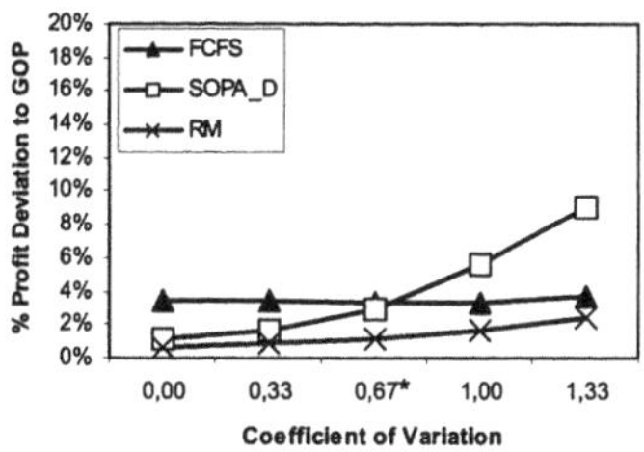

(a) Heterogeneity 10%

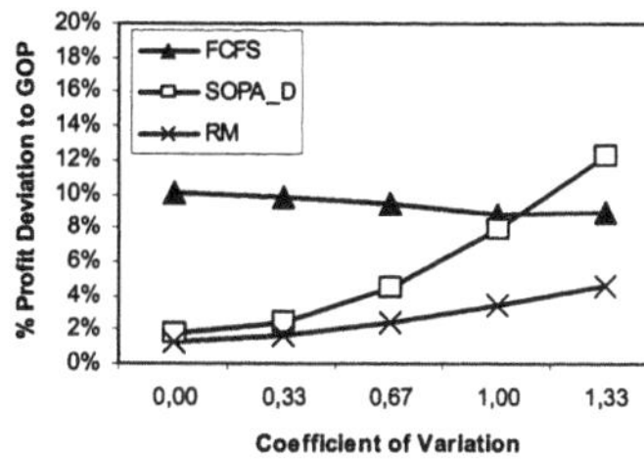

(b) Heterogeneity 20%

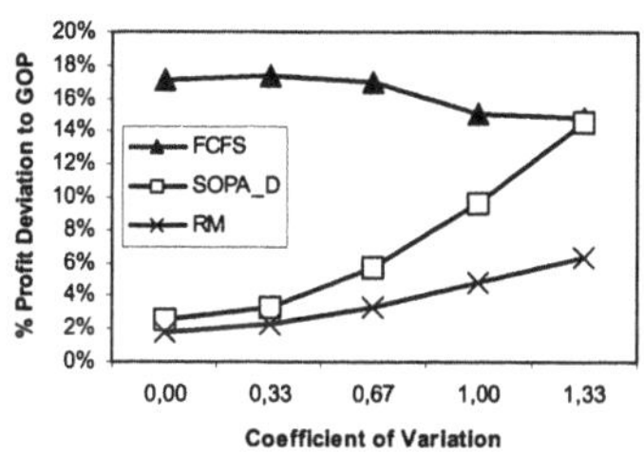

(c) Heterogeneity 30%

Figure 7.10: Varied Customer Heterogeneity for Different Levels of Demand Variability

7.2.4 Impact of Supply Shortage

Figure 7.11 displays the relative performance under different no-arrival probabilities (and—ceteris paribus—different shortage rates). Three different cases have been picked to analyze shortage: We start from a setting where FCFS and SOPA_D have an approximate equal profit ($CV = 0.67$). The influence of different shortage rates in this situation is depicted in Figure 7.11 (a). Contrasting to this, Figure 7.11 (b) shows the setting with lower demand variability ($CV = 0.33$) and 7.11 (c) shows the case with higher customer heterogeneity.

The left-hand side of each figure shows the case of supply shortage (shortage rates > 0) whereas the right side depicts the case of excess supply (shortage rates < 0). We can see in all cases that FCFS—in contrast to RM and SOPA_D—declines with decreasing shortages, regardless of whether we assume under- or oversupply. This is intuitive since the benefit of selecting among the most profitable orders is continuously decreasing with decreasing shortages. Regarding RM and SOPA_D, they also approximate the GOP value in the case of excess shortage. In the extreme case of 138% excess supply, the benefit of rationing vanishes since all orders can be satisfied so that the differences between the different approaches vanish. In the other extreme (large shortages), SOPA_D and RM benefit from their rationing strategy. While the performance of FCFS diminishes with increasing shortage, SOPA_D and RM reach higher profits when the shortage rate shifts from 21% to 41%. In Figures 7.11 (b) and 7.11 (c), both approaches outperform FCFS. Comparing the shapes of the SOPA_D and RM curves, it can be seen that in all scenarios SOPA_D is more dependent on the shortage rate, as it can only compete with FCFS in cases of very high or very low shortage. For the RM approach, we can see that it performs better than both, SOPA_D and FCFS in all cases, even in those with oversupply.

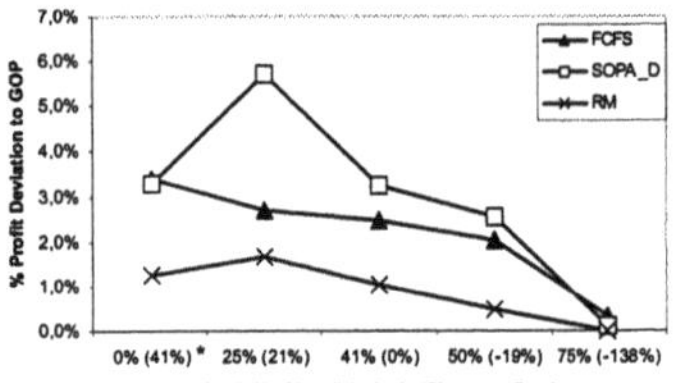

(a) $CV = 0.67$ and Low Heterogeneity

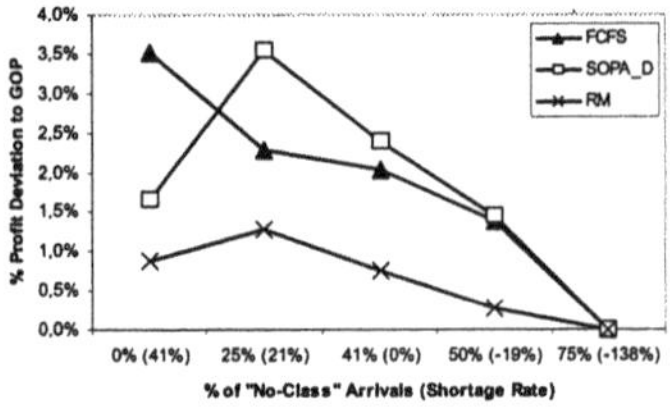

(b) $CV = 0.33$ and Low Heterogeneity

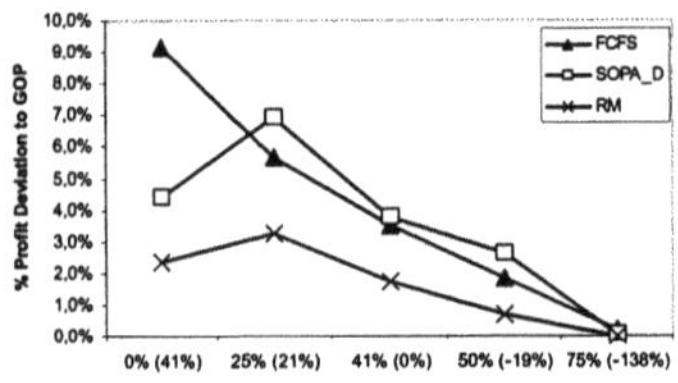

(c) $CV = 0.67$ and Medium Heterogeneity

Figure 7.11: Impact of Shortage Rate on Average Profit Deviation from GOP for Different Scenarios

7.3 Analysis of Randomized Linear Programming

The RLP approach presented in Section 5.2.2 aims at combining the general applicability of SOPA with consideration of stochastic demand. Therefore, now we focus on analyzing the effects of demand variability on the performance of RLP. We start with the base case as described in Example 7.1 and run the RLP approach with 30 iterations. In each iteration, the RLP approach draws random variates from the known demand distribution and uses them as forecasts in the allocation planning step. The second step (order promising) is done in the same way as in the SOPA_D approach.

In order to capture the effects of high demand variability, we complement the base case scenario (Poisson arrival process with a mean and variance of 10) with scenarios that follow a negative Binomial distributed process with the same mean ($\mu = 10$) but higher variances ($\sigma^2 = 64$ and 144). Furthermore, we consider a scenario with a fixed number of customers per day. As in the base case, we assume in all settings that the mean demand is known. In case of the RLP approach, we additionally assume that the variance of the demand distribution is known as well.

Given these parameters, we can calculate the resulting forecast errors. In Section 7.1.4, we result in a forecast error of 32% in the base case scenario if we assume that the mean demand is known. Accordingly, the forecast error with variance 64 is $80\% = \frac{\sqrt{64}\times 12}{120} \times 100$ and $120\% = \frac{\sqrt{144}\times 12}{120} \times 100$ with variance 144. In case of a fixed number of customers per day, we result in no forecast errors since the known mean demand is equal to the real demand. All these calculations are based on the setting of Example 7.1 in which we assume on average 10 customers per day with a fixed order quantity of 12 units (= 120 units total demand per period).

Analog to Section 7.1.3 we consider different customer heterogeneities of 10%, 30%, 50%, and 70%. The results can be seen in Figure 7.12. From the upper left hand side to the lower right hand side the variability of the demand increases. Correspondingly, the forecast errors increase as well and, hence, the AP step results in less reliable allocations. Figure 7.12 (a) shows the setting in which we have a fixed number of customers per period and, therefore, no variability. SOPA_D and RLP result in the same profits because RLP draws random variates from a distribution with no variance and therefore uses always the mean.

Like in the analysis before, FCFS is unaffected by demand variability and its curve does not seem to move from Part 7.12 (a) to 7.12 (d). This behavior is intuitive since FCFS fulfills incoming demand irrespective on fluctuations.

The profits of SOPA_D are affected negatively by increasing variability, but benefit from increasing heterogeneity. In contrast, SOPA_A seems to bene-

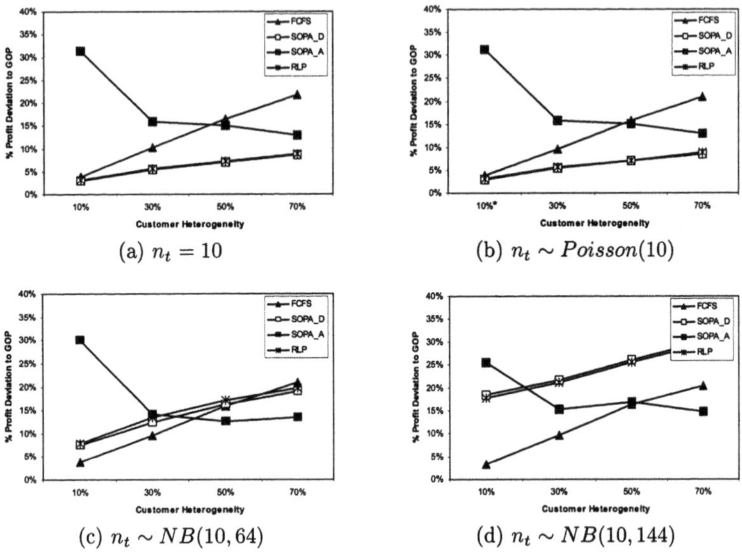

(a) $n_t = 10$ (b) $n_t \sim Poisson(10)$

(c) $n_t \sim NB(10, 64)$ (d) $n_t \sim NB(10, 144)$

Figure 7.12: RLP with Different Forecast Errors and Varied Customer Heterogeneity

fit from increasing variability in case of low heterogeneity and high demand variability. The profits of SOPA_A move from nearly 33% deviation from the optimal solution GOP with no variability to nearly 26% with 144 demand variability, while in case of high heterogeneities (70%), there is a slight deterioration from 12% to 15% deviation from GOP.

In general the RLP approach performs equally well as SOPA_D. A reason for the strong resemblance between RLP and SOPA_D is the same way of aATP consumption. Astonishingly, the more complex RLP approach brings no real benefit in contrast to SOPA_D. The consideration of the variance in the RLP approach seemingly is no suitable way to cope with stochastic demand. RLP even results in slightly less profits in case of $\sigma^2 = 64$ demand variance. However, in the last scenario with the highest considered variability ($\sigma^2 = 144$), RLP performs slightly better than SOPA_D, but on a low level which is even far away from the FCFS solution.

The results are in line with the previously mentioned findings of De Boer et al. (2002). The authors claim that the stochastic nature of the demand is already compensated by the "nested" protection levels and cannot further be improved by the RLP approach. In order to check this argument, we run additional simulations that forbid the nested consumption of ATP quantities. The setting of Figure 7.13 is in all terms equal to the one of Figure 7.12, but nested consumption is not allowed in the RLP approach and the two versions of SOPA.

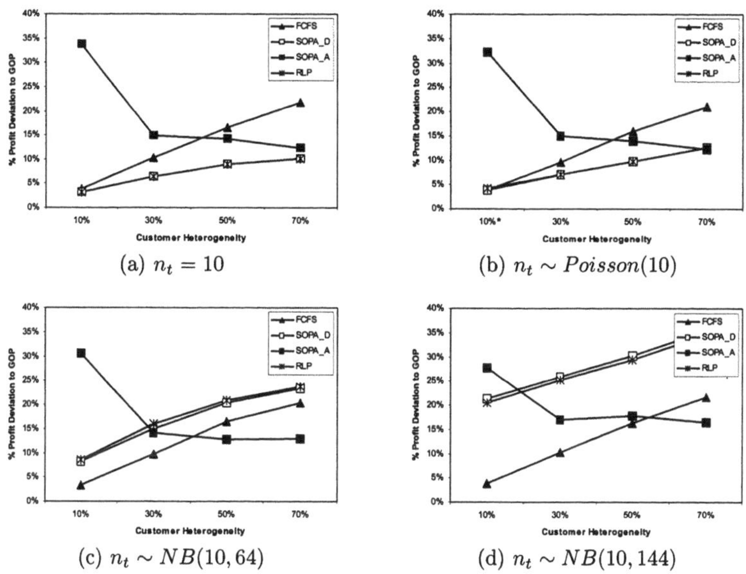

(a) $n_t = 10$

(b) $n_t \sim Poisson(10)$

(c) $n_t \sim NB(10, 64)$

(d) $n_t \sim NB(10, 144)$

Figure 7.13: RLP and SOPA with Non-Nested Order Consumption

Note that in Figure 7.13, the FCFS line is equal to the one of the previous figure but the lines of RLP and SOPA changed. In general it can be said that the prohibition of nesting leads to slightly lower profits than in the previous scenarios with nesting. However, the decrease in profits lies around 2% and is even hard to see in the figure. Refer to the data tables B.12 and B.13 for a better illustration of this issue. Interestingly, the prohibition of nesting affects all four considered scenarios in the same way, even the constant demand scenario 7.13 (a). In this respect, the claim of De Boer et al. (2002) that nesting compensates for high demand variability cannot be supported in our settings as it brings profit improvements irrespective on the level of variability.

7.4 Summary

We have seen in this chapter that the performance of demand management approaches in stochastic environments is essentially driven by the degree of customer heterogeneity and the quality of demand forecasts. The amount of supply shortage and the degree of stochasticity are further important influencing factors. In general it can be said that SOPA is beneficial in comparison with FCFS when customer heterogeneity is high and forecasts are good. However, the use of SOPA has to be carefully considered that the effort to segment customers and to create demand forecasts pays off.

The RLP approach performs similar to the analyzed SOPA_D approach. Therefore, a use of the more complex RLP instead of SOPA_D cannot be recommended, as the gathering of information about demand distribution requires much more effort.

The RM approach dominates the benchmark approaches throughout the different scenarios. However, RM requires much more effort and is dependent on certain assumptions on the demand. The use of RM can be recommended when the effort of gathering reliable demand data and spending computing time stays in a reasonable proportion to the expected profit improvements.

Chapter 8

Conclusion

In this work, we discussed the problem of how to effectively manage stochastic demand in make-to-stock manufacturing. Specifically, we considered the situation of a manufacturer who decides on the quantities he is willing to sell to different customer classes. The order acceptance decisions take into account on-hand inventory as well as already planned production quantities scheduled to arrive in the future. For each order, the manufacturer has to decide—based on its profitability—whether to accept the order, to reject it, or to backlog it against a price discount. The problem is motivated by the demand fulfillment task in advanced planning systems. A key characteristic of the problem setting is that production orders cannot be changed in the short term. This is in line with the hierarchical planning approach of most advanced planning systems and reflects the reality of many manufacturers.

We presented a literature classification and overview of research in demand management. It turned out that the majority of models considering stochastic demand focuses on make-to-order environments. We adopted ideas from the classified literature, especially from traditional revenue management approaches, and transferred them to make-to-stock manufacturing. To our knowledge, this work is the first to apply revenue management in this context.

We developed two different approaches considering stochastic demand. First, we model the make-to-stock demand fulfillment problem as a stochastic dynamic program. We proved that the optimal policy in this model has a simple, intuitive structure, which can be interpreted as an extension of the well-known booking-limit policies in classical revenue-management problems. By explicitly capturing demand uncertainty, our model differs from the rule-based deterministic models commonly underlying the demand fulfillment modules of advanced planning systems. Second, we combined conventional LP-based models with stochastic demand information by repetitively solving the LP with different random variates. This idea stems from the randomized linear programming of network revenue management problems.

We tested the models numerically and compared them against a first-come-first-served rule and against a deterministic optimization approach. Our results show that explicitly accounting for demand uncertainty significantly improves the performance of demand fulfillment. The results also show that customer differentiation can yield a substantial profit increase, in particular if differences in profitability are large across orders and if supply is scarce. In conclusion, our results highlight substantial opportunities for improving the current practice of order fulfillment in make-to-stock manufacturing.

Our models make a first step in this direction. However, many challenges remain. For the RM approach, the biggest limitation is that it is not easily scalable. For large-scale applications, the full evaluation of the value function is computationally intractable. The RLP approach, however, is applicable even in large-scale applications, but seems to bring no further benefits towards deterministic linear programming approaches. In order to gain further insight into the relative performance of different methods, they should also be compared based on empirical data, in addition to theoretical demand distributions. In addition, further analysis of the mentioned rules in Section 2.3.2 is necessary. As they are commonly applied in APS, FCFS alone is not a fair benchmark for RLP and the RM approach.

Another relevant extension to our model would be to include different customer due-dates. It is not immediately clear which effect this will have on the structure of the optimal fulfillment policy. Another direction for future research will be to include short-term price incentives, which complement the order acceptance decisions addressed here.

Appendix A

Proofs of the Structural Properties of the RM approach[1]

A.1 Proof of Proposition 5.1

We show part a) by induction. For $t = T{+}1$ the inequality holds since $V_{T+1} \equiv 0$ and since the right-hand side is non-negative for $n > m$.

Now assume that inequality a) holds for $t + 1$. We show that it also holds for t. We can rewrite

$$\begin{aligned} \Delta_m V_t(\bar{x}) - \Delta_n V_t(\bar{x}) &\leq b(n - m + \delta_{nt}(t-n) + \delta_{mt}(m-t)) \\ \Leftrightarrow V_t(\bar{x} - \bar{e}_n) - V_t(\bar{x} - \bar{e}_m) &\leq b(n - m + \delta_{nt}(t-n) + \delta_{mt}(m-t)). \end{aligned}$$

We show that this inequality holds for any given values of c and d, which implies that it also holds in expectation. To this end, let $W_t^{\bar{u}}(\bar{x}, c, d)$ denote the maximum expected profit-to-go when starting in period t with a supply vector $\bar{x}$, receiving demand d from customer class c and taking the fulfillment decision $\bar{u}$. Furthermore, let $\bar{u}_t^*(\bar{x}, d, c)$ be an optimal decision in period t under the same conditions.

Using this notation, we have to show that

$$\begin{aligned} &W_t^{\bar{u}_t^*(\bar{x}-\bar{e}_n,d,c)}(\bar{x} - \bar{e}_n, c, d) - W_t^{\bar{u}_t^*(\bar{x}-\bar{e}_m,d,c)}(\bar{x} - \bar{e}_m, c, d) \\ &\leq b(n - m + \delta_{nt}(t-n) + \delta_{mt}(m-t)). \end{aligned}$$

We show that there is a feasible decision $\bar{u}_t(\bar{x}-\bar{e}_m, d, c)$ for which this inequality holds. This suffices since $W_t^{\bar{u}_t^*(\bar{x}-\bar{e}_m,d,c)} \geq W_t^{\bar{u}_t(\bar{x}-\bar{e}_m,d,c)}$.

[1]The proofs in this chapter are part of the paper of Quante et al. (2009a)

By definition, we have

$$\begin{aligned} W_t^{\bar{u}_t^*(\bar{x}-\bar{e}_n,d,c)}(\bar{x}-\bar{e}_n,c,d) &= \sum_{i=1}^{T}(u_i^* P_t(i,c) - hx_i\delta_{it}) \\ &\quad + h\delta_{nt} + V_{t+1}((\bar{x}-\bar{e}_n) - \bar{u}^*) \\ &= \cdots + u_m^* P_t(m,c) - hx_m\delta_{mt} + \cdots + u_n^* P_t(n,c) \\ &\quad - h(x_n - 1)\delta_{nt} + \cdots + V_{t+1}(\bar{x} - \bar{e}_n - \bar{u}^*), \quad \text{(A.1)} \end{aligned}$$

where we have omitted the arguments of u_i^* for notational convenience. We now construct an appropriate feasible decision for state $\bar{x}-\bar{e}_m$. We distinguish two cases.

Case (i): $u_m^* > 0$

In this case, the decision $\bar{u}_t^*(\bar{x}-\bar{e}_n,d,c) - \bar{e}_m + \bar{e}_n$ is feasible in state $\bar{x}-\bar{e}_m$ and we get

$$\begin{aligned} W_t^{\bar{u}_t^*(\bar{x}-\bar{e}_n,d,c)-\bar{e}_m+\bar{e}_n}(\bar{x}-\bar{e}_m,c,d) &= \sum_{i=1}^{T}(u_i^* P_t(i,c) - hx_i\delta_{it}) \\ &\quad + P_t(n,c) - P_t(m,c) \\ &\quad + h\delta_{mt} + V_{t+1}((\bar{x}-\bar{e}_m) - (\bar{u}^* - \bar{e}_m + \bar{e}_n)) \\ &= \cdots + (u_m^* - 1)P_t(m,c) - h(x_m - 1)\delta_{mt} \\ &\quad + \cdots + (u_n^* + 1)P_t(n,c) - hx_n\delta_{nt} + \ldots \\ &\quad + V_{t+1}(\bar{x} - \bar{e}_n - \bar{u}^*). \quad \text{(A.2)} \end{aligned}$$

Taking the difference between Equations A.1 and A.2, the profits-to-go after period $t+1$ vanish and we are left with the difference in current profits, which equals

$$P_t(m,c) - P_t(n,c) + h\delta_{nt} - h\delta_{mt} = b(n - m + \delta_{nt}(t-n) + \delta_{mt}(m-t)),$$

by definition of P_t.

Case (ii): $u_m^* = 0$

In this case, the decision $\bar{u}_t^*(\bar{x}-\bar{e}_n,d,c)$ is feasible in state $\bar{x}-\bar{e}_m$ and we get

$$\begin{aligned}W_t^{\bar{u}_t^*(\bar{x}-\bar{e}_n,d,c)}(\bar{x}-\bar{e}_m,c,d) &= \sum_{i=1}^{T}(u_i^* P_t(i,c) - hx_i\delta_{it}) + h\delta_{mt} \\ &\quad + V_{t+1}((\bar{x}-\bar{e}_m)-\bar{u}^*) \\ &= \dots + u_m^* P_t(m,c) - h(x_m-1)\delta_{mt} + \dots \\ &\quad + u_n^* P_t(n,c) - hx_n\delta_{nt} + \dots + V_{t+1}(\bar{x}-\bar{e}_m-\bar{u}^*).\end{aligned} \tag{A.3}$$

Calculating the difference in current profits between Equations A.1 and A.3 yields

$$\begin{aligned}&-hx_m\delta_{mt} - h(x_n-1)\delta_{nt} - (-h(x_m-1)\delta_{mt} - hx_n\delta_{nt}) \\ &= h(\delta_{nt}-\delta_{mt}) \le 0,\end{aligned}$$

where the inequality follows from $n > m$. For the difference in expected future profits we obtain

$$\begin{aligned}&V_{t+1}(\bar{x}-\bar{e}_n-\bar{u}^*) - V_{t+1}(\bar{x}-\bar{e}_m-\bar{u}^*) \\ &\le b(n-m+\delta_{nt+1}(t+1-n)+\delta_{mt+1}(m-t-1)) \\ &\le b(n-m+\delta_{nt}(t-n)+\delta_{mt}(m-t)),\end{aligned} \tag{A.4}$$

where the first inequality follows from the induction assumption and the second inequality follows since A.4 is decreasing in t for $m < n$. This completes the proof of Part a).

Part b) follows immediately from Part a) by replacing $\bar{x}$ with $\bar{x}+\bar{e}_m+\bar{e}_n$ and using the definition of $\Delta_i V_t(\bar{x})$. □

A.2 Proof of proposition 5.2

We have the following equivalences

$$\begin{aligned}&P_t(m,c) - \Delta_m V_{t+1}(\bar{x}) \ge P_t(n,c) - \Delta_n V_{t+1}(\bar{x}) \\ &\Leftrightarrow P_t(m,c) - P_t(n,c) \ge \Delta_m V_{t+1}(\bar{x}) - \Delta_n V_{t+1}(\bar{x}) \\ &\overset{5.3}{\Leftrightarrow} b(n-m+\delta_{nt}(t-n)+\delta_{mt}(m-t)) + h(\delta_{mt}-\delta_{nt}) \ge \\ &\Delta_m V_{t+1}(\bar{x}) - \Delta_n V_{t+1}(\bar{x}).\end{aligned}$$

From Part a) of Proposition 5.1 we know that $\Delta_m V_{t+1}(\bar{x}) - \Delta_n V_{t+1}(\bar{x}) \leq b(n - m + \delta_{nt+1}(t+1-n) + \delta_{mt+1}(m-t-1))$. As in Case (ii) of the proof of Proposition 5.1, this implies the desired result since for $n > m$ we have $\delta_{nt+1}(t+1-n)+\delta_{mt+1}(m-t-1) \leq \delta_{nt}(t-n)+\delta_{mt}(m-t)$ and $\delta_{mt}-\delta_{nt} \geq 0$. □

A.3 Proof of Proposition 5.3 and Theorem 5.1

We show both properties jointly by induction. For $t = T$, Proposition 5.3 holds since $V_{T+1}(.) \equiv 0$ and $P_T(m,c) = P_T(n,c)$ for $m, n \leq T$.

Now assume that Proposition 5.3 holds for Period t. We first show that Theorem 5.1 then holds for Period t and subsequently that Proposition 5.3 holds for Period $t-1$.

Equation 5.6 shows that one can decompose the fulfillment decision into unit steps and that selling a given unit is beneficial if immediate profits outweigh the opportunity cost of losing this unit. Proposition 5.2 shows that there is an optimal policy $\bar{u}^*$ for which $u_i^* > 0$ implies $x_j - u_j^* = 0$ for all $j < i$. Any optimal policy that does not satisfy this property can be modified by swapping one unit of supply j against one unit of supply i. Proposition 5.2 implies that this modification does not decrease the objective function value. Therefore, one can obtain an optimal solution through a line search, starting with the earliest available supply, i.e. the smallest i, for which $x_i > 0$. The induction assumption of Proposition 5.3 shows that the objective function is concave along this search line. Therefore, one can stop the search as soon as immediate profits drop below the opportunity costs. This proves that the procedure defined in Theorem 5.1 yields an optimal policy.

We now show Proposition 5.3 for Period $t-1$. We use the same notation as in the proof of Proposition 5.1. Let $\bar{u}^1 := \bar{u}_t^*(\bar{x}, c, d)$, $\bar{u}^2 := \bar{u}_t^*(\bar{x} - \bar{e}_m, c, d)$, and $\bar{u}^3 := \bar{u}_t^*(\bar{x} - \bar{e}_m - \bar{e}_n, c, d)$ denote the optimal decisions in states $\bar{x}$, $\bar{x} - \bar{e}_m$, and $\bar{x} - \bar{e}_m - \bar{e}_n$, respectively, for a given customer class c and demand quantity d. Furthermore, let

$$A := W_t^{\bar{u}^1}(\bar{x}, c, d) - W_t^{\bar{u}^2}(\bar{x} - \bar{e}_m, c, d) \quad \text{and}$$
$$B := W_t^{\bar{u}^2}(\bar{x} - \bar{e}_m, c, d) - W_t^{\bar{u}^3}(\bar{x} - \bar{e}_m - \bar{e}_n, c, d).$$

We rewrite Proposition 5.3 for Period $t-1$ as $\Delta_m V_t(\bar{x}) - \Delta_n V_t(\bar{x} - \bar{e}_m) \leq P_{t-1}(m,c) - P_{t-1}(n,c)$ and show that

$$\begin{aligned} A - B &\leq P_t(m,c) - P_t(n,c) - h(\delta_{mt} - \delta_{nt}) \\ &\leq P_{t-1}(m,c) - P_{t-1}(n,c), \end{aligned}$$

for any values of c and d, which implies that these inequalities also hold in expectation.

The second inequality follows directly from the definition of $P_t(.,.)$ for $m < n$. For the first inequality, we distinguish three cases, based on the value of $\bar{u}^1$.

Case (i): $\bar{u}^1 \equiv 0$

Theorem 5.1 implies $\bar{u}_2 = \bar{u}_3 \equiv 0$. From the definition of W_t we get

$$\begin{aligned} A - B &= \Delta_m V_{t+1}(\bar{x}) - h\delta_{mt} - \Delta_n V_{t+1}(x - \bar{e}_m) + h\delta_{nt} \\ &\leq P_t(m, c) - P_t(n, c) - h(\delta_{mt} - \delta_{nt}), \end{aligned}$$

where the inequality follows from the induction assumption.

Case (ii): $0 < \sum_{i=1}^{T} u_i^1 < d$

Theorem 5.1 implies $\bar{u}^2 = \bar{u}^1 - \bar{e}_m$. There are two possibilities for $\bar{u}^3$. If $\bar{u}^2 \neq 0$ then $\bar{u}^3 = \bar{u}^2 - \bar{e}_n$, otherwise $\bar{u}^3 \equiv 0$. In the first case, we get

$$A - B = P_t(m, c) - P_t(n, c) - h(\delta_{mt} - \delta_{nt}).$$

In the second case, $B = \Delta_n V_{t+1}(\bar{x} - \bar{e}_m) - h\delta_{nt}$ and Theorem 5.1 implies that this value is smaller than $P_t(n, c) - h\delta_{nt}$ since it is optimal not to sell another unit of supply n. Thus, $A - B$ satisfies the desired inequality in either case.

Case (iii): $\sum_{i=1}^{T} u_i^1 = d$

Theorem 5.1 implies that either $\bar{u}^2 = \bar{u}^1 - \bar{e}_m$ or $\bar{u}^2 = \bar{u}^1 - \bar{e}_m + \bar{e}_k$ for some $k \geq n$. The first alternative leads to the same calculations as in Case (ii) above. The second alternative leaves two options for $\bar{u}^3$, namely either $\bar{u}^3 = \bar{u}^2 - \bar{e}_n + \bar{e}_l$ for some $l \geq k$ or $\bar{u}^3 = \bar{u}^2 - \bar{e}_n$. In the first case, we get

$$\begin{aligned} A - B &= P_t(m, c) - P_t(k, c) + \Delta_k V_{t+1}(\bar{x} - \bar{u}^1) \\ &\quad - P_t(n, c) - P_t(l, c) + \Delta_l V_{t+1}(\bar{x} - \bar{u}^1 - \bar{e}_k) - h(\delta_{mt} - \delta_{nt}) \\ &\leq P_t(m, c) - P_t(n, c) - h(\delta_{mt} - \delta_{nt}), \end{aligned}$$

where the inequality follows from the induction assumption. The other case regarding $\bar{u}_3$ yields $B = P_t(n, c) - h\delta_{nt}$ and therefore

$$\begin{aligned} A - B &= P_t(m, c) - P_t(k, c) + \Delta_k V_{t+1}(\bar{x} - \bar{u}_1) - P_t(n, c) - h(\delta_{mt} - \delta_{nt}) \\ &\leq P_t(m, c) - P_t(n, c) - h(\delta_{mt} - \delta_{nt}), \end{aligned}$$

where the inequality follows from the fact that it is optimal in state $\bar{x} - \bar{u}_1$ to sell an additional unit of supply k. □

A.4 Proof of Proposition 5.4

We show by induction that $\Delta_i V_{t+1}(\bar{x}) > 0$ implies $\Delta_i V_t(\bar{x}) \geq \Delta_i V_{t+1}(\bar{x})$. Since $P_t(i,c)$ is increasing in t this assures non-increasing protection levels for any i and c.

For $t = T$ the condition is empty since $\Delta_i V_{T+1}(\bar{x}) = 0$ for all i, c, and $\bar{x}$. In other words, all protection levels vanish at the end of the planning horizon.

Assume now that Proposition 5.4 holds for Period $t+1$. We show that it also holds for Period t. To this end, assume that $\Delta_i V_{t+1}(\bar{x}) > 0$. Using the Bellman recursion of V_t we have

$$\Delta_i V_t(\bar{x}) = -h\delta_{it} + E_{c,d}\left[\max\left\{P_t(i,c)\delta_{d>0}\ ;\ \Delta_i V_{t+1}(\bar{x})\right\}\right], \qquad \text{(A.5)}$$

where $\delta_{d>0}$ equals unity if $d > 0$ and zero otherwise. For $t < i$ the holding-cost term vanishes and we immediately get $\Delta_i V_t(\bar{x}) \geq \Delta_i V_{t+1}(\bar{x})$. For $t \geq i$ we rewrite (A.5) for $t+1$

$$\Delta_i V_{t+1}(\bar{x}) = -h\delta_{it+1} + E_{c,d}\left[\max\left\{P_{t+1}(i,c)\delta_{d>0}\ ;\ \Delta_i V_{t+2}(\bar{x})\right\}\right], \qquad \text{(A.6)}$$

and compare the individual terms. We have $-h\delta_{it} = -h\delta_{it+1}$ and $P_t(i,c) = P_{t+1}(i,c)$ since $t \geq i$. In addition, the induction assumption implies that $\Delta_i V_{t+1}(\bar{x}) \geq \Delta_i V_{t+2}(\bar{x})$ if the maximum in (A.6) is attained by the last term. Therefore, $\Delta_i V_t(\bar{x}) \geq \Delta_i V_{t+1}(\bar{x})$, which completes the proof. □

Appendix B

Data Tables

Table B.1: Data of Fig. 7.1

(a) Lost Sales

Cl.	FCFS	SOPA_D	SOPA_A
1	40.89%	11.76%	1.56%
2	40.52%	28.73%	31.83%
3	40.97%	77.30%	82.98%

(b) Backlogged Quantities

Cl.	FCFS	SOPA_D	SOPA_A
1	0.00%	4.28%	47.59%
2	0.00%	2.09%	60.59%
3	0.00%	1.96%	16.37%

Table B.2: Data of Fig. 7.2

(a) Early Delivery

Cl.	FCFS	SOPA_D	SOPA_A
1	58.84%	77.43%	43.99%
2	59.21%	62.95%	4.36%
3	58.82%	15.40%	0.45%

(b) On Time Delivery

Cl.	FCFS	SOPA_D	SOPA_A
1	0.27%	6.53%	6.86%
2	0.27%	6.23%	3.22%
3	0.20%	5.35%	0.20%

Table B.3: Data of Fig. 7.3

Cl.	GOP	FCFS	SOPA_D	SOPA_A
1	2,617,006	2,515,394	2,535,015	1,231,004
2	2,617,006	2,515,394	2,544,101	1,767,756
3	2,617,006	2,515,394	2,543,725	1,774,840
4	2,617,006	2,515,394	2,540,218	1,849,463
5	2,617,006	2,515,394	2,539,859	1,860,748
6	2,617,006	2,515,394	2,535,119	1,882,588
7	2,617,006	2,515,394	2,533,737	1,870,950
8	2,617,006	2,515,394	2,531,967	1,894,752
9	2,617,006	2,515,394	2,531,083	1,894,894
10	2,617,006	2,515,394	2,533,138	1,900,758

Table B.4: Data of Fig. 7.4

Cl.	FCFS	SOPA_D	SOPA_A
1	3.88%	3.13%	52.96%
2	3.88%	2.79%	32.45%
3	3.88%	2.80%	32.18%
4	3.88%	2.93%	29.33%
5	3.88%	2.95%	28.90%
6	3.88%	3.13%	28.06%
7	3.88%	3.18%	28.51%
8	3.88%	3.25%	27.60%
9	3.88%	3.28%	27.59%
10	3.88%	3.21%	27.37%

Table B.5: Data of Fig. 7.5

(a) Heterogeneity 10%

Cl.	FCFS	SOPA_D	SOPA_A
1	3.88%	3.13%	52.96%
2	3.88%	2.79%	32.45%
3	3.88%	2.80%	32.18%
4	3.88%	2.93%	29.33%
5	3.88%	2.95%	28.90%
6	3.88%	3.13%	28.06%
7	3.88%	3.18%	28.51%
8	3.88%	3.25%	27.60%
9	3.88%	3.28%	27.59%
10	3.88%	3.21%	27.37%

(b) Heterogeneity 30%

Cl.	FCFS	SOPA_D	SOPA_A
1	10.24%	9.67%	54.44%
2	10.24%	5.42%	12.52%
3	10.24%	5.38%	14.69%
4	10.24%	4.91%	13.61%
5	10.24%	5.01%	8.50%
6	10.24%	5.27%	10.09%
7	10.24%	5.28%	10.11%
8	10.24%	5.32%	9.52%
9	10.24%	5.36%	9.70%
10	10.24%	5.27%	9.55%

(c) Heterogeneity 50%

Cl.	FCFS	SOPA_D	SOPA_A
1	16.29%	15.63%	54.40%
2	16.29%	8.28%	10.51%
3	16.29%	7.23%	13.49%
4	16.29%	6.33%	12.16%
5	16.29%	6.50%	7.80%
6	16.29%	6.94%	8.78%
7	16.29%	6.76%	8.07%
8	16.29%	6.94%	8.05%
9	16.29%	7.02%	7.37%
10	16.29%	6.90%	7.36%

(d) Heterogeneity 70%

Cl.	FCFS	SOPA_D	SOPA_A
1	21.61%	21.08%	52.63%
2	21.61%	10.41%	9.04%
3	21.61%	8.63%	12.76%
4	21.61%	7.47%	10.53%
5	21.61%	7.81%	6.60%
6	21.61%	8.40%	7.66%
7	21.61%	8.02%	7.14%
8	21.61%	8.05%	6.07%
9	21.61%	8.31%	6.37%
10	21.61%	8.20%	5.94%

Table B.6: Data of Fig. 7.6

(a) Forecast Error 0%

Cl.	FCFS	SOPA_D	SOPA_A
1	3.88%	1.94%	52.96%
2	3.88%	0.36%	33.43%
3	3.88%	0.15%	31.04%
4	3.88%	0.10%	30.00%
5	3.88%	0.06%	29.13%
6	3.88%	0.04%	28.66%
7	3.88%	0.03%	28.33%
8	3.88%	0.02%	27.67%
9	3.88%	0.02%	27.19%
10	3.88%	0.02%	26.83%

(b) Forecast Error M

Cl.	FCFS	SOPA_D	SOPA_A
1	3.88%	3.13%	52.96%
2	3.88%	2.79%	32.45%
3	3.88%	2.80%	32.18%
4	3.88%	2.93%	29.33%
5	3.88%	2.95%	28.90%
6	3.88%	3.13%	28.06%
7	3.88%	3.18%	28.51%
8	3.88%	3.25%	27.60%
9	3.88%	3.28%	27.59%
10	3.88%	3.21%	27.37%

(c) Forecast Error 50%

Cl.	FCFS	SOPA_D	SOPA_A
1	3.88%	4.54%	52.96%
2	3.88%	5.42%	31.21%
3	3.88%	5.41%	23.94%
4	3.88%	5.61%	21.51%
5	3.88%	5.40%	19.60%
6	3.88%	5.24%	16.87%
7	3.88%	5.63%	15.84%
8	3.88%	5.54%	13.90%
9	3.88%	6.01%	13.69%
10	3.88%	5.54%	13.13%

(d) Forecast Error 100%

Cl.	FCFS	SOPA_D	SOPA_A
1	3.88%	8.88%	52.96%
2	3.88%	11.79%	17.47%
3	3.88%	11.07%	16.21%
4	3.88%	11.63%	14.84%
5	3.88%	11.74%	11.49%
6	3.88%	12.10%	11.02%
7	3.88%	12.39%	11.14%
8	3.88%	12.58%	10.19%
9	3.88%	13.59%	11.16%
10	3.88%	12.49%	9.55%

Table B.7: Data of Fig. 7.7

Backlogging Costs	GOP	FCFS	SOPA_D	SOPA_A
0	2,799,229	2,515,394	2,701,440	2,788,465
1	2,713,034	2,515,394	2,638,449	2,606,074
2	2,683,542	2,515,394	2,608,421	2,231,926
3	2,666,971	2,515,394	2,590,617	1,760,303
4	2,655,540	2,515,394	2,579,133	1,253,369
5	2,646,701	2,515,394	2,569,319	1,112,489
6	2,639,198	2,515,394	2,563,497	1,556,233
7	2,632,968	2,515,394	2,558,761	1,682,605
8	2,627,311	2,515,394	2,554,074	1,702,957
9	2,621,976	2,515,394	2,548,068	1,745,037
10	2,617,006	2,515,394	2,543,725	1,774,840

Table B.8: Data of Fig. 7.8

(a) Lost Sales

Cl.	GOP	FCFS	SOPA_D	RM
1	1.82%	38.65%	7.82%	14.62%
2	32.73%	40.40%	29.45%	26.91%
3	86.41%	38.53%	83.62%	76.89%

(b) Backlogged Quantities

Cl.	GOP	FCFS	SOPA_D	RM
1	2.62%	0.00%	2.84%	3.10%
2	1.51%	0.00%	2.62%	1.45%
3	0.03%	0.00%	1.04%	0.00%

Table B.9: Data of Fig. 7.9

CV	GOP	FCFS	SOPA_D	RM
0.00	17,890.36	17,265.44	17,682.46	17,768.62
0.33	17,851.67	17,229.71	17,553.97	17,694.21
0.67	17,843.03	17,247.27	17,327.95	17,635.90
1.00	17,748.89	17,164.66	16,767.71	17,449.12
1.33	17,440.88	16,803.89	15,880.23	17,031.49

Table B.10: Data of Fig. 7.10

(a) Heterogeneity 10%

CV	FCFS	SOPA_D	RM
0.00	3.49%	1.17%	0.68%
0.33	3.48%	1.68%	0.88%
0.67	3.33%	2.91%	1.16%
1.00	3.28%	5.58%	1.69%
1.33	3.65%	9.10%	2.37%

(b) Heterogeneity 20%

CV	FCFS	SOPA_D	RM
0.00	10.04%	1.72%	1.25%
0.33	9.77%	2.44%	1.63%
0.67	9.42%	4.50%	2.45%
1.00	8.84%	7.95%	3.47%
1.33	8.89%	12.21%	4.63%

(c) Heterogeneity 30%

CV	FCFS	SOPA_D	RM
0.00	17.07%	2.50%	1.73%
0.33	17.28%	3.32%	2.26%
0.67	16.95%	5.71%	3.29%
1.00	15.10%	9.58%	4.86%
1.33	14.82%	14.57%	6.31%

Table B.11: Data of Fig. 7.11

(a) $CV = 0.67$ and Low Heterogeneity

Shortage Rate	FCFS	SOPA_D	RM
0% (41%)	3.38%	3.28%	1.24%
25% (21%)	2.70%	5.73%	1.64%
41% (0%)	2.47%	3.23%	1.02%
50% (-19%)	2.03%	2.56%	0.49%
75% (-138%)	0.31%	0.10%	0.00%

(b) $CV = 0.33$ and Low Heterogeneity

Shortage Rate	FCFS	SOPA_D	RM
0% (41%)	3.52%	1.66%	0.89%
25% (21%)	2.29%	3.53%	1.28%
41% (0%)	2.03%	2.39%	0.76%
50% (-19%)	1.38%	1.44%	0.28%
75% (-138%)	0.01%	0.00%	0.00%

(c) $CV = 0.67$ and Medium Heterogeneity

Shortage Rate	FCFS	SOPA_D	RM
0% (41%)	9.18%	4.41%	2.36%
25% (21%)	5.64%	6.93%	3.25%
75% (-138%)	3.50%	3.75%	1.71%
41% (0%)	1.83%	2.63%	0.66%
50% (-19%)	0.23%	0.07%	0.00%

Table B.12: Data of Fig. 7.12

(a) $n_t = 10$

Heterogeneity	FCFS	SOPA_D	SOPA_A	RLP
10%	3.81%	1.65%	32.60%	1.65%
30%	10.28%	3.34%	14.81%	3.34%
50%	16.47%	4.37%	13.79%	4.37%
70%	21.78%	5.11%	12.45%	5.11%

(b) $n_t \sim Poisson(10)$

Heterogeneity	FCFS	SOPA_D	SOPA_A	RLP
10%	3.83%	2.98%	31.24%	3.19%
30%	9.65%	5.50%	15.86%	5.64%
50%	15.90%	7.05%	15.07%	7.20%
70%	20.97%	8.62%	12.92%	8.81%

(c) $n_t \sim NB(10, 64)$

Heterogeneity	FCFS	SOPA_D	SOPA_A	RLP
10%	3.40%	7.45%	29.98%	7.87%
30%	9.77%	12.42%	14.15%	13.49%
50%	16.46%	16.26%	12.63%	17.04%
70%	20.37%	18.98%	13.45%	19.65%

(d) $n_t \sim NB(10, 144)$

Heterogeneity	FCFS	SOPA_D	SOPA_A	RLP
10%	3.83%	18.59%	25.56%	17.75%
30%	10.33%	21.65%	15.41%	21.23%
50%	16.36%	26.08%	16.87%	25.56%
70%	21.63%	30.00%	14.78%	29.50%

Table B.13: Data of Fig. 7.13

(a) $n_t = 10$

Heterogeneity	FCFS	SOPA_D	SOPA_A	RLP
10%	3.81%	3.17%	33.69%	3.17%
30%	10.28%	6.45%	14.92%	6.45%
50%	16.47%	8.94%	14.15%	8.94%
70%	21.78%	10.10%	12.34%	10.10%

(b) $n_t \sim Poisson(10)$

Heterogeneity	FCFS	SOPA_D	SOPA_A	RLP
10%	3.83%	3.93%	32.23%	4.12%
30%	9.65%	7.02%	14.97%	6.99%
50%	15.90%	9.75%	14.01%	9.70%
70%	20.97%	12.66%	12.32%	12.59%

(c) $n_t \sim NB(10, 64)$

Heterogeneity	FCFS	SOPA_D	SOPA_A	RLP
10%	3.40%	8.18%	30.56%	8.65%
30%	9.77%	14.96%	14.05%	16.01%
50%	16.46%	20.26%	12.81%	20.81%
70%	20.37%	23.29%	13.01%	23.65%

(d) $n_t \sim NB(10, 144)$

Heterogeneity	FCFS	SOPA_D	SOPA_A	RLP
10%	3.83%	21.37%	27.81%	20.57%
30%	10.33%	25.92%	17.04%	25.21%
50%	16.36%	30.28%	17.90%	29.45%
70%	21.63%	35.50%	16.51%	34.63%

Bibliography

Agrawal, Narendra, Stephen A. Smith. 1998. Estimating negative binomial demand for retail inventory management with unobservable lost sales. *Naval Research Logistics* **43**(6) 839–861.

Anderson, Eric T., Gavan J. Fitzsimons, Duncan Simester. 2006. Measuring and mitigating the costs of stockouts. *Management Science* **52**(11) 1751–1763.

Arslan, Hasan, Stephen C. Graves, Thomas Roemer. 2007. A single-product inventory model for multiple demand classes. *Management Science* **53**(9) 1486–1500.

Ball, Michael O., Chien-Yu Chen, Zhen-Ying Zhao. 2004. Available-to-promise. David Simchi-Levi, S. David Wu, Zuo-Jun Shen, eds., *Handbook of Quantitative Supply Chain Analysis - Modeling in the E-Business Era*, chap. 11. Kluwer Academic Publishers, 447–483.

Barut, Mehmet, V. Sridharan. 2005. Revenue management in order-driven production systems. *Decision Sciences* **36**(2) 287–316.

Bitran, Gabriel, René Caldentey. 2003. An overview of pricing models for revenue management. *Manufacturing & Service Operations Management* **5**(3) 203–229.

Boyd, Andrew. 1998. Airline alliance revenue management. *OR/MS Today* **25**(5) 28–31.

Boyd, E. Andrew, Ioana C. Bilegan. 2003. Revenue management and e-commerce. *Management Science* **49**(10) 1363–1386.

Buttle, Francis. 2004. *Customer relationship management*. 1st ed. Butterworth Heinemann, Oxford.

Chan, L. M. A., Z. J. Max Shen, David Simchi-Levi, Julie L. Swann. 2004. Coordination of pricing and inventory decisions: A survey and classification. David Simchi-Levi, S. David Wu, Zuo-Jun Shen, eds., *Handbook of Quantitative Supply Chain Analysis - Modeling in the E-Business Era*, chap. 9. Kluwer Academic Publishers, 335–392.

Chen, Chien-Yu, Zhen-Ying Zhao, Michael O. Ball. 2001. Quantity and due date quoting available to promise. *Information Systems Frontiers* **3**(4) 477–488.

Chen, Chien-Yu, Zhenying Zhao, Michael O. Ball. 2002. A model for batch advanced available-to-promise. *Production and Operations Management* **11**(4) 424–440.

Chiang, Wen-Chyuan, Jason C. H. Chen, Xiaojing Xu. 2007. An overview of research on revenue management: current issues and future research. *International Journal of Revenue Management* **1**(1) 97–128.

De Boer, Sanne V., Richard Freling, Nanda Piersma. 2002. Mathematical programming for network revenue management revisited. *European Journal of Operational Research* **137**(1) 72–92.

De Véricourt, Francis, Fikri Karaesmen, Yves Dallery. 2002. Optimal stock allocation for a capacitated supply system. *Management Science* **48**(11) 1486–1501.

Defregger, Florian, Heinrich Kuhn. 2007. Revenue management for a make-to-order company with limited inventory capacity. *OR Spectrum* **29**(1) 137–156.

Ding, Qing, Panos Kouvelis, Joseph M. Milner. 2006. Dynamic pricing through discounts for optimizing multi-class fulfillment. *Operations Research* **54**(1) 169–183.

Ehrenberg, A. S. C. 1959. The pattern of consumer purchases. *Applied Statistics* **8**(1) 26–41.

Elmaghraby, Wedad, Pinar Keskinocak. 2003. Dynamic pricing in the presence of inventory considerations: Research overview, current practices, and future directions. *Management Science* **49**(10) 1287–1309.

Fischer, Markus E. 2001. *"Available-to-Promise": Aufgaben und Verfahren im Rahmen des Supply Chain Management*. Theorie und Forschung Band 704, Wirtschaftswissenschaften Band 63, Roderer, Regensburg.

Fleischmann, Bernhard, Herbert Meyr. 2004. Customer orientation in advanced planning systems. Harald Dyckhoff, Richard Lackes, Joachim Reese, eds., *Supply Chain Management and Reverse Logistics*, chap. 3. Springer, 297–321.

Fleischmann, Bernhard, Herbert Meyr, Michael Wagner. 2008. Advanced planning. Hartmut Stadtler, Christoph Kilger, eds., *Supply Chain Management and Advanced Planning*, 4th ed. Springer, Berlin, Heidelberg, 81–106.

Fleischmann, Moritz, Joseph Hall, David Pyke. 2004. Smart pricing: Linking pricing decisions with operational insights. *Erim report series research in management* .

Gordon, Valery, Jean-Marie Proth, Chengbin Chu. 2002. A survey of the state-of-the-art of common due date assignment and scheduling research. *European Journal of Operational Research* **139**(1) 1–25.

Guerrero, Hector H., Gary M. Kern. 1988. How to more effectively accept and refuse orders. *Production and Inventory Management Journal* **29**(4) 59–63.

Gupta, Diwakar, Lei Wang. 2007. Capacity management for contract manufacturing. *Operations Research* **55**(2) 367–377.

Ha, Albert Y. 1997a. Inventory rationing in a make-to-stock production system with several demand classes and lost sales. *Management Science* **43**(8) 1093–1103.

Ha, Albert Y. 1997b. Stock-rationing policy for a make-to-stock production system with two priority classes and backordering. *Naval Research Logistics* **44**(5) 457–472.

Harris, Frederick H., Jonathan P. Pinder. 1995. A revenue management approach to demand management and order booking in assemble-to-order manufacturing. *Journal of Operations Management* **13**(4) 299–309.

Hill, Terry. 2000. *Manufacturing Strategy*. 3rd ed. McGraw-Hill, Boston, Mass.

Hoekstra, Sjoerd, Jac E. Romme. 1992. *Integral Logistic Structures: Developing Customer-Oriented Goods Flow*. McGraw-Hill, London.

Jalora, Anshu. 2006. Order acceptance and scheduling at a make-to-order system using revenue management. Ph.D. thesis, Texas A&M University.

Kalyan, Vibhu. 2002. Dynamic customer value management: Asset values under demand uncertainty using airline yield management and related techniques. *Information Systems Frontiers* **4**(1) 101–119.

Kambil, Ajit, Eric van Heck. 2002. *Making Markets: How Firms Can Design and Profit from Online Auctions and Exchanges*. Harvard Business School Press, Boston.

Keskinocak, Pinar, Sridhar Tayur. 2004. Due-date management policies. David Simchi-Levi, S. David Wu, Zuo-Jun Shen, eds., *Handbook of Quantitative Supply Chain Analysis - Modeling in the E-Business Era*, chap. 12. Kluwer Academic Publishers, 485–547.

Khouja, Moutaz. 1999. The single-period (news-vendor) problem: Literature review and suggestions for future research. *Omega* **27**(5) 537–553.

Kilger, Christoph, Herbert Meyr. 2008. Demand fulfilment and ATP. Hartmut Stadtler, Christoph Kilger, eds., *Supply Chain Management and Advanced Planning*, 4th ed. Springer, Berlin, Heidelberg, 181–198.

Kilger, Christoph, Michael Wagner. 2008. Demand planning. Hartmut Stadtler, Christoph Kilger, eds., *Supply Chain Management and Advanced Planning*, 4th ed. Springer, Berlin, Heidelberg, 133–160.

Kimms, Alf, Robert Klein. 2005. Revenue Management im Branchenvergleich. *Zeitschrift für Betriebswirtschaft* **1** 1–30.

Kimms, Alf, Michael Müller-Bungart. 2007. Simulation of stochastic demand data streams for network revenue management problems. *OR Spectrum* **29** 5–20.

Kleijn, Marcel J., Rommert Dekker. 1998. An overview of inventory systems with several demand classes. Econometric institute report 9838/a, RSM Erasmus University.

Klophaus, R. 1998. Revenue Management: Wie die Airline Ertragswachstum schafft. *Absatzwirtschaft* **Sondernummer Oktober** 146–155.

Kocabıyıkoğlu, Ayşe, Ioana Popescu. 2005. Joint pricing and revenue management with general stochastic demand. Working paper, INSEAD.

Kolisch, Rainer, Danilo Zatta. 2006. Revenue-Management in der Sachgüterproduktion. *Marketing Journal* **12** 38–41.

Kuhn, Heinrich, Florian Defregger. 2004. Revenue Management in der Sachgüterproduktion. *Wirtschaftswissenschaftliches Studium* **5** 319–324.

Kumar, Sameer, Jared L. Frederick. 2007. Revenue management for a home construction products manufacturer. *Journal of Revenue & Pricing Management* **5**(4) 256–270.

Lautenbacher, Conrad J., Shaler Jr. Stidham. 1999. The underlying markov decision process in the single-leg airline yield-management problem. *Transportation Science* **33**(2) 136–146.

Lawless, Jerald F. 1987. Negative binomial and mixed poisson regression. *The Canadian Journal of Statistics* **15**(3) 209–225.

Lee, Young M. 2006. Simulating impact of available-to-promise generation on supply chain performance. *WSC '06: Proceedings of the 38th conference on Winter simulation*. Winter Simulation Conference, Monterey, California, 621–626.

Mantrala, Murali K., Surya Rao. 2001. A decision-support system that helps retailers decide order quantities and markdowns for fashion goods. *Interfaces* **31**(3) 146–165.

Manugistics. 2002. Enterprise profit optimization. URL `http://www.manugistics.com/documents/epo_whitepaper.pdf`.

Matsumoto, Makoto, Takuji Nishimura. 1998. Mersenne twister: A 623-dimensionally equidistributed uniform pseudorandom number generator. *ACM Transactions on Modeling and Computer Simulation* **8**(1) 3–30.

McGill, Jeffrey I, Garrett van Ryzin. 1999. Revenue management: Research overview and prospects. *Transportation Science* **33**(2) 233–256.

Melchiors, P., R. Dekker, M.J. Kleijn. 2000. Inventory rationing in an (s, Q) inventory model with lost sales and two demand classes. *Journal of the Operational Research Society* **51**(1) 111–122.

Meyr, Herbert. 2008. Clustering methods for rationing limited resources. Lars Mönch, Giselher Pankratz, eds., *Intelligente Systeme zur Entscheidungsunterstützung*. SCS Publishing House e.V., 19–32.

Meyr, Herbert. 2009. Customer segmentation, allocation planning and order promising in make-to-stock production. *OR Spectrum* **31**(1) 229–256.

Meyr, Herbert, Heidrun Rosič, Christian Seipl, Michael Wagner, Ulrich Wetterauer. 2008a. Architecture of selected APS. Hartmut Stadtler, Christoph Kilger, eds., *Supply Chain Management and Advanced Planning*, 4th ed. Springer, Berlin, Heidelberg, 349–366.

Meyr, Herbert, Michael Wagner, Jens Rohde. 2008b. Structure of Advanced Planning Systems. Hartmut Stadtler, Christoph Kilger, eds., *Supply Chain Management and Advanced Planning*, 4th ed. Springer, Berlin, Heidelberg, 109–116.

Mild, Andreas, Martin Natter, Thomas Reutterer, Alfred Taudes, Jürgen Wöckl. 2006. Retail revenue management. Peter Schnedlitz, Renate Buber, Thomas Reutterer, Arnold Schuh, Christoph Teller, eds., *Innovationen in Marketing und Handel*. Linde, Wien, 124–143.

Möllering, Karin T., Ulrich W. Thonemann. 2007. An optimal critical level policy for inventory systems with two demand classes. Tech. rep., University of Cologne.

Neslin, Scott A. 2002. Sales promotion. Barton A. Weitz, Robin Wensley, eds., *Handbook of Marketing*, chap. 13. Sage Publications, London, 310–338.

Optiant. 2007. URL `http://www.optiant.com`.

Pak, Kevin, Nanda Piersma. 2002. Airline revenue management: An overview of OR techniques 1982-2001. Econometric Institute Report 256, Erasmus University Rotterdam.

Petruzzi, Nicholas C., Maqbool Dada. 1999. Pricing and the newsvendor problem: A review with extensions. *Operations Research* **47**(2) 183–194.

Pibernik, Richard. 2005. Advanced available-to-promise: Classification, selected methods and requirements for operations and inventory management. *International Journal of Production Economics* **93–94** 239–252.

Pibernik, Richard. 2006. Managing stock-outs effectively with order fulfilment systems. *Journal of Manufacturing Technology Management* **17**(6) 721–736.

Pibernik, Richard, Prashant Yadav. 2009. Inventory reservation and real-time order promising in a make-to-stock system. *OR Spectrum* **31**(1) 281–307.

Porteus, Evan L. 2002. *Foundations of Stochastic Inventory Theory*. Stanford University Press.

Quante, Rainer, Moritz Fleischmann, Herbert Meyr. 2009a. A stochastic dynamic programming approach to revenue management in a make-to-stock production system. Working paper, Vienna University of Economics and Business Administration.

Quante, Rainer, Herbert Meyr, Moritz Fleischmann. 2009b. Revenue management and demand fulfillment: Matching applications, models, and software. *OR Spectrum* **31**(1) 31–62.

Rehkopf, Stefan. 2006. *Revenue Management-Konzepte zur Auftragsannahme bei kundenindividueller Produktion*. 1st ed. DUV.

Rehkopf, Stefan, Thomas Spengler. 2004. Revenue management in a make-to-order environment. H. Fleuren, D. den Hertog, Kort P., eds., *Operations Research Proceedings 2004*. Springer, 470–478.

Rohde, Jens, Herbert Meyr, Michael Wagner. 2000. Die Supply Chain Planning Matrix. *PPS Management* **5** 10–15.

Rohde, Jens, Michael Wagner. 2008. Master planning. Hartmut Stadtler, Christoph Kilger, eds., *Supply Chain Management and Advanced Planning*, 4th ed. Springer, Berlin, Heidelberg, 161–180.

SAP Help Portal. 2008. URL `http://help.sap.com`.

Scarf, Herbert. 1960. The optimality of (s,S) policies for the dynamic inventory problem. K. J. Arrow, S. Karlin, P. Suppes, eds., *Mathematical Methods in the Social Sciences*. Stanford University Press, Stanford, California, 196–202.

Schneeweiß, Christoph. 2003. *Distributed decision making*. 2nd ed. Springer.

Schwendinger, j. 1979. Master production scheduling's available-to-promise. *APICS Conference Proceedings* 316–330.

Sharman, Graham. 1984. The rediscovery of logistics. *Harvard Business Review* **62**(5) 71–79.

Silver, Edward A. 1981. Operations research in inventory management: A review and critique. *Operations Research* **29**(4) 628–645.

Silver, Edward A., David F. Pyke, Rein Peterson, eds. 1998. *Inventory Management and Production Planning and Scheduling*. 3rd ed. Wiley.

Smartops. 2007. URL `http://www.smartops.com`.

Specht, Dieter, Christian M. F. Gruß. 2007. Revenue Management Ũ eine Strategie für die Produktion in der Automobilindustrie? Dieter Specht, ed., *Strategische Bedeutung der Produktion: Tagungsband der Herbsttagung 2006 der Wissenschaftlichen Kommission Produktionswirtschaft im VHB*, 1st ed. DUV, Wiesbaden, 61–72.

Spengler, Thomas, Stefan Rehkopf, Thomas Volling. 2007. Revenue management in make-to-order manufacturing – an application to the iron and steel industry. *OR Spectrum* **29**(1) 157–171.

Stadtler, Hartmut. 2008. Purchasing and material requirements planning. Hartmut Stadtler, Christoph Kilger, eds., *Supply Chain Management and Advanced Planning*, 4th ed. Springer, Berlin, Heidelberg, 217–230.

Stadtler, Hartmut, Christoph Kilger, eds. 2008. *Supply Chain Management and Advanced Planning*. 4th ed. Springer, Berlin, Heidelberg.

Swann, Julie L. 1999. Flexible pricing policies: Introduction and a survey of implementation in various industries. Contract report, General Motors Corporation.

Talluri, Kalyan T., Garrett J. van Ryzin. 1999. A randomized linear programming method for computing network bid prices. *Transportation Science* **33**(2) 207–216.

Talluri, Kalyan T., Garrett J. van Ryzin. 2004. *The Theory and Practice of Revenue Management*. Kluwer Academic Publishers.

Tempelmeier, Horst. 2006. *Inventory Management in Supply Networks. Problems, Models, Solutions*. 1st ed. Norderstedt: Books on Demand.

Teunter, Ruud H., Willem K. Klein Haneveld. 2008. Dynamic inventory rationing strategies for inventory systems with two demand classes, poisson demand and backordering. *European Journal of Operational Research* **190**(1) 156–178.

Vakali, Athena, Lefteris Angelis, Dimitra Pournara. 2001. Internet based auctions: a survey on models and applications. *ACM SIGecom Exchanges* **2**(1) 6–15.

Vollmann, Thomas E., William L. Berry, D. C. Whybark. 2005. *Manufacturing Planning and Control for Supply Chain Management*. 5th ed. Mcgraw-Hill.

Weatherford, Lawrence R., Samuel E. Bodily. 1992. A taxonomy and research overview of perishable-asset revenue management: Yield management, overbooking, and pricing. *Operations Research* **40**(5) 831–844.

Whitin, T. M. 1955. Inventory control and price theory. *Management Science* **2**(1) 61–68.

Yano, Candace Arai, Stephen M. Gilbert. 2003. Coordinated pricing and production/procurement decisions: A review. Amiya K. Chakravarty, Jehoshua Eliashberg, eds., *Managing Business Interfaces: Marketing, Engineering and Manufacturing Perspectives*, chap. 3. International Series in Quantitative Marketing, Kluwer Academic Publishers, Norwell, Massachusetts, 65–103.

Forschungsergebnisse der Wirtschaftsuniversität Wien

Herausgeber: Wirtschaftsuniversität Wien –
vertreten durch a.o. Univ. Prof. Dr. Barbara Sporn

Band 1 Stefan Felder: Frequenzallokation in der Telekommunikation. Ökonomische Analyse der Vergabe von Frequenzen unter besonderer Berücksichtigung der UMTS-Auktionen. 2004.

Band 2 Thomas Haller: Marketing im liberalisierten Strommarkt. Kommunikation und Produktplanung im Privatkundenmarkt. 2005.

Band 3 Alexander Stremitzer: Agency Theory: Methodology, Analysis. A Structured Approach to Writing Contracts. 2005.

Band 4 Günther Sedlacek: Analyse der Studiendauer und des Studienabbruch-Risikos. Unter Verwendung der statistischen Methoden der Ereignisanalyse. 2004.

Band 5 Monika Knassmüller: Unternehmensleitbilder im Vergleich. Sinn- und Bedeutungsrahmen deutschsprachiger Unternehmensleitbilder – Versuch einer empirischen (Re-)Konstruktion. 2005.

Band 6 Matthias Fink: Erfolgsfaktor Selbstverpflichtung bei vertrauensbasierten Kooperationen. Mit einem empirischen Befund. 2005.

Band 7 Michael Gerhard Kraft: Ökonomie zwischen Wissenschaft und Ethik. Eine dogmenhistorische Untersuchung von Léon M.E. Walras bis Milton Friedman. 2005.

Band 8 Ingrid Zechmeister: Mental Health Care Financing in the Process of Change. Challenges and Approaches for Austria. 2005.

Band 9 Sarah Meisenberger: Strukturierte Organisationen und Wissen. 2005.

Band 10 Anne-Katrin Neyer: Multinational teams in the European Commission and the European Parliament. 2005.

Band 11 Birgit Trukeschitz: Im Dienst Sozialer Dienste. Ökonomische Analyse der Beschäftigung in sozialen Dienstleistungseinrichtungen des Nonprofit Sektors. 2006

Band 12 Marcus Kölling: Interkulturelles Wissensmanagement. Deutschland Ost und West. 2006.

Band 13 Ulrich Berger: The Economics of Two-way Interconnection. 2006.

Band 14 Susanne Guth: Interoperability of DRM Systems. Exchanging and Processing XML-based Rights Expressions. 2006.

Band 15 Bernhard Klement: Ökonomische Kriterien und Anreizmechanismen für eine effiziente Förderung von industrieller Forschung und Innovation. Mit einer empirischen Quantifizierung der Hebeleffekte von F&E-Förderinstrumenten in Österreich. 2006.

Band 16 Markus Imgrund: Wege aus der Insolvenz. Eine Analyse der Fortführung und Sanierung insolventer Klein- und Mittelbetriebe unter besonderer Berücksichtigung des Konfigurationsansatzes. 2007.

Band 17 Nicolas Knotzer: Product Recommendations in E-Commerce Retailing Applications. 2008.

Band 18 Astrid Dickinger: Perceived Quality of Mobile Services. A Segment-Specific Analysis. 2007.

Band 19 Nadine Wiedermann-Ondrej: Hybride Finanzierungsinstrumente in der nationalen und internationalen Besteuerung der USA. 2008.

Band 20 Helmut Sorger: Entscheidungsorientiertes Risikomanagement in der Industrieunternehmung. 2008.

Band 21 Martin Rietsch: Messung und Analyse des ökonomischen Wechselkursrisikos aus Unternehmenssicht: Ein stochastischer Simulationsansatz. 2008.

Band 22 Hans Christian Mantler: Makroökonomische Effizienz des Finanzsektors. Herleitung eines theoretischen Modells und Schätzung der Wachstumsimplikationen für die Marktwirtschaften und Transformationsökonomien Europas. 2008.

Band 23 Youri Tacoun: La théorie de la valeur de Christian von Ehrenfels. 2008.

Band 24 Monika Koller: Longitudinale Betrachtung der Kognitiven Dissonanz. Eine Tagebuchstudie zur Reiseentscheidung. 2008.

Band 25 Marcus Scheiblecker: The Austrian Business Cycle in the European Context. 2008.

Band 26 Aida Numic: Multinational Teams in European and American Companies. 2008.

Band 27 Ulrike Bauernfeind: User Satisfaction with Personalised Internet Applications. 2008.

Band 28 Reinhold Schodl: Systematische Analyse und Bewertung komplexer Supply Chain Prozesse bei dynamischer Festlegung des Auftragsentkopplungspunkts. 2008.

Band 29 Bianca Gusenbauer: Öffentlich-private Finanzierung von Infrastruktur in Entwicklungsländern und deren Beitrag zur Armutsreduktion. Fallstudien in Vietnam und auf den Philippinen. 2009.

Band 30 Elisabeth Salomon: Hybrides Management in sino-österreichischen Joint Ventures in China aus österreichischer Perspektive. 2009.

Band 31 Katharina Mader: Gender Budgeting: Ein emanzipatorisches, finanzpolitisches und demokratiepolitisches Instrument. 2009.

Band 32 Michael Weber: Die Generierung von Empfehlungen für zwischenbetriebliche Transaktionen als gesamtwirtschaftliche Infrastrukturleistung. 2010.

Band 33 Lisa Gimpl-Heersink: Joint Pricing and Inventory Control under Reference Price Effects. 2009.

Band 34 Stefan A. Zopf: Analyse der Potentiale und Effekte des Ingredient Brandings und dessen Einfluss auf die Markenstärke. 2009.

Band 35 Dagmar Kiefer: Multicultural Work in Five United Nations Organisations. An Austrian Perspective. 2009.

Band 36 Gottfried Gruber: Multichannel Management. A Normative Model Towards Optimality. 2009.

Band 37 Rainer Quante: Management of Stochastic Demand in Make-to-Stock Manufacturing. 2009.

Band 38 Franz F. Eiffe: Auf den Spuren von Amartya Sen. Zur theoriegeschichtlichen Genese des Capability-Ansatzes und seinem Beitrag zur Armutsanalyse in der EU. 2010.

www.peterlang.de